Contemporary Politics

Series editors

David Beethem
Bob Jessop
John Keane
Anne Sassoon

Already published

The Context of British Politics
David Coates

The Noble Lie
The British constitution and the rule of law
Ian Harden and Norman Lewis

The Power of the Powerless
Citizens against the state in central-eastern Europe
Vaclav Havel et al.
Edited by John Keane

After Full Employment
John Keane and John Owens

Contradictions of the Welfare State
Claus Offe
Edited by John Keane

The Myth of the Plan
Lessons of Soviet planning experience
Peter Rutland

Gramsci's Politics
Anne Showstack Sassoon

Women and the State
The shifting boundaries of public and private
Edited by Anne Showstack Sassoon

Women and the Public Sphere
A critique of sociology and politics
Edited by Janet Siltanen and Michelle Stanworth

In preparation
Introduction to Soviet Politics
Peter Rutland

The Noble Lie

*The British constitution
and the rule of law*

Ian Harden and
Norman Lewis

Foreword by Sir Douglas Wass

Hutchinson

London   Melbourne   Sydney   Auckland   Johannesburg

Hutchinson Education

An imprint of Century Hutchinson Ltd

62-65 Chandos Place, London WC2N 4NW

Century Hutchinson Australia Pty Ltd
PO Box 496, 16-22 Church Street, Hawthorn, Victoria 3122, Australia

Century Hutchinson New Zealand Ltd
PO Box 40-086, Glenfield, Auckland 10, New Zealand

Century Hutchinson South Africa (Pty) Ltd
PO Box 337, Bergvlei 2012, South Africa

First published 1986
Paperback edition first published 1988

© Ian Harden and Norman Lewis 1986

Set in 10 on 12 point Linotron Times

Printed and bound in Great Britain by
Anchor Brendon Ltd, Tiptree, Essex

British Library Cataloguing in Publication Data

Harden, Ian
    The noble lie: the British constitution
    and the rule of law.
    1. Great Britain—Constitutional law
    I. Title   II. Lewis, Norman
    344.102'2   KD3989
ISBN 0 09 172997 1 paper

'How, then, might we contrive one noble lie to persuade if possible the rules themselves, but failing that the rest of the city?' Plato

'To create a Good Society where men can be themselves remains a task not for tinkers but for tailors.' Martin Hollis

Contents

Foreword

This is an important and exciting book. It is about the interface between law and politics, about the legitimacy of political authority and about the adequacy of the component parts of our constitution to safeguard the citizen, both as an individual and as a member of society, from arbitrary acts of government. It is not a book which will appeal to many politicians, and it will certainly offend, or at the least disturb, many lawyers; for it makes each category pointedly aware of the account in a democratic society it should take of the claims and assertions of the other.

The case for constitutional reform is much in vogue. The incorporation of the European Convention on Human Rights in our domestic legislation, the introduction of a form of proportional representation into our electoral system, some revision of the role and functions of the Second Chamber, even the duties and rights of the sovereign in regard to the appointment of the Prime Minister – all these are now the subject of informed debate. The authors of this book do not deny the importance of these issues, but their canvas goes much wider. Indeed their purpose is nothing less than to challenge the very assumptions upon which a century ago Dicey formulated his specification of our constitution – a specification which constitutional lawyers and political scientists alike still largely take as the final word on the subject.

On the Diceyan formulation, the twin pillars of the constitution are an omnicompetent Parliament and an independent judiciary administering the common law. The two pillars are quite separate and are seen as having different purposes. Neither seeks to interfere with the other. In particular the judiciary assumes minimal competence in political matters; in return for this forbearance, the politicians do not concern themselves greatly with the accountability of the judges or with the archaic way in which they are appointed. If the judiciary is today not quite as timid in relation to executive government as it was thirty years ago, it still displays a strong distaste for challenging political authority. At most it ventures into the field of the formal procedures followed by ministers in exercising the powers conferred upon them. It seeks simply to establish whether those procedures have violated any aspect of the common law. The distancing of the judiciary from anything approaching a challenge to substantive political decision has left the way clear for executive government in this country to enjoy a power and a freedom which is unrivalled in the liberal democratic world. Thanks to the enforcement of strict party discipline in the House of Commons and the minimal financial and reforming powers of the House of Lords, there is in practice little formal check on arbitrary government. There is no statutory requirement for the government to give reasons for most of its decisions; no duty is laid upon it to publish or give access to information on which decisions are made; no rules apply to the internal processes followed in reaching decisions or govern the mechanisms by which deals are struck between public authority and private interest groups. There is no prescriptive procedure for the consultation of wider 'constituencies' than those the government chooses to identify and prefer. The only hard obligation on the government is to seek the endorsement of the electorate at large when Parliament is dissolved.

The authors of this book cannot accept a state of affairs which affords so many opportunities for arbitrary – and perverse – government, for the brushing aside of criticism and objection, and for the following of processes which are a denial of Rousseau's conception of democracy as the realization of human capacities through participation in public life. They acknowledge that governments have not always sought to rule with minimum interference from those outside the charmed circle. The creation of Departmental Select Committees in 1979 was a bold move in the direction of allowing Parliament to investigate and comment on how Whitehall is run. The statutory provisions for land use planning lay obligations on ministers which are a model from the point of view of public participation. The powers given to the Social Security Advisory Committee to enable it to fulfil its role, and the duty laid on the Secretary of State in regard to any advice the committee may tender similarly earn the authors' approval. But they see these examples as oases in a desert of closed and secretive government.

That the Diceyan concept of the constitution has survived the emergence of a dominant all-pervasive state and a large public sector is perhaps due to the fact that those who have held public office have refrained from abusing the powers which their command over Parliament has conferred on them. Whether the exercise of arbitrary power was tempered by reflections that office was not a permanent entitlement and that one day the governors would be the governed, or whether it was checked by the unwritten custom that in a democracy the majority should always pause before overriding the articulated protests of the minority, the anxiety concerning arbitrary government was less acute a generation ago than it is today. It is true that as long ago as 1929 the Lord Chief Justice of the day was writing of administrative government as 'The New Despotism' and that the proliferation of subordinate legislation after the Second World War gave rise to concern at the time at the freeing of the executive from parliamentary scrutiny. But certainly in regard to policy-making there was a disposition to promote open public debate before introducing major reform. The Royal Commission was one recognized instrument in this process. In 1986 it is perhaps significant that no Royal Commission has been appointed for nearly ten years; and the terms of reference and composition of those independent inquiries which have been set up have taken on a highly prejudiced form, almost as though they were designed to ensure that the government's policy preferences would be confirmed. Conviction politics has inevitably sharpened the issue of arbitrary power. But, as the authors of this book demonstrate, the danger of arbitrary power was inherent in the very narrowness of the view we took of constitutional legitimacy.

Other countries, both those with a Westminster-style government and those with a presidential system, have set constitutional bounds on arbitrary power. In the last dozen years Australia has enacted a series of measures designed to bring administrative decisions under independent review. The United States has a much longer tradition of oversight of executive authority, but even there there have been important developments recently to bring about a more participatory democracy. The 1977 Government in the Sunshine Act circumscribes what can be dealt with by Federal agencies without the public having an opportunity to be present and it lays down firm rules to be followed when closed sessions are held, together with provision for judicial review. And both Australia and the United States, like many advanced countries, have enacted legislation which gives the public a right of access to most official information.

With the experience of other countries in mind, the authors set out their own prescription for reform in the United Kingdom. More openness in government requires a Freedom of Information Act. Greater accountability requires government departments to have to show evidence, certainly if challenged in the courts, that they have given reasoned consideration to all material factors and issues in coming to decisions. Deals between government and private interests would be put in the public domain. Departments would be required to ensure that consultation was conducted not with just a few powerful interest groups, but with all who had a view to express. Acts of omission, no less than acts of commission, would become subject to judicial review.

All this would require of the judiciary a far less passive and acquiescent role than they have become accustomed to. They would have to take what the Americans dub a 'hard look' at rules and policy decisions, and satisfy themselves much more rigorously than is now the case that ministers and public authorities generally had observed all the proper procedures, had taken account of all the relevant facts and had come to a reasonable conclusion. The law would develop from its current narrow *gesellschaft* model into a more socially purposive instrument for achieving a participatory form of government.

At the institutional and legislative level there would be an Administrative Procedure Act laying down generally for public bodies the requirements they would have to meet in conducting business; and overseeing the whole new arrangement would be a Standing Administrative Conference whose broad remit would be to study the efficiency, adequacy and fairness of the administrative procedures of government and to propose changes.

Most of this will be strong meat for our politicians, our lawyers and our public officials. Life is difficult enough, they will say, without having to complicate it with an elaborate set of rules for conducting departmental business, for consulting widely and for having to account for every action or lack of action. The judges will see endless scope for conflict with elected political authority and with it the spectre of their own position being put under scrutiny. With opposition from such diverse and powerful quarters there may be little expectation of early acceptance of these reforms by those whose consent would be essential.

Is it realistic to suppose that a programme on these lines is a practicable item on the political agenda? I believe that it, or something like it, is. It must be evident to most people involved in public affairs that in a mature developed democracy, effective government is possible only on the basis of a large measure of consensus on the part of those affected. Government by fiat may be possible in the short run, but sooner or later the fiat has to be seen by the public to be reasonable, fair, well-directed and relevant. Policies endure only to the extent that they are widely tolerated, whether they are liked or not. The introduction of norms of conduct in government designed to secure greater acceptance of public decisions and a greater perception that the decisions are reasonable and well thought out may therefore lead eventually to a more stable system of decisions and great continuity of public policy. One day this will be seen by the politicians to be an issue which can arouse popular enthusiasm and electoral support. As Abba Eban once said, 'When all else has failed, men will try reasonableness.'

Part One
The Constitutional Heritage

1   Introduction

Dicey and the rule of law

It has long seemed to us that the time for recasting argument concerning those two enduringly influential chimerae, the 'rule of law' and the 'British constitution' was over-ripe. 1985 was the centenary of the appearance of Albert Venn Dicey's vastly authoritative *Introduction to the Study of the Law of the Constitution*,[1]* so it seemed an opportune moment for a reappraisal. We are convinced that discourse surrounding these two powerful ideas has become hidebound by dated concepts and outmoded political theory.

Many, if not most, commentators would now distance themselves to varying degrees from the text of Dicey's work, arguing that whatever the validity of his original analysis, it had been overtaken by events or was clearly the product of an excessively Whiggish cast of mind.[2] Nevertheless, in many ways Dicey's terms of debate still constitute the ruling paradigm: they are the point of departure, the standard against which to judge constitutional propriety. His account, however threadbare, still occupies the high ground of British constitutional theory and we believe it is now time for others to seize the heights.

Our approach is novel because we contest the accepted meanings given to 'law', 'the rule of law' and even 'the constitution', not out of intellectual chic, but because Dicean formulations are very much a product of their age in being both markedly positivistic and empiricist. This is hardly surprising given the influence of John Austin on Dicey's thinking and the pervasive hold which particular notions of

---

* Superior figures refer to the references at the ends of chapters.

scientific analysis of the social world enjoyed during that period. We shall not elaborate on the contentious nature of either positivist or empiricist ways of working at this point,[3] but it is worth stressing that, although Dicey's work is perhaps known only to a small proportion of the population, the views with which it is associated inform much political rhetoric and characterize much of British cultural life. Moreover, even the most contemporary work on the constitution can still locate its arguments within Dicean parameters.[4] In other words, even where Dicey's constitutional diagnoses are disputed, there is a marked tendency to accept the contours of his investigation and with them many of the hidden theoretical assumptions.

We have no doubt that Dicey struck a contemporary chord but in doing so he appealed to ideals and sentiments about government which transcend the historical moment he was concerned to describe. He wrote as if his assessment constituted the necessary embodiment and the natural resting place of those ideals and sentiments. It was of course no more than a staging-post in the development of the British polity and state, albeit one which in many respects was particularly well settled. Since that time, the nature of the British state has been transformed, although little in the way of conscious and active remodelling of our high political institutions has taken place. Over the last century seemingly endless and infinitely subtle shifts of role have been absorbed by the executive branch of government, which is not the subject of any systematic constitutional body of legal accountability.

The danger with Dicey's conflation of nineteenth-century constitutional arrangements and *the* rule of law is that, if we freeze the latter notion into the institutional background of a particular period, we abandon its larger flavour. If it then becomes *as description* the ruling paradigm for discussing constitutionality and the rule of law, it can only work in opposition to an effective analysis of contemporary constitutional conditions by suppressing the fact that there are underlying propositions and beliefs that inform the idea itself. The Dicean concept is the archetype of what modern American writers have styled 'legal formalism', the main danger of which is to disguise if not suppress 'the inevitably political and redistributive functions of law'.[5]

The ideals and sentiments about government which inspired allegiance to the highly connotative notion of the 'rule of law' may or may not have been accurately encapsulated for the nineteenth century by the Dicean formulation. Yet such a formulation, however modernized, amended or embellished, fails to convey either descriptive, explanatory or cultural message a century later. Some version of a rule of law, and some notion of constitutionality are nevertheless an enduring feature of how the British people think about the way they are governed and how they would describe their collective political world-view in more reflective moments. We believe that constitutional law and theory have largely failed to come to terms either with embedded notions of constitutionality in a modern setting or with a descriptive account of the behaviour of constitutional actors. Our charge is that, at best, students of the British constitution have failed to provide an adequate anatomy of constitutional behaviour. At worst they have so dessicated our collective public enterprise as to deprive it of all sense of moral purpose or direction. The rule of law is an ancient ideal, the roots of which can be traced back at least as far as classical Greece. In European societies in general, and particularly in Britain, it has come to encapsulate a complex moral aspiration: the legitimacy of public power.

Outline of the argument

One of our prime concerns will be to provide, within settled traditions, a model for producing an anatomy of legitimate public power – a cast of constitutional actors and roles. This alone would be something of an advance on what is currently available and would produce an outline description of a programme for more detailed work on our system of constitutional law. Our model takes as its starting-point the largely uncontested notion of the omnicompetence of Parliament.

When we say 'uncontested', we do not mean that the idea of parliamentary omnicompetence would satisfy the sociologist or political scientist, still less the natural lawyer or moral philosopher. Rather we mean that, in so far as we have any clear constitution at all, parliamentary omnicompetence is axiomatic. The logic of this simple proposition invites us to examine the notion of 'delegated omnicompetence' since it is undisputed that a legislative assembly is incapable of managing the affairs of a modern welfare/capitalist state unaided. The nature and forms of implicit and explicit delegation are highly complex. Nevertheless they can be stated with relative simplicity at a number of recognizable points on a spectrum of public behaviour patterns.

Given the absence of an entrenched Bill of Rights (and leaving aside the problems of European Community and human rights law), the conventional wisdom is that Parliament may enact whatever legislation it sees fit. Given also that the initiative for almost all legislation comes from government ministers, then it is obvious that the executive branch of government, acting in effect as the agent of an omnicompetent legislature, is afforded enormous power and influence. Again, we would emphasize that we are not concerned to identify the empirical constraints on this power and influence. For the constitutional lawyer then, and indeed the constitutional scholar generally, it is necessary to trace the network of constitutional agency relationships flowing from Parliament through the executive. This provides a theoretical basis for much of what is commonplace in the literature – for example, description of the behaviour patterns and influence of civil servants and other directly appointed or anointed agents of the executive. These include the numerous quasi-governmental agencies, the significance of whose rapid growth in Britain and elsewhere, especially since the Second World War, has increasingly occupied scholarly attention.[6] In addition, the notion of delegated omnicompetence allows us to look for other behaviour patterns of the executive, which are in many cases not directly restrained by legislation or judicial pronouncement. We therefore include in our description of the power and influence of constitutional actors all the new property of largesse, grant and state aids as well as the better evidenced idea of the 'contract state'.[7]

This model also implies that the legitimate behaviour patterns of the 'delegates', themselves the site of constitutionally significant activity, must be considered and described in as systematic a way as possible. Leaving aside for the time being the concept of legitimacy, our model necessitates something that is largely missing in the constitutional law literature – a description of the networked, semi-formal, semi-structured, unstructured and informal dealings of the executive and its agents. The theme is developed at length in Part Two where we include in our constitutional anatomy such phenomena as corporatism, lobbying, *ex parte* negotiations and a range of devices which are generally less structured than the most visible consultative practices.

Perhaps even more interestingly, this analysis leads us to develop the issue of executive *inaction*, a matter which, as we shall see, has begun to occupy the United States Federal courts in the administrative law field. This is in one sense to do no more than to provide an institutional examination of that darling of the 1960s and early 1970s, discretion. As all public lawyers know, discretion includes the freedom *not* to act as well as to act. Judicially imposed constraints on discretion include the necessity to take proper considerations into account and to exclude those which a court would regard as improper. What we propose is that the logic of these doctrines be extended to provide an institutional framework for an analysis of the actual responsibilities of an omnicompetent executive, thereby taking into account the world of 'private government' and its relationship with the 'public' domain. It is also to give constitutional consideration to what has elsewhere been called the 'new feudalism'.[8] This is too intricate an argument to be developed in an introduction and we shall leave the issue stated baldly at this time.

One of the achievements we hope to have to our credit by the end of this essay is to have produced a new descriptive and analytical model of constitutionally legitimate action in Britain.

Legitimate public action

Now it may be thought that examining and exposing the scope of political and public action is a proper activity for constitutionalists, whether lawyer or otherwise, and that that is to end the matter. However, there has not always been agreement on what it means properly to describe the British constitution. Indeed much of the novelty of Dicey's seminal work was his emphasis on 'conventions' of the constitution which had previously not occupied such a central textual position. Similarly, the pivotal position Walter Bagehot ascribed to the cabinet broke new ground and caused a considerable shift in the emphasis adopted by students of the constitution.[9]

Perhaps the laxest attitude to describing the constitution was that of Sir Ivor Jennings whose constitutional analysis can only be described as exceedingly relativist since he inclined to the view that a description of the British constitution is necessarily a subjective matter – 'a writer on the British constitution selects what seems to him to be important'.[10] For all the richness of his scholarship, we would not seek to defend this particular position of Sir Ivor's, for any description of the constitution needs some kind of organizing or analytical framework and those commonly adopted are, to say the least, a matter of theoretical controversy.[11]

A constitution speaks to, and is the touchstone for, the legitimacy of government and governing arrangements. In many countries the issue is specifically addressed in a constitutional document, but in Britain we have approached the matter in a characteristically inarticulate and incoherent manner. Constitutional constancy is represented by the 'rule of law' which, as ruling ideology, has in some mysterious way stood for the 'best interests of the nation'. Yet the latter have been seen to be served by a succession of different, dominant ideas: the common law, the sovereignty of Parliament and some minimum version of representative democracy. All seem now to have finally become indispensable to our constitutional framework. The expression 'the rule of law', having served many masters, is now probably acceptable shorthand for this cluster of credos.

If we are to regard a constitution, any constitution, as a set of institutional arrangements for securing the boundaries and the conduct of public life then considerable doubt must attach to the adequacy of leading accounts of the British system. Since we are aware of no constitutional theory which posits a model closely related to our own, a little time needs to be spent explaining why we are led where we are. Although our model is logically implicated in the constitutional and political axiom of parliamentary omnicompetence, we still need to say a little about the justification for the way we have chosen to draw our extended anatomy.

The notion of mapping or describing public activities is inspired not just by idle curiosity but because public power is a phenomenon with which all citizens by definition have a right to be concerned: it is power exercised on their behalf. Furthermore, to be concerned with describing the contours of public life is to be committed to Sir Karl Popper's 'open society' if the method of science is indeed such that the empirical testing of hypotheses needs to be as overt an affair in the social as in the natural world.[12] Furthermore, most transcendental arguments require openness as a concomitant of purposive rational action,[13] and although we are committing ourselves to an examination of what the British hold to be *their* underlying expectations, we doubt if they would really wish to exclude themselves from the stage of world citizenship. It is difficult to avoid the conclusion that an open and accessible public domain is a fundamental requirement, and that the withholding of information has to be justified as a special case. We shall not argue this point fully in the Introduction, but merely outline some of the considerations which cause us to insist that such mapping of public constitutional power is itself legitimate and the result of legitimation demands. It should also be added that openness as a desideratum must be associated with the question of rendering an account. We develop our ideas of accountability in Part Three, especially in Chapter 8.

First, we argue that *any* notion of representative government implies that choice of representative is paramount. If the choosing exercise is intended to be meaningful, then the intentions of the various candidates and their views of current and past conditions need to be available. In periodic elections, those making the decision to withdraw or continue to support a candidate need information on the candidate's record. Even if we accept a version of representative democracy which accords the representative the right to exercise his or her own best judgement, it is difficult to see how the choosing exercise is to be invested with meaning if we have no opportunity to examine the behaviour patterns of candidates and their agents. This implies an essentially open system *at all times* if the elective exercise is to make democratic sense *at any time*. We shall return to this theme, especially in Chapter 9.

Second, the traditional guarantors of an open polity and of the rule of law (ministerial responsibility to Parliament and an independent judiciary) do not provide the knowledge our analysis shows to be required. Again, and this is a point we shall argue more fully, if *public* power has any special qualities or features, then more effective guarantees need to be forged.

In our view these two items lock together to form a third, namely, that there are a number of contradictions involved in the various strands of traditional constitutional theory. These need to be drawn out and exposed if we are to gain any insight into what it means to speak of constitutionality within a British setting. The absence of first principles in an obvious constitutional sense, the absence of clear starting stalls, produces tensions and uncertainties and theoretical and institutional inconsistencies. Moreover in light of their absence, can we be heard to say that public power in Britain has *no* legitimation foundations, has no inner certainties, has no set of ruling expectations? It would in our view be both brute and brutal so to argue and indeed underneath the rhetoric of 'common sense', 'collective experience' and 'organic growth' lurks an inarticulate belief system which characterizes our system of government. The rule of law, elastic though it may be, comes as close as anything to signposting our expectations about the nature of our unique compact. Even the now traditional concern with constitutional conventions springs to our aid for, whether they are regarded as law or positive morality or classifiable in some other way, they are an earnest that there is a proper and legitimate way to conduct public life. This honouring of conventions is normally allied to expectations as to the *kind* of substantive laws we can anticipate, at least at the level of the personal freedoms, an attachment to 'natural justice' and more generally a collective opposition to arbitrariness and retroactivity. What this amounts to is that there is a set of *immanent* expectations or beliefs, roughly equatable with the concept of the rule of law which lend colour to the ideas lying behind the notion of the British constitution. This leads us to a discussion of the broad theoretical approach we have chosen to adopt in this essay.

An immanent critique is one which seeks to identify the major claims or beliefs of a group or order and to subject them to different degrees of scrutiny. The first stage is to examine the logical interrelationships between the various claims to control for consistency and internal 'fit'. If a broad degree of fit is established then one problem is removed. If, however, some degree of dissonance appears then any implications of the contradictions so exposed must be addressed.

Stage two is to examine the relationship between claim and reality – to set the exposed beliefs against the empirical world. Once more the object of the exercise is to examine the degree of 'mesh' or disjuncture. Such an approach is beset with difficulties but, although we are conscious that the elusiveness of constitutional principle in Britain renders such an approach inherently fragile and unstable, that same elusiveness seems to us to make it inevitable.

In recent years something approximating to this theoretical model has been used by the critical legal studies movement in the United States but it owes its major inspiration to the work of Adorno and Horkheimer.[14] In particular the critical legal studies movement has adopted Horkheimer's definition of 'immanent criticism' as the confrontation of 'the existent, in its historical context, with the claim of its conceptual principles, in order to criticise the relation between the two and thus transcend them'.[15]

It is a common, though not a necessary, theme of immanent critique that the exposure of contradictions internal to a system's own dynamics might trigger off a dialectical process whereby a new level of demands or expectations causes the system or group to move into a new higher gear. As such it is associated with reformist or radical tendencies.[16] In constitutional terms, this may not be thought inappropriate in so far as the expectations of citizenship are unlikely to remain static. We shall return to this thesis in due course but there seems to us little doubt that constitutional debate is especially beset by tensions and contradictions in Britain.

The pragmatic development of British political and governmental institutions and practices has meant that alongside expectations about openness, democracy, public accountability and the like there have developed strong traditions and practices concerning the day-to-day doing of the nation's business which live very uneasily with those expectations. The result is that appeals to loyalty to the British public way of life have rolled together inconsistent themes and expectations. At the general rhetorical and hegemonic level these appeals have been remarkably successful in that for the most part a stable political system has run alongside a remarkably stable social order. Indeed, both citizen and stranger seem convinced that we must in some sense have 'got it right' and most particularly that we are a nation which in a very special way lives under the law. Whatever sense of admiration and wonder we may feel about the stability of British social and political institutions, the claim to be a nation living under law cannot be rationally sustained. In earlier times those who were on the receiving end of the dissonance between expectation and reality occasionally cried 'foul'.[17] We would anticipate more and more disaffection in contemporary Britain given the enormous complexity of a set of governmental relations which have not been readdressed in the light of first principles.

There are genuine conflicts between ideas such as responsible public power, open debate, mandate (an extremely cloudy notion whose rhetorical appeal is none the less extremely strong), what ministerial responsibility has come to represent, notions of public confidentiality and most obviously the almost universally condemned Official Secrets Acts. These latter phenomena are usually presented as either legitimate accompaniments of, or necessary exceptions to, the general openness and the 'lawfulness' of the constitution. In fact the events of the last hundred years have been so momentous as to cloud, at least in the public mind, the nature of the British constitution, the rule of law, and what it means to live in a democracy.

Our contention is that there are immanent expectations of a system of open and accountable government which run deep in the British people and that the rhetoric and claims made for our system of government foster such expectations. Yet these expectations square ill with the contemporary constitutional and political scene. If this is correct then we need to map out the anatomy of our modern system of public power or constitutional behaviour to establish how far the expectations and claims to which we have referred are at odds with reality. We shall argue that a revised rule of law can expose public and constitutional activity more accurately than is traditionally the case in constitutional writings. In this event debate surrounding constitutionality should conform more closely to the ideals which have informed the notion of the rule of law throughout most of British history.

The overriding problem besetting a modern analysis of the British constitution is that the complexity of the task has often been obscured by the images created by previous writers. In particular there has been a tendency to conflate a number of issues which, though closely associated, rationally retain separate identities. Thus to speak of constitutionality is to address moral, political and practical concerns. Citizens implicitly engage in all these forms of analysis by accepting legitimation claims while those in authority do the same by making those legitimation claims. In fact constitutional analysis is the announcement of a vision of citizenship. However, to address the problem of constitutionality is also to engage in a social scientific activity. We have chosen to connect the social scientific and the citizenship activities through the adoption of the theoretical perspective of immanent critique. This, we believe, is both more coherent and more honest than standard constitutional theory which, while touching on all of these concerns, has usually done so in a way which affects to be social scientific while actively seeking to exlude at least the moral and political dimensions. This is evidenced by Dicey's inability to say anything about how conventions come into being and by Jennings's overt relativism when speaking to underlying values or principles. This is not unconnected with the methodology or theory of most constitutional writers: *viz*. legal positivism. This often takes the form of an opposition to natural law in favour of value-free conceptual inquiry. However, whereas social science positivism more generally is commonly an exercise in un- ashamed epistemological empiricism, asserting the theory- neutrality of facts, legal positivism more closely resembles what Collingwood terms 'intuitive realism'. In other words, it operates upon the basis of presuppositions (or concepts) which are simply unexposed and unaddressed.[18]

We shall seek to rework the notion of the rule of law by showing that appeals to it, slippery concept though it be, transcend particular historical moments and justifications. Certain minimum conditions need to obtain in order to appeal to it as a 'master ideal',[19] and the complexity of modern political and governmental institutions has left those conditions behind. This is partly, we shall argue, because of allegiance to a dated concept of law itself which tends to equate legality with the legal system of an epoch which more or less coincided with the time of Dicey's writing. Such a notion of legality is one among several yet it is appealed to as if it were the only one capable of producing order and accountability. It does no such thing and we shall indicate how it needs to be replaced as the ruling legal paradigm.

A revised concept of law and its handmaiden, 'legality' or the 'rule of law', will allow us to show how the gap between the master ideals and current political and constitutional practice can be bridged. This analysis leads the constitutionalist to a programme of institution-building for the construction of rational discourse, for the construction of constitutional openness and accountability primarily through the medium of what American Federal administrative law has termed the 'hard-look doctrine'.

We should at the outset make one point clear. The focus of this essay is to a major extent on collective decision-making mechanisms but this does not mean that individual or human rights are unimportant. On the contrary there is and must be an irreducible sphere of individual entitlements as a necessary aspect of human self-realization and development.[20] However, these issues already enjoy a relatively high visibility in the literature, albeit that they are poorly dealt with in constitutional practice. Furthermore, we believe that individual rights can flourish best in an atmosphere of collective and social well-being. This collective atmosphere forms the focus for most of what follows.

This introduction has largely been occupied with developing our ideas on the rule of law and the constitution at a fairly general level. What follows is divided into three. Part One, which tills much of the ground to which this introduction has staked an initial claim, we have called 'The constitutional heritage'. In Part Two 'The business of governing', we describe the behaviour of political and governmental institutions and make an attempt to analyse that behaviour against the claims of traditional doctrine. In so doing we take 'delegated omnicompetence' as a central theme and seek to explain the behaviour of Parliament's 'agents by implication'. This is practically coterminous with what we have called the 'disinte-grated state'. Development of this theme allows us to describe both action and inaction; decision-making and non-decision-making. In Part Three we address ourselves to 'Reconstitutionalizing the business of governing' in which we show how a revised concept of law could contribute to advancing the principles of constitutional legitimation which we believe most people would accept as a key part of our national cultural heritage.

References

1   References throughout are to the 9th edn with an introduction by Professor E. C. S. Wade (Macmillan 1939).
2   See, e.g. E. C. S. Wade's introduction to the 9th edn and, more impressive to our minds, Sir Ivor Jennings, *The Law of the Constitution*, 5th edn (Cambridge University Press 1966).
3   Though see e.g. W. G. Runciman, *A Treatise on Social Theory*, vol. 1 (Cambridge University Press 1983) at pp. 5, 11 and *passim*; A. Ryan, *The Philosophy of the Social Sciences* (Macmillan 1970) esp. pp. 13, 102, 103; T. S. Kuhn, *The Structure of Scientific Revolutions* (Chicago UP 1962) and most scintillatingly R. M. Collingwood, *An Essay on Metaphysics* (Clarendon 1940) esp. ch. 14 on 'Positivist metaphysics'.
4   See e.g. Geoffrey Marshall, *Constitutional Conventions* (Clarendon 1984).
5   See e.g. Morton J. Horwitz, *The Transformation of American Law 1780–1860* (Harvard University Press 1977) at p. 266.
6   See A. Barker (ed.), *Quangos in Britain* (Macmillan 1982).
7   See T. Daintith, 'The Executive power today' in J. Jowell and D. Oliver (eds.), *The Changing Constitution* (Oxford University Press 1985); C. A. Reich, 'The new property', *Yale Law Journal*, **73**, pp. 733–87; Bruce L. R. Smith, 'Accountability and independence in the contract state', in B. L. R. Smith and D. C. Hague, *The Dilemma of Accountability in Modern Government* (Macmillan 1971). For an earlier treatment see Don K. Price, *Government and Science* (New York University Press 1954), ch. 11 'Federalism by contract'.
8   G. Poggi, *The Development of the Modern State* (Hutchinson 1978) esp. ch. VI, 'State and society under liberalism and after'.
9   W. Bagehot, *The English Constitution*, first published 1867, 2nd edn 1872; our references will be to the Fontana edition, with an introduction by R. H. S. Crossman (1963).
10   *The Law of the Constitution*, p. 37.
11   See e.g. Sir Kenneth Wheare, *Modern Constitutions* (Oxford Univer-

sity Press 1966), esp. ch. 1 and G. Marshall, *Constitutional Theory* (Clarendon 1971), *passim*.

12 See *The Open Society and its Enemies*, 2 vols., 5th edn (RKP 1966) esp. vol. 1, pp. 172–7.

13 See in particular Alan Gewirth, *Reason and Morality* (Chicago University Press 1978) e.g. pp. 212, 243, 244.

14 Roberto M. Unger, 'The critical legal studies movement', *Harvard Law Review*, **96** (1983), pp. 561–675; David Held, *Introduction to Critical Theory* (Hutchinson 1980).

15 M. Horkheimer, *Eclipse of Reason* (New York: Seabury Press 1974), p. 182.

16 D. M. Trubek, 'Complexity and contradiction in the legal order', *Law and Society Review*, **11**, (1977), pp. 529–69.

17 See e.g. John Brewer and John Styles (eds.), *An Ungovernable People: the English and their law in the seventeenth and eighteenth centuries* (Hutchinson 1980).

18 Collingwood, ch. 5.

19 Philip Selznick, *Law, Society and Industrial Justice* (New York: Russell Sage Foundation 1969) p. 28. He is speaking here of 'legality' but elsewhere he makes it clear that legality and the rule of law are coterminous.

20 Gewirth, *Reason and Morality*.

2 The rule of law: a chequered history

We might well have chosen to describe this volume as an essay in constitutional jurisprudence for reasons which we think are well described by Nonet and Selznick:

Where we look for the foundations of law, the sense we make of the legal process, and the place we give law in society – all profoundly affect the shape of the political community and the reach of social aspirations. There is a need we think to make these implicit concerns more central in jurisprudential inquiry, to encourage a renewed appreciation of the interplay of legal theory and social policy. By policy we have in mind not detailed prescriptions but basic perspectives that determine how public purposes are defined and how practical alternatives are perceived. Jurisprudence gains focus and depth when it self-consciously considers the implications it has for action and institutional design. Philosophical analysis, in turn, helps ensure that basic issues of policy are closely examined, not buried under unscrutinised assumptions and perspectives.[1]

We agree too that, characteristically, legal theories are built upon implicit theories of authority,[2] a view also espoused by E. C. S. Wade in his review of Dicey's influence when he remarked that Dicey knew and understood full well that all lawful authority in the state is legal authority. Dicey's mistake was to believe that one organ, the courts, were capable of restraining the legal excesses of the others and to make this the focus of his analysis when in reality what ought to have been given most centrality was the extent of the 'lawful' powers of the administration that escaped effective judicial oversight. It is upon this limited view of administration, according to Wade, that Dicey's interpretation of the rule of law rested.[3] We can only wonder that this relatively old insight has not been the subject of programmatic development by constitutional lawyers in Britain.

In the United States the critical legal studies movement has argued that the first stage in examining the relationship between law and broader social forms is to understand the nature of the social ideals which law is thought to foster. That done, it is vital to examine, empirically and theoretically, the purported relationship between legal institutions and these ideals. The broad appeal being canvassed here links, rather curiously perhaps, E. C. S. Wade and a figure in the critical legal studies movement such as David Trubek in calling for immanent critique of their respective legal orders; an inquiry into the fundamental assumptions which breathe life into those orders.[4] Wade was prepared to argue that underneath the elaborate organization of our governmental machinery there rests a fundamental faith in a democratic form of government. This gave rise in his view to beliefs, sentiments, principles or prejudices which are firmly entrenched in public opinion.[5]

These contentions reinforce our view that the rule of law is an ideal which transcends particular periods in a nation's history. More especially, it transcends the legitimacy of any given institutional devices impleaded as vindications of the supremacy of the rule of law. Such institutional devices, in our case of the parliamentary and judicial varieties, are indeed part of and central to the vindication of any version of the rule of law. Even so, they cannot necessarily be expected to function unaided and in unchanged form regardless of political, economic, social and administrative developments. Such guarantees need constant encashing through a process of relating institutions to ideals in an atmosphere of candour and a spirit of genuine inquiry.

Part of the problem has been, in our view, that described by Jennings when he observed that the principles of constitutional law established by the courts primarily denote a simple acceptance of the constitution of the 1689 Revolution Settlement.[6] Institutions and practices which have grown up since that time have frequently not received formal recognition in legislation nor have the courts incorporated them into the 'common law'.

A more recent commentator has echoed these sentiments by arguing in *In Search of the Constitution* that appeals to the forms of the past do little to control the substance of contemporary power.[7] Johnson reminds us that we are guilty of projecting the present into the past if we imagine that even at the time of the vindication of limited monarchy and of parliamentary rights in 1689, the claims made on behalf of Parliament were already identical with those made two hundred years later. The discovery or rediscovery of fundamentals is the pressing requirement. Once it is met, the constitutional programme becomes much clearer to draw up:

since the dominant approach to the rule of law has been empirical and procedural, it should not in theory be difficult to change the methods and procedures so that a new correspondence is established between the ideal and the reality. In other words, it is not denied that the positivism of the traditional English mode of thinking about the rule of law contained an important hold on realities which it would be well to preserve. The crucial addition which needs to be made is to bring back into the conception of the rule of law something of the dimension of a Commonwealth under the guidance of law. This could be achieved only if these matters were to be considered more politically, and if an effort were made to see the uses of law as one aspect of the problem of establishing and maintaining political authority.[8]

We shall have more to say of the relationship between constitutional law and the overall polity in due course.

The idea and the ideal of law display essential insights into Western systems of thought and belief and, some would argue, into what it means to be human. Within these traditions some notion of legal autonomy[9] informs most conceptions of the rule of law, together with the dominant idea that the state must not fall permanently hostage to a faction lest the exercise of citizenship be impeded.[10]

English legal history is replete with illustrations of the importance of these arguments. Long before the revolutionary settlement, itself an occurrence of major moral symbolism, state law was seen as having significant importance for advancing social ideals. The medieval state was in part characterized by strong moral idealism: honest manufacture, just prices, fair wages, reasonable profits were legally mandated requirements. There is strong support for the view that even commerce and industry, far from being understood as a market exchange of commodities, were seen at that period in terms of relationships between people: thus the often-remarked reference to 'status' as an informing legal concept.[11] It was only considerably later that the dominance of a different, marketist, individualist ideology saw the ideals embedded in the rule of law transferred from a clear substantive morality to something much more loosely based in procedures and institutions with only a cloudy civil libertarian notion of substantive morality remaining.

The change from a belief in the moral ideal of law to its market version, best expressed in freedom of contract, was not of course peculiar to Britain.[12] Indeed Anglo-American utilitarianism was always in danger of adopting an impoverished view of human nature, an essentially atomistic conception of human beings as voters in an electoral system or consumers in a market system, and of overlooking the need to expand imagination and establish a sense of civic duty through a theory of political education and culture.[13] Be that as it may, although the rule of law became the 'golden metwand' of collective life and enjoyed genuine significance, it was nevertheless seen to be full of vagueness and ambiguity.[14] It has remained difficult to pin down but has undoubtedly enjoyed central legitimating force. What it has not evoked in recent times is an attempt to relate its general constituent principles to the problems of modern administration in such a way as to redefine its contemporary nature.

The rule of law is a highly connotative, value-laden idea and as such must be sharply differentiated from *a* rule of law, a specific norm or guide to action. It speaks to a belief in the kind of polity which seeks to subordinate naked power and to elevate civic order and rational progress. It implicitly rejects the idea of immunity from criticism, of being above collective institutions rather than facilitating their operation. Legality assumes a shared sphere of legitimate action and has come to be concerned with the procedures for the emergence of policies and rules.[15] As the rule of law it can be regarded as an essential part of the 'moral heritage of the West'.[16] It is the central legitimating feature of organized public life – the supreme constitutional principle.

What is logically entailed in claims relating to the rule of law is that we should examine the principles which underlie our legal and historical traditions with a view to elucidating the more specific behaviour of institutions and comparing ruling ideals with institutional arrangements that supposedly embody these ideals in practice.[17] The common habit of assuming an organizing theory for describing laws or the constitution without articulating it and making it available for criticism unfortunately obscures debate about constitutional fundamentals. This practice is too often accompanied by a tendency to see the jurist or constitutional lawyer as merely reporting what people say and think about what they do rather than accounting for the data through a critical interpretation. This 'positivistic' account is based upon the misconception that there is a strict separation between conceptual facts and values and fails to acknowledge that institutions and systems come into existence through human agency so that we are bound sensibly to ask why they were brought into existence and how they are operating. To reject positivistic accounts is to insist that a law or a constitution consists not necessarily or merely in posited rules or posited conduct but in a concept of shared public purposes.[18]

For the legal fraternity in particular, though perhaps for constitution-watchers in general, positivism is what underlies their art when practised at its most rigorous. In its undisciplined form it partakes of what Collingwood called 'intuitive realism' which is the assumption that knowledge amounts to the simple intuition or apprehension of things confronting us 'which absolutely and in themselves just are what we "intuit" or "apprehend" them as being'.[19]

Positivism, for Collingwood, is the belief that social knowledge can be scientific only through first ascertaining and then classifying 'facts', the ascertainment exercise being the job of the senses. It represents the failure to come to terms with the understanding that answers depend upon questions and that neither are self-presenting. To quote Collingwood again:

The science of psychology had been founded centuries ago on the recognition that by means of our senses we never observe any facts at all, we only undergo feelings. Here positivism ignored the whole history of modern thought and reverted in a single jump to a long-exploded error of the Middle Ages.

In other words the claim that scientific thought has no presuppositions would only be a tenable proposition if the work of observing facts were done by the senses without any assistance from the intellect.[20]

The dominance of positivism, the outcome of a fascination with the supposed methods and empiricist logic of natural science, has had serious repercussions for Anglo-American political systems. The positivist outlook has tended to emphasize contingency and to advocate a method of detail which consists of treating wholes by separating them into their parts and breaking every question into pieces before attempting to resolve it. This disposition to analyse wholes into specific, discrete parts is alien to the emphasis upon the interrelationships among parts contained in the concept of either 'the state' or of 'the constitution'. The capacity of institutions consciously to foster larger purposes is seriously impaired in this tradition, a fact which is strongly connected with the differences between 'state' and 'non-state' societies.[21]

We do not intend to delay our exposition by theoretical elaboration of positivist and non-positivist schools of social science for we shall make our case about constitutional analysis specifically and at length. Our minor excursus relates only to the implications of positivist assumptions for legal and constitutional scholars and our main concern is to bring their often inarticulate adoption to public attention. Yet perhaps we should dwell on one further aspect of classical social science which has large implications for our whole design. It is the tendency to what Habermas has called the 'scientization of politics' or 'technicism' and is perhaps a modern morality play built around Weber's concept of bureaucratic rationality.[22] The connections between particular theoretical positions and the driving impulse of modern complexity towards instrumental, technical outcomes is somewhat tortuous but it is much more likely that technical outcomes which are not the product of politicial choice will predominate where first principles are not constantly and openly addressed. Where there is a failure to relate the beliefs and sentiments which underlie the constitutional enterprise (i.e. where the rule of law is not the guiding spirit of inquiry) to working patterns of public behaviour then the claims of technical expertise tend to undermine the legitimacy of public criticism.[23]

To diminish or underpresent the nation's heritage of constitutional ideas is to accentuate the likelihood that the state's task will be seen as that of managing the firm after the fashion of the contemporary large corporation. The connections between the various phenomena we have so far outlined and the general analysis underlying much of the rest of this essay are so strong that we think it worthwhile to extend the argument a little.

The vacuum left by the devaluation of ideology . . . is filled not by a renewal of open-ended discourse but by an appeal to economic, technological and managerial 'expertise'. And to supply that expertise or to control its employment in the conduct of rule does not seem a job parliament can adequately do. Instead, the job falls mainly to the professional civil service, which enlists the support of research institutes, planning units, and consultative bodies manned chiefly by the 'scientific estate' and by spokesmen for the larger corporations and other interest groups. As a result, administrative decisions are increasingly articulated in a language that effectively screens them from parliamentary criticism and public debate, and that frequently provides a convenient cover for the interests actually dictating those decisions.[24]

In Part Two of the book we argue in some depth that this is a fairly accurate characterization of contemporary British government, and that our traditional institutional devices fail precisely to produce open discourse or to ensure that the underlying rationale of the concept of the rule of law is maintained. Legislation in the modern world has largely lost its pristine properties of specificity and open declaration. Instead it favours loose-textured enabling provisions or measures of an administrative nature given the form of law in order to legalize the expenditures they involve and to shield ministers and civil servants from having to take political or personal responsibility for them. This was precisely the danger which E. C. S. Wade detected in the acceptance of Dicey's version of the rule of law, for such behaviour is 'lawful' in a narrow sense but offends the spirit of legality in every salient particular. This is why Dicean judicial guarantees were so flawed, a matter to which we turn in Chapter 7. Hidden, implicit or reified assumptions conspire to cloud the reality of governmental conduct and to intertwine technical and political outcomes. By unpacking the essential characteristics of the rule of law, by returning to first principles, we should be in a better position to examine current public behaviour patterns against the inner claims and necessities.

The rule of law and democracy

The seventeenth-century constitutional settlement was based on the ideas of a representative Parliament and the common law protection of individual rights. Although Dicey formulated this as the sovereignty of Parliament and the rule of law there is no doubt that the settlement has in more recent times been strongly associated with democratic sentiments. Indeed even in earlier periods the notion obtained that law in some sense or another emanated from consensual or representative quarters. What is interesting too is that the notion of lawfulness and legality has never during this millennium been associated in England with the idea of force *in itself* but rather with 'auctoritas' or legitimate power. This has taken subtly different forms at different periods while the notion of the rule of law has been the authorizing constancy during these political shifts. Bracton's writings, for instance, reflected the medieval idea that law, whether of God or man, rules the world and that kings and potentates live under its sway. This notion, axiomatic among the lawyers of the fourteenth and fifteenth centuries was expressed on the continent of Europe and periodically in Britain, in the idea of a supreme fundamental law which no power in the state could change and only the lawyers could interpret. We shall also see that the common law became idealized at various periods in very similar terms, though by Dicey's time the idea of government under law had largely become associated in Britain with the more homely notion of a law subject to the control of Parliament.

The dominance of rule of law sentiments has been such that only in the Stuart period was this form (i.e. Parliament and the common law) of the theory of the supremacy of law seriously questioned.[25] Down through the years to its formulation by Dicey the doctrine came to mean the supremacy, not only of the common law, but of the whole law of England, so long as Parliament sees fit to leave it unchanged.[26] Associated with these developments is, of course, the theory of parliamentary sovereignty but its history and acceptance have been somewhat chequered and contested. Indeed the nature and effects of the revolution were such that there was for some time considerable reluctance to accept all the consequences of a pure theory of sovereignty. As Holdsworth says, the results of the settlement meant not only that Parliament became the dominant partner in the constitution but that the constitutional rights of the subject, for which Parliament had always stood, assumed a greater importance than the theory of sovereignty itself.[27] Here we find a particular illustration of our argument that institutions and systems come into play through human agencies and for specific purposes and that their behaviour has accordingly to be judged in light of those purposes. The supremacy of Parliament came to be invested with expectations about what should be done with that supremacy and about the terms of Parliament's trusteeship. One does not have to side with Locke in the belief that political society was founded precisely to safeguard some such constitutional rights[28] in order to accept that a brute and unencumbered version of the theory of sovereignty never took root in England.[29] Indeed, not only was there a plausible case for holding that the revolution was a restoration of the ancient constitution of the Lancastrian Kings[30] but even John Austin, the high priest of both legal positivism and sovereignty is remembered, *inter alia*, for having stated that members of the House of Commons were merely trustees for the body by which they are elected and appointed.[31]

Austin's views did not go uncontested[32] but English constitutional commentaries indicate that sovereignty, the rule of law, representative government and its later manifestation, democracy, were all highly contentious notions. That the constitutional foundations of Britain are difficult to uncover is not in dispute; but nor is the fact that this is in large measure owing to an inability to secure agreement on *what version* of shared public purposes should be adopted. This is merely an aggravated example of the problem of interpretation of constitutional underpinnings which obtains even for more modern written constitutions containing some degree of moral entrenchment.[33] Indeed the 'classical' versions of democracy in the Western tradition generally are by no means homogeneous.

Many different and incompatible doctrines have been presented under this label even if only modern material is considered and pejorative usages are discarded. Schumpeter for example defined the 'classical' theory of democracy as 'that institutional arrangement for arriving at political decisions which realizes the common good by making the people itself decide issues through the election of individuals who are to assemble in order to carry out its will'.[34] This he considered, in Bagehotian fashion, to demand a level of rationality in debating issues which the ordinary person does not possess. Furthermore, Schumpeter drew the distinction later elaborated by Berlin between democracy and liberal ideals and interests.[35] He thus sought to demote democracy from an ideal conception of legitimate government to a mere 'institutional arrangement for arriving at political decisions in which individuals acquire the power to decide by means of a competitive struggle for the people's vote'.[36]

Critics of Schumpeter have sought to deny the existence of any single 'classical' theory of democracy, distinguishing between a utilitarian, instrumental, view of representative government as the best political shell for the harmonious pursuit by individuals of their own private interests and the conception, associated with Rousseau and J. S. Mill, of democracy as the realization of human capacities through participation in public life.[37] Both the critics of Schumpeter and those who followed his lead in developing an account of democracy as a set of procedures for choosing leaders seem to have agreed, however, on one central issue. That is that *representative* democracy necessarily entails decision-making by governing elites so that 'our only recourse is to rely on the good graces of those who wield a great amount of power not to abuse it'.[38] Whatever larger understanding of the nature and purposes of public life may be attributed to British constitutional arrangements, the pessimistic conclusion that representative procedures can have little impact upon the 'iron law of oligarchy' is fundamentally at odds with the claims of our constitutional heritage. At the very least we must not assume *a priori* that such pessimism is warranted. It is the job of constitutional lawyers to address questions of institutional and procedural design creatively with J. S. Mill's 'grand difficulty' of politics in view – the reconciliation of elite rule with accountability to the many.

There are many reasons why we as a nation and as constitutional scholars have not been used to dwelling on 'the beliefs, sentiments, principles or prejudices' which underlie public purposes, but if we are to uncover the doings of our political processes and provide a critical interpretation of them then that cast of mind needs to be set aside. The point has been well made in one of the most sentient constitutional essays of the post-war years:

to recapture a sense of institutions as the expression of values, as the translation of procedural norms into stable relationships which can then be directed to the achievement of substantive purposes ... would be a foundation for the revival of a constitutional understanding and of a tradition of constitutional argument. . . .

A constitution is indeed a corset for those who seek power: that is its rationale. But constitutional principles are not corsets for the political discourse of a free society: they are the necessary condition for having any discourse at all about how purposes are to be fulfilled in that society.[39]

Although the purposes to be fulfilled may change over time, ideas about the framework for establishing and implementing such purposes continue to run constantly through different epochs as catalysts. The notion of government under law, of the rule of the law, is the most enduring of these and seems at most periods to be the touchstone for obligation and for claims to legitimate the polity. Indeed, where conduct offensive to the rule of law is equated with unconstitutionality it is seen to mean something more than a breach of convention or even of 'law' narrowly conceived. It is conduct contrary to the traditions and spirit of a free people whose constitution is the expression of community values. Now if this seems to confuse the relationship of law to the political compact it is because of a failure to come to terms with a sufficiently expansive concept of law, a matter which we treat in Chapter 3. We would not be the first to observe that at a high enough level of abstraction all law and all government are politics.[40]

The rule of law has done service under a number of different regimens and has been the vindication of a number of different claims at different times. This is not to argue that the rule of law is mere rhetoric but rather that it has tended to be shorthand for legitimation claims in widely different sets of circumstances. That a society should be informed by cogent ideals relating to order, rule-governed behaviour, opposition to arbitrariness, looser or stronger versions of accountability – but that such congeries of beliefs should gain expression in different ways and conjure up different expectations at different times – should occasion no surprise. This seems to be precisely what has happened in Britain, though we shall argue that the present is a period of dissonance in the relationship between the ideals and their forms of expression.

As an illustration, we might remind ourselves that when the principle of representation was in its infancy those who were selected acted not on behalf of people, but of property. Even after it became understood that they attended Parliament as much for the object of consulting on national affairs as for that of supplementing the financial resources of the Crown, their influence for a long time remained slight.[41]

The terminology of the Great Reform Act of 1832, speaking as it did of the 'representation of the people', attested the victory of a constitutional principle more revolutionary than the enlargement of the electorate introduced by the Act itself. However, by the mid nineteenth century representative government had come to be regarded as coincident with representative democracy.[42] Similarly, we could cite the transformation of Parliament from its pre-revolutionary role into the central focus of national government: from its seventeenth-century position as the place where local interests were pursued it had become by the late nineteenth century the site of party government where competing national programmes were contested. Simultaneously, the law of the predominantly rural and aristocratic society of the eighteenth century was recast and adapted to the needs of the predominantly industrial and increasingly democratic society of the nineteenth century.[43]

Parliament, the executive and the rule of law

The language of government under law and the representative nature of Parliament are constant themes in English constitutional history but at each point the appeals which they represent tend to disguise the reality of public power to a greater or lesser extent. Thus Maitland pointed out that the reign of Edward IV represented what has come to be called 'the new monarchy' although the limits of royal power erected in earlier centuries remained as they were. In the changed circumstances the king was beginning to discover that parliamentary institutions could be made the engines of his will.[44] We shall show in Part Two that the modern executive long ago mastered this particular art, though the rhetorical appeals to the authority of Parliament are just as regularly made.

The incremental and pragmatic development of British constitutional politics has plainly contributed greatly to this state of affairs. Douglas Ashford has, as a transatlantic observer, keenly appreciated this, though as a student of government he retains considerable affection and respect for the stability of British institutions. He singles Britain out among modern democracies for not laying down clear principles concerning the interrelationships of key political actors and institutions and for saying too little generally about executive obligation. The undisturbed history of social and political life is a major cause of the subordination of principle to pragmatism and of the failure clearly to distinguish societal consensus from the specific conduct of government. This tradition not only conceals the ability to judge how well elite consensus affects policy-making but effectively disenfranchises British electors who 'are only free at the moment they cast their ballots' not being possessed, so to speak, of reserved powers.[45] Furthermore, however strong public support for the British system of government in the abstract, the regular patterns of governmental behaviour are largely a mystery to the average elector who no doubt would wish to have the accommodation of interests and lobbies put upon an observable footing rather than going along with the pretence that no such relationships exist.[46]

It is not difficult to illustrate how political legitimation in Britain, or giving substance to the rule of law, has been more or less consciously kept off the agenda. In the nineteenth century the trappings of modern democracy were superimposed on an existing constitutional structure, and a modern administration similarly grafted on to pre-existing patterns of government. Because no real crisis of legitimacy occurred, the need to pledge inalienable rights, to set firm limits to the exercise of executive power or to speak specifically to tailored forms of redress against the state was never felt to be as strong a need in Britain as elsewhere.

Given the British genius for maintaining political stability, questions concerning the inner content of notions like the rule of law were never seriously posed, although even some of our most sober constitutional scholars pay implicit homage to the constitutional role of the people.[47] For such a role to be meaningful it seems to us that at the very least the ability to scrutinize power in the light of performance is required. The basic transition which is needed is from a blanket certification of the *source* of power to a sustained justification of its *use*.[48] Among legal constitutional scholars Sir Ivor Jennings, because he operated upon the real difficulties of the constitution so much more openly than most of his contemporaries, exposed most clearly the inadequacies of constitutional theory in relation to this issue. The principles of 1689 became for him the accepted theory of democracy whereby ultimate power must reside in a representative assembly: such assembly guaranteeing the conditions upon which it, and therefore the electorate, are able to make informed judgements. That is, of course, precisely what we do not possess, and recognition of this state of affairs caused him subsequently to engage, as we have already noted, in a mass of incoherent propositions including the assertion that 'strictly speaking . . . there is no constitutional law in Great Britain; there is only the arbitrary power of Parliament'.[49] Now there is widespread agreement, at least among political scientists, that even setting aside the deficiencies of this proposition as constitutional aspiration it is neither a current operational truth nor a remotely possible one. Whatever the motives of policy-makers themselves, the complexity of decisions and their unforeseen consequences make plenary decision-making largely impracticable.[50]

There is little argument that such difficulties beset all modern legislatures and all modern governments, but British constitutional institutions disguise these facts more than almost any other Western democracy, while our claims for freedom under the law are among the most insistent. E. C. S. Wade argued in 1939 that the political supremacy of Parliament as a law-making organ was becoming more and more of a fiction and the state of affairs he was describing has since become even more complicated.

What we find then is that most serious commentators speak the general language of accountable nationhood, of underlying expectations, while finding it extraordinarily difficult to identify constitutional guarantees. Rather, the institutional apparatus remains remarkably stable while periodically local debates rage which are accommodated by gestures little or large but rarely of a fundamental kind. Even these have a habit of being swallowed whole by the executive supremacy of different periods and ages.

Emden, for example, speaks generally of a problem of institutional accountability and refers to the fact that the growth of party politics and party government was intended to democratize a process which would otherwise ensure that the House of Commons lay at the mercy of the occupant of the throne. Yet he observed, as have others, the degeneration of party as a potential democratic instrument. The concept of 'mandate' Emden saw as a form of *restriction* of the tyranny of party government, but he was remarkably uncertain as to its ambit, just as years before the ambit of the prerogative had been the subject of intense debate. Everyone was in agreement that those in control had to be in some measure or by some means accountable – it was simply a question of how precisely it was to be achieved.[51] The following remarks are instructive in this regard:

> though it is rarely formulated as a conventional rule the most obvious and undisputed convention of the British constitutional system is that Parliament does not use its unlimited sovereign power of legislation in an oppressive or tyrannical way. That is a vague but clearly accepted conventional rule resting on the principle of constitutionalism and the rule of law. . . .
>
> [A]lthough [conventions] . . . do not always modify legal powers, the major purpose of the domestic conventions is to give effect to the principles of governmental accountability that constitute the structure of responsible government.[52]

What Geoffrey Marshall has identified in these passages is a major, if not the major strain of our immanent set of cultural beliefs. Nowhere is it entrenched that Parliaments will not behave in an oppressive fashion nor can we find scripture referring or relating to the principles of governmental accountability, but we are assured that they are the essence of the rule of law. In this respect we entertain no doubts that Marshall as constitutional authority is at one with popular clamour. However, British governments do periodically behave oppressively, and the governmental machine at large can scarcely be regarded as being systematically accountable.

Parliament, institutions, the rule of law and accountability

When Poggi spoke of Parliament being 'shunted away' from the effective centre of a country's life he was not speaking just about

Britain, yet in Britain Parliament retains a peculiar importance as the chief institutional link between the citizenry and the state. Bagehot, in effect, saw the function of the Commons as neither to legislate nor to administer, but to elect a business-like board to rule the country and then to keep an eye on its proceedings.[53]

Now keeping an eye on things and rendering government accountable in a systematic way are plainly two different things. It may be that we do not want executive power to be accountable in any effective sense, in which case we can simply concur with Crossman's paraphrase of Bagehot that

Good government depends on the discovery of some device for inducing into the masses a respect for their superiors, and persuading them not to use the power of the majority in order to overthrow law and order. It is the main task of political science, Plato says, to work out the technique through which the acquiescence of the many in the rule of the few can be achieved.[54]

On the other hand, if we do not subscribe to the concept of 'the noble lie' – if we are serious about the rule of law – then we shall need to examine the facts of public power against institutional responses for according it some measure of respect. The British constitutional record is very mixed with a whole series of pragmatic responses to developments and pressures superimposed upon remarkably stable institutions. British constitutional history is littered with changes which were often accompanied by extremely dubious, not to say spurious, rhetoric while managing occasionally to effect tangible improvements. The revolution of 1688 for example would have seemed a good deal less glorious to the mass of the people had they been told that one of its primary objectives was to preserve the property rights of the aristocracy. However, as the eighteenth century wore on and the landed aristocracy itself became increasingly associated with the executive branch of government, the very measures they had obtained to protect themselves against the Crown began to be used against them by the people. No doubt Whig historians may have exaggerated the impartiality of the judges and the integrity of the rule of law, but neither was wholly mythical.[55]

E. P. Thompson has identified the paradox whereby the rule of law was used by the powerful to lend the rhetoric of legitimacy to their hegemony during the eighteenth and nineteenth centuries even though it had earlier enjoyed a nobler parentage. Yet ironically, at a later stage, they were forced to come to terms with its powerful symbolism in order to preserve their own self-image.[56]

Legal autonomy then, quite leaving aside the content of the substantive law, has had a chequered and not consistently principled history. In this respect it resembles so much else that partakes of our constitutional heritage. Atiyah has spoken of England stumbling into the modern administrative state without design and even contrary to the inclinations of most Englishmen. Even the lawyers were not aware of the revolution that had taken place as legislation multiplied, for in substantial measure the vast new body of law was not enforced by lawyers at all. Its implementation lay, in the first instance, in the hands of the new bureaucracy, the new administrative staff and their expert advisers who were multiplying so rapidly in the middle of the century.[57]

This extraordinary growth was largely overlooked by Dicey, so much so that Lord Hewart's famous polemic against *The New Despotism* published in 1929, seemed to operate on the assumption that the administrative state was exclusively a product of the twentieth century.[58] In fact, constitutional institutions have been remarkably stable throughout these many vicissitudes and parliamentary sovereignty has maintained its cultural and popular pre-eminence. Power though, has moved elsewhere while the inner nature of the rule of law has not been readdressed in institutional terms to examine processes of genuine accountability. It has to be admitted that British society has retained a high degree of confidence in the system. This, however, is almost certainly because citizens remain unaware of its workings.[59]

The central traditions and institutions of our stable polity would be in no way imperilled by the introduction of methods of institutional accountability complementary to Parliament. These would be directed to ensuring that choices were made in an atmosphere of genuine information about alternative courses of action. This after all is what is logically entailed by a representative democracy.

The rule of law: a summary

The rule of law is symbolic: it is a transcendent phenomenon in that, although its symbolism is appealed to in different ways at different times, it is almost always shorthand for some interpretation of the inner meaning of a polity. It speaks for the general will of the nation or nations, such will making different demands at different periods. It is, in any event, highly connotative. In the England of the fifteenth century its force was that the king was always subordinate to a higher law of somewhat uncertain provenance.[60] The doctrine had been recognized in some form or another from a very early period in English history and was usually associated with the idea that some version of justice according to law was due to all. Whether or not the rule of law was seen as a bridle on royal power, it had for very long periods been seen as the bond uniting the various parts of the body politic.[61] After the revolution, ostensibly a contest between King and Parliament, the doctrine became clearly associated with the idea of the Lockean liberal state. Even these ideas however had deep roots within English intellectual and political life which were occasionally seen as a local encashment of a universal legal order.[62]

The rule of law is a symbol of the legitimating force of the whole notion of constitutionality, which nevertheless undergoes substantial periodic alteration while clinging to the same rhetoric. The medieval notion of the rule of law, for instance, informed the spirit of the American revolution and held sway in that country for some considerable time before the classical liberal traditions overtook the older habits of mind. The prerevolutionary versions of the concept in both countries partook of the view that society and government were locked into an organic union, that government was subject to fundamental law and that the legal, political and religious realms intermingled. Horwitz has shown how the unalloyed doctrines were eventually distilled in nineteenth-century America, but in Britain theories of sovereignty less enamoured of Lockean contract had already transmuted the rule of law into something very different indeed. The language in which it was celebrated remained, however, substantially unaltered.[63]

The post-Lockean version of the rule of law, associated as it was with the views of the classical liberal theorists, conflated legitimacy, legality and, not least, legal autonomy. The form of law became itself 'the golden metwand', the 'potent fiction'. Thereafter and for many years, the contrast between a law-based and a lawless polity was the contrast between rule-governed and non-rule-governed behaviour, the latter being equated with arbitrariness. The autonomy of the legal order began to play a role in legitimating capitalist society in that a logically formal legal order appeared as a neutral and autonomous source of normative guidance which lent authority to the liberal state.[64] Power and authority were thereby rendered impersonal and fair, not at the command of any particular faction of society. As a formal ideal, the rule of law was seen as demanding that governmental power must be exercised within the constraints of rules that apply uniformly to general classes of persons or acts. The institutional aspect of this idea is the autonomous judiciary and the concept *nulla poena sine lege*, no punishment without a law.[65]

As has frequently been remarked, this is to say nothing of the substantive nature of the ideal, and therein resides the classic weakness of reliance on the form of law, understood merely as a set of authoritative rules. This weakness is rescued in orthodox doctrine by appeals to a universally accessible legislature, for the rule of law in its revised sense requires that laws be made by a procedure to which everyone might have reason to agree in his or her own self-interest. More especially, it insists that each person participate somehow in the process of law-making. It is therefore expected that the legal order will possess the attribute of substantive autonomy: it will represent a balance struck among competing groups rather than the embodiment of the interests and ideals of a particular faction.[66]

Each of the major planks of the liberal version of the rule of law proves on examination to be largely fictitious. Not only does it ignore the realities of power and influence within the social system at large, but in the British context the notion of equal access to decision-making through Parliament is largely mythical. Contemporary decision-making processes are significantly insulated from democratic politics and consequently demean the larger civic expectations. Even the older experiences of British politics failed to match the idealized versions, for the difference between the theory and practice of representation was considerable.[67] In the Elizabethan period legislation was promoted and opposed on behalf of boroughs, crafts, companies and individuals, often in a context of intensive lobbying. This is in spite of the fact that in origin the rule-based, classical, version of the rule of law depended on a view of contractual marketism that was intimately connected with equal freedoms, choice and a strong degree of decentralization. That is, after all, precisely what contract in its purest form ought to achieve. Indeed both contract and property rights may be seen as the embodiment of a relatively decentralized economic order which clearly offers some resistance to concentrations of arbitrary power. In some quarters this system is still viewed as directly allied to the cause of freedom and even as part of the necessary definition of freedom itself.[68]

In spite of the great expectations invested in such a system and, indeed, in spite of its manifest achievements, material discrepancies and irregularities of a high order can play havoc with any version of the rule of law based upon even the slimmest notions of free and equal citizenship. However, in the development of our argument it is important to understand that it would be a mistake to invest one single jurisprudential theory with all the hopes and aspirations of the rule of law. Thus in the time of Blackstone, or even Coke for that matter, the British constitution and English law were a mosaic of enactments and customs and conventions which, because they came from all periods of English history, represented divergent ideas taken from many periods of that history.

Be that as it may, for all the changes that have taken place since the nineteenth century in political, industrial and social structures we seem to have become stuck in a constitutional time-warp. The state still functions in our time within and through political and juridical forms derived from the liberal-democratic nineteenth-century constitution. It does so to an extent sufficient partly to disguise and partly to limit the changes in the substance of the political process, but at the same time it modifies and distorts the forms themselves.[69]

Given that Bagehot had observed and remarked upon this state of affairs in the middle of the nineteenth century, it is odd that so little has been made of it by constitutional lawyers since that time. For when speaking of the cleavage between the 'dignified' and the 'efficient' parts of the constitution he identified the emergence of 'a disguised republic' which had largely been successful in concealing from the masses the revolutionary shift of power that had taken place behind the constitutional facade.[70] What is missing is a rigorous examination of the institutional machinery operating behind the facade. It needs to be readdressed in the light of the underlying sentiments implied by a rule of law idiom which denies the possibility of caprice, faction and closet.

The manifest failure of our legal structure to come to terms with the realities of contemporary operational power is not a unique failure. It is reflected across most Western systems of government.

The 'crisis' of autonomous law exists because law, particularly in its conceptual structures, has not yet adapted to the exigencies of a highly differentiated society. Legal doctrine is still bound to the classical model of law as a body of rules enforceable through adjudication. The legal order lacks a conceptual apparatus adequate for the planning and social policy requirements that arise in the interrelations among specialized social subsystems.[71]

None the less, that the problems we identify are general problems of modernity does nothing to justify the failure of our legal system to provide an adequate response to the problem of citizen reenfranchisement and the needs of a mature institutional learning system.

Constitutional accountability: a thin gruel

We have shown that constitutional accountability in Britain has normally been thought of either in terms of the ability to recall governments and appoint replacements periodically (the ability of Parliament to call decision-making to account); or of the guarantees afforded by the common law and the judges; or some combination of these two. It seems clear to us that none of these nor any combination of them has produced or is likely to produce such accountability, whether or not the fact is popularly understood. That it is widely understood by the inquiring is hardly in doubt, though when attention is periodically drawn to this state of affairs the position always seems about to be miraculously improved. For example, it has become evident to a growing number of people that parliamentary redress of grievances does not match up to the dignified claims for its authority, especially in the period since the end of the Second World War. Yet, since the 1960s this observation has not infrequently been accompanied by suggestions that the judiciary, previously perceived as somewhat constitutionally un-adventurous, might be about to restore the balance in favour of the citizen.[72] This was especially felt to be the case when judicial constitutional torpor was apparently being stirred by a series of decisions in the 1960s which subjected a tribunal to judicial review even in the face of a statutory exclusion clause, quashed a minister's decision for failure to promote the purpose of the statute which conferred the power on him, and imposed traditional norms of fair procedure on a decision-making process affecting an individual.[73] As we shall outline in Chapter 7, not only was this never likely to prove an adequate substitute, but it has resolutely proven not to be so. This is nowhere more marked than in the failure of the courts to structure discretion by developing a general duty to give reasons for decisions. Even so, the fact that it was felt necessary to disguise the diminution of parliamentary prestige is itself an important recognition of the force of rhetoric in British constitutional lore, most strikingly of course in relation to the rule of law ideal.

Delivery, as opposed to rhetoric, seems to move in cycles with particular gains being observable at various times, only for further developments in the structure and practices of government to create new forms of unaccountability. This in turn is followed by rhetorical assurances of further concessions and renewed appeals to the reawakened power of the most recently underplayed component of the constitutional settlement. For instance, prior to universal suffrage the rule of law and the constitution were guaranteed by the common law (and after 1701 by an independent judiciary). With the rise of mass parties and democratization of the suffrage parliamentary sovereignty unsurprisingly became the guarantor of constitutional accountability with Parliament itself as the universal provider. Thus the major state developments which were occurring went unnoticed, unremarked or were presumed to be magically taken care of by institutional machinery developed hundreds of years earlier. We discuss later the powerful networks of decision-making in Britain which are woven into a pattern of relationships with the executive power. Suffice it to say at this point that Middlemas's study of *Politics in Industrial Society*[74] indicates how a massively powerful strain in twentieth-century British politics went substantially undetected as a major force in the British state. Although it was fairly late before 'corporatism' became a political buzzword in Britain, many commentators were exposing the inability of traditional institutions to provide accountability which the conventional wisdom assumed:

in a period when effective power in all spheres of life – economic, social, political – is being concentrated in fewer and fewer hands, parliamentary control of the executive has been steadily decreasing, without being replaced by other methods of democratic control.[75]

The natural response was to see the equilibrium being restored by reassertion of the powers of the judiciary. No serious attempt to mould the judiciary into a constitutional force adequate to control the executive was made after the opportunity to re-examine the whole of administrative law was rejected by the Wilson government in 1969 in favour of a limited inquiry into remedies. The subsequent history of the reform of administrative law we leave over to Chapter 7. Before that, however, an excursus on the nature and symbolism of the common law should help to piece together the component parts of the peculiarly British rule of law form.

The courts and the common law

The two pillars of the revolution settlement and the central aspects of the orthodox version of the rule of law are, as we have seen, the supremacy of an elected Parliament and an independent judiciary administering the common law. We have argued that periodically, as one of the two pillars has shown itself to be on the verge of crumbling, defenders of the orthodoxy have sought to demonstrate just how strongly reinforced the other has been. Subsequently the process is reversed but at all times one or the other, and occasionally both, will offer the contemporary guarantee of all things secure and just.

'The common law' is one of those most effective of all pieces of mystification. Almost to the same extent as the rule of law itself, it has been invested in Britain with magical powers and its rhetoric has at times even echoed what Rousseau called the general will.

There is no doubt that the concept of traditional, 'common' law, administered by an independent judiciary played a vital, perhaps *the* vital role in promoting the idea of legal autonomy, a matter we have already touched upon. In performing this task its significance should not be underestimated and its importance in marginalizing arbitrary power, particularly within the immediate historical context of its emergence, must not be underplayed. None the less it has over the centuries been invoked by those wielding effective power within the community as some kind of universal redeemer. It became to arbitrariness and partisan government what the Christian cross affects to be to vampires. This, needless to say, was to claim too much.

Dicey, in addressing the containment of governmental excesses, spoke both of judicial control and of ministerial responsibility to Parliament. But, as we have noted, his emphasis was very substantially upon the former, and in particular on individual liberty of action and how it is guarded by the courts. His argument was that the courts afford remedies for all illegalities by whomsoever committed, and that these were at least as effective as the guarantees contained in a formal constitution of the continental European type.[76]

For Dicey then the rules of law which inform the constitution were not the source but the consequence of the rights of individuals as defined and enforced by the courts. The principles of private law had through Parliament and the courts been extended so as to determine the position of the Crown and its servants and thus the constitution was the result of the ordinary law of the land.[77] Now this was never strictly true but in any event the vast administrative apparatus of the state was not only different in kind from power exercised by ordinary individuals but for the most part was largely unsupervised by the courts. Being also suffused with fairly broad areas of discretion it was therefore already in Dicey's own sense, to a considerable extent 'arbitrary'. This is in spite of the fact that the rule of law had come to mean the supremacy not only of the common law and the rest of the law of England which Parliament had seen fit to leave undisturbed, but also regular law as opposed to arbitrary power, prerogative or even wide discretionary authority of government.[78]

Dicey clearly associated the common law with the assertion of 'the rights of the nation'. This is unsurprising given Dicey's general acceptance of the revolution settlement as the basis of the constitution. Parliamentary leaders during the seventeenth century began to see that the independence of the judiciary was the sole security for the maintenance of the common law which was nothing else but the rule of established customs modified only by Acts of Parliament, that process occurring by some unspoken law of natural balance. When Chief Justice Coke battled in the seventeenth century for the power of the judiciary he saw himself as asserting the rights of the nation and, although he was ultimately unsuccessful, the common law did achieve a remarkable recuperation. This was assisted by the Act of Settlement which according to Holdsworth gave the courts the great position which they occupy in the modern constitution. This process was the touchstone of the rule of law in that an independent judiciary was simultaneously able to protect the sacred liberties of the subject, to inculcate a law-abiding habit in the nation by dint of their impartiality, and to ground the authority of the state in the rule of law as opposed to the rule of men. This linkage of the common law, the general will of the people, and the rights of the nation to the existence of an independent judiciary lent credibility to the real governance of the nation by Parliament.[79]

Within this framework the expectation of the common lawyers was that Parliament would leave the central features of the common law largely untouched so that the common law of the constitution would continue to guarantee individual liberty, liberty of discussion, freedom of assembly and rights of property. E. C. S. Wade in his introduction to Dicey, speaks to the partial continuation of this silent understanding by pointing out that although a vast body of administrative law and practice had begun to submerge the older accords, at least general libertarian traditions had been maintained. It does not need us to show the ungrounded optimism of this latter observation since the importance of the remark lies in the association of an idealized common law with at least some major proportion of the symbolism associated with the rule of law.

A weakening of the old libertarian accords was visible even to Wade, yet it was in identifying the massive changes in the nature of the administrative state that he was able to exemplify the glaring deficiencies of the orthodox version of a state under law. The common law, he argued, rested upon an individualistic conception of society and lacked the means of enforcing public rights as such, particularly where a framework of regulation has, for its object, the welfare of the public as a whole or at least a large section of it.[80] The implications of this remark are twofold. First, in terms of a commitment to open and accountable structures, in the absence of rigorous administrative law procedures the common law has little or nothing to say. Second, and this is an associated item, if the rule of law amounts to a faith in the nation rendering an account unto itself through law, then our concept of what constitutes the legal must be expanded to include the whole of legitimate institutional public power. We shall address this vital argument in Chapter 3.

The revolutionary settlement had proceeded upon the basis that a reconstituted Parliament would work in harness with a re-invigorated common law, administered (ultimately) by an independent judiciary. Such common law would not be lightly countermanded in its essentials for it was, after all, an emanation of social prehistory. The common law in Coke's time was certainly of great antiquity and, being the only law which England had ever known, it was necessarily 'immemorial' and to that extent hallowed.[81] This symbolism was retained, and no doubt nurtured by parliamentarians who were looking to buttress their own legitimacy. At a much later period legitimacy began to be provided by universal suffrage and a universal franchise. When Parliament in turn was criticized for its lack of consensual deliberation and accountability then the vindication became once again the common law and the judiciary. What we see then is a kind of yo-yo dialectic. The common law was at all times an essential component of the rule of law which operated as an extraordinarily potent fiction whose influence has only recently been examined closely. It was not all it claimed to be, yet it clearly did serve to protect the liberties of citizens sufficiently to carry enough conviction to act as a larger legitimating symbol.

As E. P. Thompson and others have shown, the common law and the rule of law were not simply crudely-based class instruments of justice:

When seventeenth and eighteenth-century Englishmen thought of the law, they thought not only of the criminal law and its preoccupation with theft, but of the common law in its broadest sense and of the body of regulation and equitable practice which oiled the social mechanism and mediated disputes of all kinds, including those that occurred within as well as between classes.[82]

Thus the widespread acceptance of the law was in no small measure owing to the fact that it constrained authority and limited those who tried to manipulate the legal process. Had it been purely a means of legitimizing private power and initiatives it could never have gained the hold on the popular imagination which it achieved. So powerful was the symbolism that when legal due was denied to a clamouring citizenry it was capable of behaving in a distinctly lawless fashion.[83] None the less, an appeal to this common prescription should not be allowed to conceal the considerable divergencies of opinion about what the rule of law entailed. There were also celebrated incidents in English history where legal claims also operated as competing statements about and attempts to achieve a particular sort of polity.[84] Thus the common law/rule of law culture could be seen as synonymous with the legitimacy of the political order, and constitutional machinery (the inner resonance of law) may usefully be seen as a method of enfranchising competing interests, as between citizens and their organizations and the larger state apparatus. This is a matter about which we shall have much to say later.

In concluding this section we wish to underline the fact that, although the guarantee of the English compact has been seen to be some kind of mix or fusion of the common law and an elected assembly, there is little real doubt that effective power in the last two hundred years has flowed through Parliament. Holdsworth might well argue that the supremacy of the common law was guaranteed by Parliament and that the common lawyers could safely leave Parliament with custody of the common law traditions, but this was a claim increasingly difficult to sustain as time wore on. Even Dicey recognized implicitly that the supremacy of law had become the supremacy of Parliament. His response was to claim that, provided the legal sovereign is a parliamentary assembly, exercises of 'arbitrary sovereign power' assume the form of regular legislation and maintain in no small degree the real no less than the apparent supremacy of the law.[85] Dicey would no doubt have been horrified to know that Hegel could have associated himself with this sentiment without any difficulty.

Choice, democratic form and polity

Little we have said concerning the gap between the rule of law orthodoxy and the realities of the administrative state is really very new; it is its relatively tardy discovery by legal scholars that should cause surprise. Even a century or more ago the relationship between the public and the private spheres was not quite what orthodoxy proclaimed and no real attempts were made to afford information to the public at large about the complexities of the newly-emergent administrative state. We now realize, for instance, that when the first railway companies were created in the nineteenth century not only were accounting requirements rudimentary in the extreme but governments positively rejected demands for public auditing to protect shareholders.[86] Such opposition to formal canons of accountability is rarely highlighted in constitutional texts which offer little invitation to examine the historical links between public and private behaviour.

More than a hundred years on, we are faced with an even greater degree of public/private interpenetration, continued secrecy, some active institutional concealment, little change in the machinery of accountability and a most formidable elaboration of the agenda of government. To cope with this agenda, calls for increased skills both in policy formation and execution and reform must be sought as much in political institutions as in administrative systems.[87] Periodically we shall speak to the matter of freely accessible information in a democracy and it may be as well to state our position clearly and firmly at the outset. Freedom of information is a prerequisite of a free society and any form of democratic polity. This *sine qua non* of a constitutional order cannot be undermined by reference to exceptions regarding state security, commercial sensitivity or the like, for exceptions need to be justified by reference to the central criterion of open debate freely conducted on the basis of full information. Choosing representatives, parliamentary control, or accountability in any of its many forms are shams without familiarity with the record of government. This is what we meant when we said in Chapter 1 that freely accessible information as a general and essential proposition was a necessary entailment of claims about the British constitution. It must be the case that representative democracy entails choosing with the fullest information available or the game is rigged at the outset. The logic of choice also assumes that freely accessible information must characterize the political process *systematically* or the periodic choice once again runs the risk of being rigged by whoever is withholding the information. The logic of the rhetoric then requires freedom of information, though we are patently denied it in the British practice of government. On the public level we operate to *prevent* free trade in information and on many occasions our political processes have encouraged or at least empowered active concealment. On occasion information about British government can be discovered by British citizens only with the help of United States freedom of information legislation. In retirement, of course, even the most senior of civil servants will admit that the British obsession with secrecy is indefensible but its continued practice contemporaneously allows the flouting of democratic traditions and the encouragement of general incompetence.[88]

When a select committee of the House of Commons can attack a government white paper on expenditure on the basis that the information contained is inadequate and that economic projections are absurd, and yet fail to prevent Treasury prescriptions being forced on an unwilling House of Commons which is then treated to even scantier information in subsequent years, then something is seriously wrong.[89] And yet, as problems multiply and objectives become more ambitious, government requires more organizational support, touches a wider range of interests, requires more information, and needs more careful monitoring of its activities.[90]

The larger dimension of constitutionality

The issue of freedom of information represents not only a crucial aspect of an immanent critique of the legitimation claims of the British constitution but also has broader implications for the nature of constitutionality in all modern societies. Adopting what he terms the 'dialectically necessary method' of analysing the logical implications of what it is to be a being capable of action, Alan Gewirth argues that certain minimum conditions of accountability, which he designates the 'method of consent', must be met for any society to be regarded as truly human. This involves the constitutional requirement that each person is able to discuss, criticize and vote for or against the government of the day and to work actively with other persons in groups of various sizes to further perceived political objectives including the redress of socially-based grievances. However, he goes on to say that these minimum conditions need to be buttressed in a contingent or circumstantial but continuing process which relates to continuing problems of redistributive justice.[91] He is here making a moral defence of arguments which have also been put forward by a number of social theorists, most consistently perhaps Habermas, that free constitutions are a kind of organized competition between alternative views and policies, which Habermas calls discourse and of which a general election is simply the culmination. Provided that a hard look is taken at the areas of major controversy it is a contingent matter as to the form of many of the institutional arrangements for securing the conditions. Nonet and Selznick go so far as to say that the problems under analysis in this section are largely evolutionary and that evolutionary legal responses are a necessary concomitant. They adopt the view that democracy is shorthand for an array of principles which reveal the capacity of a system to address the problems of seeking the consent of the governed. The increasing complexity of the public sphere requires that we move from legitimation of a casual or sporadic form to legitimation in depth. This means exposing power and policy-making to scrutiny in the light of performance.[92]

People in a democracy should then be free to learn what facts they please about their own system of government. Moreover, choice in its most complete sense connotes antecedent informed deliberation between alternatives and a reasoned decision based on that deliberation.[93] A single assembly in modern conditions is incapable of examining ranges of policies and policy alternatives and to this extent the peculiarly British cultural and historical traditions exacerbate the problems which any modern democracy could expect to face. The complexity of modern systems is also such that a deep-structured democracy is necessary for a society's own learning processes. Not only are our parliamentary institutions currently inadequate to the performance of these tasks, but our legal system has also failed to come to terms with such requirements. Modern societies need to inform themselves of the range of issues and interests which group life requires and unless a legal order provides a wholly different approach to the allocation of access to decision-making processes then there is little prospect that conditions for the rule of law in a modern setting will be met. What is needed is a theory of the public interest that can enhance the rationality of political discourse. Instead, what tends to lie behind our constitutional axioms is a system of power politics which deals in raw conflict and the less than open accommodation of special interests. If we are to match our inner expectations and redeem the claims which are embedded deep within the concept of the rule of law, a set of forms aimed at encouraging an open learning process is necessary.[94] Let us conclude this chapter with an attempt to bring up to date one major strain of Dicey's defence of rule of law orthodoxy: *viz.* the absence of arbitrary behaviour. If arbitrariness is, even in substantial measure, equatable with unaccountable conduct then we shall need to address the concerns attendant upon it in light of contemporary patterns of bureaucratic discretion.

Discretion and arbitrariness

There can be little doubt that the absence of wide discretionary power which, for Dicey, was essentially the same as opposition to arbitrary conduct, was so closely associated with the rule of law and the British constitution that they became almost indistinguishable concepts. What might be thought extraordinary is not that Dicey and his contemporaries could unite to oppose unaccountable discretion and the possibility of factions holding the nation hostage but that he was unaware of the existence of such possibilities in the England of his time. The likely explanation is that Dicey saw the constitution in terms of individual liberties and nothing else: the *powers* of authorities as such, the overall legitimate conduct of the new bureaucracies seemed outwith his analysis altogether. Regardless of the accuracy of his faith in the fact of British civil liberties, it was laissez-faire that seemed to him to represent the cornerstone of constitutional guarantees. The judges would or should protect the individual's right to pursue his or her own self-interest. Not only was this analysis defective and short-sighted but it was accompanied by the stated belief that individuals would be well protected by the English constitution provided that, they did 'not meddle in politics'.[95] This statement, extraordinary in itself, says volumes about the relationship between laws and constitutions and between laws and political structures; matters of which we shall have more to say, particularly in Chapter 7.

By 1915 Dicey seemed, according to some, to have had something of a change of heart, though our reading is that he was too
wedded to old faiths to be able to come to terms with the modern
state. True, he had begun to observe the transfer of decision-
making processes from the courts to the executive and he lamented
that such transference of authority was sapping the foundation of
that rule of law which had for him and preceding generations been a
leading feature of the British constitution. Yet even so, he was able
to dissemble to a remarkable degree in, for example, adding that
by becoming involved in matters of welfare and commerce, the state
was really engaged in business like any other private manufacturer,
and that everyone knew that such trading could not be conducted
according to constitutional principles. Business was business and
the business of governing something else besides! On the other
hand he was clearer than many later commentators that ministerial
accountability to Parliament or to cabinet was a very feeble guarantee against action which evades the authority of the law courts.
None the less, at the end of the day, the courts of law (not to
mention the possibility of impeachment!) would save us from the
scourge of *droit administratif*,[96] that system of continental
European administrative law which Dicey had so mischaracterized.

The general failure to analyse the relationship between the
principles underlying the rule of law and the less than accountable
state of the British polity should now be clear. The administrative
state had arrived if not without notice, then at least without adequate announcement. If Dicey and other lawyers of his generation
had not been so enslaved by the narrow law concept to which they
were firmly anchored their exegesis of British constitutional law
might have been very different indeed. For, after all, the difference
between judicial and administrative agencies is not fundamental in
that both apply the law to individual cases and thereby exercise a
discretion.[97] Failure to understand that simple proposition is likely
to mean that safeguards are too rarely attached to the behaviour of
administrative bodies. As we have seen, it can be argued that
Dicey's most serious error was his inability to come to terms with
the broad policy powers which the new state had reposed in the
administrative machine.

It has become common ground that regulation and state tutelage
have increased dramatically since the time of Dicey's writing and
that the number and power of officials has similarly increased. What
has not always seemed to follow is the necessity for increasing

popular control as a concomitant, rather than an injunction to the masses not to 'meddle' in politics. What we should be proclaiming is that the rule of law, when closely scrutinized, requires that we oppose arbitrary and untrammeled behaviour whatever its provenance and whatever conceptual shape it assumes; that fair procedures, rational discourse and being called to account for public behaviour are of its essence. Even if valid lines can be drawn between adjudication and administration it is clear that the two phenomena are simply different points on a spectrum. Perhaps, as Selznick has argued, administration entails a weaker commitment to legality but it does not follow that legality is foreign to the ethos of administration.[98] We ought by now to accept the lucid analysis of this fake dichotomy which Lauterpacht presented to public lawyers more than fifty years ago.

He explained that attempts to establish a rigid line of demarcation between judicial and administrative justice had proved inevitably unsuccessful. The futility of these efforts was seen to be even more obvious than in the parallel attempt to find a clear line of demarcation between the legislative and judicial function. The difference between judicial and administrative adjudications, far from being of a fundamental character, is to a large extent grounded in the historical experience of absolutist and bureaucratic states, wherein the rule of executive departments was tantamount to the reign of arbitrariness. Remove the judicial safeguards from ordinary courts and they will become administrative bodies. Add these safeguards to the latter and they will become courts of law in all but name. Although the identification of administrative justice with the absence of law may be explained historically and psychologically as a reaction against the shortcomings and dangers of purely administrative decisions, there is no warrant for the view that the latter stands outside the realm of law or that it ever should.[99]

Where does this lead us? First it is clear that arbitrariness is the declared enemy of the rule of law and that arbitrary behaviour is and has been extensive in Britain if one examines the whole state apparatus and its informal understandings with private power configurations. Furthermore, given the contemporary map of public power a simple appeal to rule-governed behaviour is not a sufficient condition of rediscovering the ancient ideal. In spite of a strongly rooted historical attachment to the belief that the establishment of rules will banish arbitrary and despotic power[100] we should not be easily beguiled. Thus, not only must the concept of arbitrary behaviour be closely scrutinized but it must be placed against a contemporary map of public power to test the currency of conformity to the rule of law. We must abandon the idea that arbitrary behaviour consists only in the tyrannical oddities of absolutist rule and recognize that rules, for instance, are made arbitrarily when appropriate interests are not consulted and when there is no clear relation between the rule enunciated and the end to be achieved. Rules are arbitrary when they reflect confused policies, are based on ignorance or error and when they suggest no inherent principles of criticism. They are arbitrary when the legal system, broadly described as the institutionalization of legitimate public power, is incapable of taking account of new interests and circumstances and adapting to change.[101]

We shall argue later that no guarantee against arbitrary conduct can be assured where courts adopt a 'crystal-ball' approach to the resolution of tough questions. This, the essentially 'soft' form of judicial review inherent in the *Wednesbury* test,[102] discussed in Chapter 7, still dominates administrative law doctrine in Britain. To adopt an American approach, we can say that the unsolved problem of regulatory reform is to perfect an interest-representation model which will import political checks into the administrative arena.[103] It is not only regulation *per se* which needs such an infusion to overcome problems of excessive discretion and potentially arbitrary behaviour, but the whole governmental process and in particular the executive/administrative machine. In order to construct institutions for accountable behaviour and open discourse and learning we require an independent model of administrative decision-making.[104] We develop suggestions concerning the nature of such an independent model in Chapters 8 and 9 and need only say at this point that until the administrative process is subjected to a procedure which has at its heart a concern for fairness, accuracy and acceptability then the canons of even the traditional version of the rule of law will not have been observed.

References

1 *Law and Society in Transition: Toward Responsive Law* (New York: Harper and Row 1978) p. 3.
2 ibid., p. 4.
3 A. V. Dicey, *Introduction to Law of the Constitution*, 9th edn (Macmillan 1939) p. lxxiii.

4   D. M. Trubek, 'Complexity and contradiction in the legal order', *Law and Society Review*, **11** (1977), 529 at 546.

5   Dicey, p. lxxiii.

6   Sir Ivor Jennings, *The Law of the Constitution* 5th edn (CUP 1959) p. 116.

7   Nevil Johnson, *In Search of the Constitution* (Methuen 1977).

8   ibid., p. 149.

9   On which see Nonet and Selznick *passim* and R. M. Unger, *Law in Modern Society* (Macmillan 1976).

10   R. M. Unger, 'The critical legal studies movement', *Harvard Law Review*, **96** (1983), p. 561 at 588–9.

11   Sir William Holdsworth, *A History of English Law*, 4th edn, vol. II (Methuen/Sweet and Maxwell 1936) p. 468.

12   Morton J. Horwitz, *The Transformation of American Law 1780–1860* (Harvard University Press 1977).

13   Kenneth Dyson, *The State Tradition in Western Europe* (Martin Robertson 1980), p. 198; and see C. B. Macpherson, *The Political Theory of Possessive Individualism* (OUP 1962).

14   Dicey, pp. 186–7.

15   Selznick, *Law, Society and Industrial Justice* (New York: Russell Sage Foundation 1969), p. 11.

16   G. Poggi, *The Development of the Modern State* (Hutchinson 1978) p. 148.

17   Unger, 'The critical legal studies movement', p. 588. In fact this internal or immanent critique can be grounded in more utopian or transcendental fashions too; there is bound in our view to be a coincidence between them, as see Alan Gewirth, *Reason and Morality* (Chicago University Press 1978), e.g. p. 23; J. Habermas, *Communication and the Evolution of Society* (Heinemann 1979), e.g. pp. 16, 100.

18   See Thomas Morawetz, *The Philosophy of Law* (Macmillan 1980), pp. 9–14 and ch. 1 generally for an account of positivism which is largely used by him in contrast to 'naturalism' or natural law and not primarily as a Comptean version of a science of man as opposed to say rationalist or pragmatist versions; on which see generally Ted Benton, *Philosophical Foundations of the Three Sociologies* (RKP 1977).

19   R. G. Collingwood, *An Essay on Metaphysics* (Clarendon 1940) p. 34.

20   ibid., pp. 144–6.

21   See Dyson, *The State Tradition in Western Europe*, esp. pp. 4–7.

22   See generally M. Rheinstein (ed.), Weber's *Law in Economy and Society* (1954), and more specifically D. M. Trubek, 'Max Weber on law and the rise of capitalism', *Wisconsin Law Review* (1972) 720.

Jurgen Habermas's writings are replete with these arguments but see esp. *Toward a Rational Society* (Heinemann 1971), ch. 5.

23 Nonet and Selznick, p. 43

24 Poggi, pp. 142–3.

25 Holdsworth, *A History of English Law*, vol. X. (Methuen/Sweet and Maxwell 1938), pp. 647–8. See also F. W. Maitland, *The Constitutional History of England* (Cambridge University Press 1955) p. 99.

26 Holdsworth, vol. X, p. 649.

27 Holdsworth, vol. VI, 2nd edn (Methuen/Sweet and Maxwell 1937) pp. 284–6.

28 *Two Treatises of Government* (Cambridge University Press 1960). See esp. Second Treatise ch. IX 'Of the ends of political society and government'. Though the revolution of 1689 *was* expressed in terms of an original contract between King and people; see Maitland, esp. pp. 283–4.

29 Holdsworth, vol. X, pp. 528–31.

30 Maitland, p. 388.

31 *Jurisprudence*, 4th edn (2 vols., Murray 1879), vol. 1, p. 253.

32 See Dicey, p.75.

33 See R. Dworkin, *Taking Rights Seriously* (Duckworth 1977).

34 J. A. Schumpeter, *Capitalism, Socialism and Democracy* (Allen and Unwin 1943), p. 250.

35 Isaiah Berlin, *Four Essays on Liberty* (Oxford University Press 1969).

36 Schumpeter, p. 269.

37 C. Pateman, *Participation and Democratic Theory* (Cambridge University Press 1970); P. Bachrach, *The Theory of Democratic Elitism* (University of London Press 1969).

38 Bachrach, p. 63. See also ibid., pp. 87, 102 and Pateman, p. 20.

39 Johnson, *In Search of the Constitution*, pp. 147–8.

40 Jennings, p. 74.

41 C. S. Emden, *The People and the Constitution*, 2nd edn (Clarendon 1956), pp. 1–3.

42 ibid., pp. 2–3.

43 Holdsworth, vol. xi.

44 Maitland, p. 199.

45 Douglas Ashford, *Policy and Politics in Britain* (Blackwell 1981), p. 11.

46 See e.g. A. J. Beattie, 'The two party legend', *Political Quarterly*, **45**, 288 at 289.

47 Geoffrey Marshall and Graeme C. Moodie, *Some Problems of the Constitution* 5th edn (Hutchinson 1971), p. 16.

48 Nonet and Selznick, p. 56 (original italics).

49 Jennings, p. 65. See also pp. 107, 316–17.

50   Ashford, p. 6

51   See Emden generally but ch. 12 in particular regarding 'Parties and the people'; on the prerogative see Holdsworth, vol. X esp. p. 527.

52   Geoffrey Marshall, *Constitutional Conventions* (Clarendon 1984), pp. 9, 18.

53   Poggi, p. 144; R. H. S. Crossman, introduction to W. Bagehot, *The English Constitution* (Fontana 1963), p. 19.

54   ibid., p. 27.

55   P. S. Atiyah *The Rise and Fall of Freedom of Contract* (Clarendon 1979), p. 13.

56   E. P. Thompson, *Whigs and Hunters* (Penguin 1975), p. 269.

57   Atiyah, p. 236.

58   Lord Hewart, *The New Despotism* (Benn 1929).

59   Johnson, pp. 136–7.

60   Maitland, p. 198.

61   Holdsworth, vol. II, p. 253.

62   See e.g. Christopher Hill, *Intellectual Origins of the English Revolution* (Oxford 1965), pp. 109–10.

63   See e.g. Maitland, pp. 100–1, and Horwitz, *passim*.

64   See Max Weber, *Economy and Society*, G. Roth and C. Wittich (eds.) (New York: Bedminister Press 1968) esp. pp. 941–54.

65   Trubek, 'Complexity and contradiction in the legal order'.

66   Unger, *Law in Modern Society*, p. 178.

67   Samuel H. Beer, *Modern British Politics*, 2nd edn (Faber and Faber 1982), p. 7.

68   Unger, *Critical Legal Studies*, p. 655.

69   Poggi, p. 121.

70   Bagehot, p. 15.

71   N. Luhmann, quoted by G.Teubner, 'Substantive and reflexive elements in modern law', *Law and Society Review*, **17** (1983), 239 at 271.

72   Marshall and Moodie, p. 81.

73   *Anisminic v Foreign Compensation Commission* [1969] 2 AC 147; *Padfield v Minister of Agriculture* [1968] AC 997; *Ridge v Baldwin* [1964] AC 40.

74   K. Middlemas, *Politics in Industrial Society* (Andre Deutsch 1979).

75   Crossman, introduction to Bagehot p. 46.

76   Dicey, p. lxxviii.

77   ibid., p. 203.

78   Holdsworth, vol. x, esp. p. 649.

79   See Holdsworth, vol. x, pp. 644–5; Dicey, p. 228; Maitland, pp. 300–1.

80   Dicey, pp. lxx, lxxii.

81   See e.g. Brian P. Levack, *The Civil Lawyers in England 1603–41* (Clarendon Press 1973), p. 146.

82   John Brewer and John Styles, (eds.), *An Ungovernable People: the*

English and their law in the seventeenth and eighteenth centuries (Hutchinson 1980), p. 19.

83 ibid.
84 John Brewer, 'The Wilkites and the law 1763–4', in Brewer and Styles (eds.), esp. at p. 131.
85 Dicey, p. 237.
86 Atiyah, p. 248.
87 Peter Self, *Administrative Theories and Politics* (Allen and Unwin 1972), p. 290.
88 See e.g. Peter Kellner and Lord Crowther-Hunt, *The Civil Servants* (MacDonald Futura 1980), pp. 170, 188–9, 280–1; Sir Douglas Wass, *Government and the Governed* (CRKP 1984) pp. 83–100.
89 See Kellner and Crowther-Hunt, p. 247.
90 Ashford, p. 7.
91 *Reason and Morality*, esp. pp. 308–9.
92 Nonet and Selznick, *Toward Responsive Law*, p. 56.
93 Gewirth, p. 31.
94 See e.g. Habermas, *Communication and the Evolution of Society*, p. 186; Nonet and Selznick, esp. p. 118.
95 'The development of administrative law in England', *Law Quarterly Review*, **31** (1915), pp. 148–53.
96 Dicey, p. lxxiii.
97 ibid., pp. 136–7.
98 *Law, Society and Industrial Justice*, p. 16.
99 H. Lauterpacht, *The Function of Law in the International Community* (Clarendon 1933), p. 387.
100 Brewer and Styles, p. 12.
101 See e.g. Selznick, pp. 12–14, Gewirth, p. 53.
102 *Associated Provincial Picture Houses Ltd. v Wednesbury Corporation* [1948] 1 KB 223.
103 B. Boyer, *Fifty Years of Regulatory Reform in the United States*, Paper to Conference on Regulation in Britain (Oxford 1983).
104 P. R. Verkuil, 'Judicial review of informal rulemaking', *Virginia Law Review*, **60** (1979), pp. 185–239.

3 Politics and polity: the role of law

Having outlined the orthodox Dicean conception of the rule of law and having argued that it has tended to hijack or colonize our larger constitution we need now to re-examine some of the critical claims upon which it was founded. The highly positivistic Dicean account has been instrumental in divorcing legal analysis from constitutional fundamentals. By reifying an historically contingent form of constitutional practice, it has discouraged investigations concerning moral and political purpose and has conflated constitutional scholarship and a specific legal and economic tradition. We hope we have exposed the bankruptcy of this account of the compact existing between the British people and their history and in particular to have shown that neither British political institutions – including 'autonomous' courts of law – nor the collective claims made about our world-view, make larger sense except in terms of their commitment to choice, to debate, to accounting for the conduct of public business and to answerability to the plenary constituency which is the nation.

Before we are in a position to signpost the regeneration of the rule of law in modern conditions, we need to examine the generic relationships between the political and the legal orders and the public and societal realms, in order to address the symbiosis between constitutionality and legitimation. A central aspect of this exercise will be to develop and explain our earlier references to an enlarged concept of law, which is crucial to much of what we have to say.

The cleavage between law and politics

Part of the difficulty in encouraging constitutional lawyers in Britain to engage in institution-building to assist in meeting constitutional claims and expectations is that the orthodox paradigm irrationally

separates out 'law' from 'politics'. Furthermore, the limitations of
the rule of law concept have been paralleled by the narrowness of
British perspectives on 'law' itself which has rarely been seen as
possessing the larger sense of *Recht* or *droit*.[1] This theme will form
the major part of the next section but first let us return to the
cleavage between law and politics which is associated with, but of
course not the same as, the drawing of a clear distinction between
public and private spheres of life, between state and society.

In the medieval period it was almost impossible to defend a sharp
division between the realms of law, politics and religion. It was the
development of legal autonomy and theories of liberal individualism that, by separating out the state and the individual bearer of
legal rights, made possible the identification of separate legal and
political territories. In Britain the need to distinguish clearly between a sovereign assembly and the independent administration,
both of the common law itself and of the assembly's amendments to
the common law, was a necessary part of the constitutional settlement. In the United States of America Tudor or medieval attitudes
towards the mingling of law and politics were reflected to a considerable degree in the constitution and for various reasons were
more resilient than was the case in Britain. Nevertheless the historical conditions were becoming ripe by the end of the eighteenth
century for a radical revision of former attitudes which eventually
affected the USA as well as Britain but in circumstances where the
constitution allowed for the possibility of an eventual reemergence
of the old ideas:

By creating a neutral and apolitical system of legal doctrine and legal
reasoning free from what was thought to be dangerous and unstable
redistributive tendencies of democratic politics, legal thinkers hoped to
temper the problem of the 'tyranny of the majority'. Just as nineteenth-
century political economy elevated the market to the status of the paramount institution for distributing rewards on a supposedly neutral and
apolitical basis, so too private law came to be understood as a neutral
system for facilitating voluntary market transactions and vindicating injuries to private rights. The hostility to statutes expressed by nineteenth
century judges and legal thinkers reflected the view that state regulation of
private relations was a dangerous and unnatural public intrusion into a
system based on private rights.[2]

One does not have to share Horwitz's view as to motive to accept
that the Dicean model of the rule of law effectively embodied an

ideology. 'Autonomous law', as Nonet and Selznick label it, embodies standards that general public consent, authenticated by tradition or by constitutional process, has removed from political controversy. This legal heritage meant that the judges and therefore the law were insulated from the struggle for political power and uncontaminated by political influence. Now, whereas we have already allied ourselves to a faith in the autonomy of an aware judiciary, this simple-minded orthodox duality evades all the most intellectually demanding dilemmas. There is, in this model, no possibility of law being seen as part of a surrogate political process which contributes to problem-solving and enfranchises contending interests in the policy-making arena. Designing legal institutions to carry out political purposes more competently is by definition out of order.[3]

That this state of affairs does not represent an enduring feature of British constitutional history is evidenced by Maitland's account of the role of land law under feudalism. Public and political rights and duties of all kinds were inextricably blended with private rights in land, 'so that the constitution of Parliament, of the law courts, all seemed in a way to be an appendix to the law of real property'.[4] We shall see in addressing the vexed issue of the public/private divide that even in the headiest days of the pre-eminence of the Dicean paradigm a clean break between law and politics was never possible, but the fact that the contrary belief has been so strongly held has meant that legal processes have contributed less to the pursuit of public purposes than might have been in the general interest.

The central theme of this book is that a revised concept of law and constitutionality should inform a public, reasoned decision-making process so that barriers which define the spheres of influence of law, administration and politics are broken down in order to foster the deployment of resources necessary for collective learning and hence for rational and efficient policy-making.[5] The danger of tyranny or injustice lurks in unchecked power rather than in blended power *per se*. Since power in Britain is, as we shall see, blended to an extraordinary degree, our revised rule of law needs to construct machinery for the better imposition of checks as well as to ensure efficiency through a mutual learning process. A necessary precondition for achieving this is an expanded concept of law, which accepts the interlocking of legal and political processes without actually erasing the boundaries between them:

As a political actor [government] assumes responsibility for deciding what ends are to be pursued and what resources it is prepared to commit in dealing with problems. . . . But government must then proceed as a *legal* actor, to establish the agencies and mechanisms by which public ends will be furthered. In principle ... these institutions [should be] designed to bring maximum objectivity to the elaboration of public policy.[6]

By adopting this analysis we do not seek to replace politics by law but to harness legal institutions to explore and facilitate policy-making and create the optimum conditions for political choice. These conditions are ultimately constitutional matters of a high order. They also impinge upon the nature and legitimate extent of public action so that we shall have to relate problems of constitutionality or legitimacy to the vital question of the public/private divide. As we have explained, our attention is focused on the collective conditions of public life. We shall not organize our discussion of the distinction between public and private around the idea of substantive individual human rights against the state. Such rights are certainly important, but the quality of political life depends crucially upon the institutional atmosphere in which it takes place – this is the context for all other rights and shapes the nature of the state.[7] As far as the traditional political liberties are concerned specific institutional conditions are required for their realization. Thus if it is argued that a congeries of rights necessary for civic competence is demanded of advanced democracies – rights such as the right to life and physical integrity, the right to mental equilibrium and a feeling of confidence as to the general possibility of attaining one's goals, the right to act on the basis of the fullest possible information and so on – then social institutions need to be constructed in such a way as at least not to obstruct the achievement of such ends.[8] Again, if we regard voluntary, non-noxious, action as a general good then we shall need to regard behaviour caused by forced choices as unacceptable – as being involuntary. Consequently an agent – and public actors are constitutional agents *par excellence* – must neither withhold information from nor deceive a recipient concerning relevant circumstances lest consent to transactions be rendered involuntary. Information and what Alan Gewirth calls 'consent procedures' must be guaranteed by the constitutional structure of the state so that institutions assist the attainment of the rights regarded as fundamental.[9]

We have already said enough to make it clear that we are

unpersuaded by arguments concerning the sharp cleavage between the legal and the political realms. We do not however, argue that a high degree of judicial autonomy is anything but a primary necessity, a matter which we shall address in due course. Rather we believe both that standards of rational discursive justice need to be further imported into the political decision-making process and that a constitutionally aware judiciary constitutes the strongest guarantee against arbitrariness and colourability. It is in our view the strongest hope we have for ensuring a contemporary deliverance of the rule of law.

The public/private divide

Constitutionality, the legitimate atmosphere for public action, naturally poses questions concerning the boundaries between the public and the private sphere. Whatever constitutes the public sphere, it is clear that action within it should accord with settled constitutional principles, specifically in relation to procedural matters. As to substantive behaviour that will amount to a local or contingent issue unless, of course, one asserts some version of natural law and/or fundamental human rights. Although we agree with almost all of Gewirth's arguments in relation to the latter issue we shall, as we have indicated, pass them over in favour of examining the institutional implications of immanent British constitutional expectations.[10] The relation of the public sphere to private behaviour, varying as it may over time, needs equally to be characterized by settled principles. Given that in Britain these must, according to our earlier arguments, be constituted by canons of openness and accountability, information should be available about the relationships, the tensions between the boundary fences, and the degree of compenetration occurring between 'state' and 'society' at any given time.

Unfortunately, the dominance of Dicean notions of constitutionality has meant that this mapping exercise has not been systematically attempted by British constitutional lawyers who have thereby ensured that much essentially public behaviour has gone unscrutinized, at least in an overt institutional sense. For present purposes, since we shall not discuss what ought to be characterized as the irreducible core of 'private' action and since we shall marginalize the civil liberties component of an 'immanent' set of British constitutional claims, we here merely address our central constitutional axiom: *viz.* parliamentary omnicompetence. This axiom is now in effect reduced to the *realpolitik* of executive omnicompetence so that *in constitutional theory at least*, ministers may make private business public business. There is no area (European Community and human rights law aside) of social life where the public writ cannot 'constitutionally' run. Now from moment to moment the empirical progress of the public writ could and should be traced to describe the extent and forms of the compenetration of public and private. Legal institutions are currently defective in that they fail to bring these salient relationships to light. In particular they fail to expose the informal relationships between ministers and 'private' actors, a consistent theme of the remainder of this essay. However, above and beyond this example, we believe we can trace a more general intellectual concealment of the symbiosis between public and private interests.

(For the classic liberal state described by Dicey, a clear distinction between public and private was a crucial aspect of its legitimacy. The primary function of the public sphere was to facilitate the activities of the private. According to this tradition, the public sphere operated according to democratic principles while the hierarchy and dominations that characterized the private sphere were both explained by the market and to some extent justified by its principles and were in any event not legitimately the subject of public action.[11])

The corollary was that legal thought was concerned to create a clear separation between constitutional, criminal and regulatory law (in short, public law) and the law of private transactions – torts, contracts, property and commercial law.[12] What is not always appreciated is that this development by no means characterized English law over the longer run. It was historically specific and according to Holdsworth was in no small measure owing to surrender to the economic proposals of Adam Smith and his successors. We have already noted that a very detailed regulatory regime characterized much of British commerce and industry during the early part of the eighteenth century. This included, for example, regulations regarding the treatment of apprentices, the payment of wages, for the settlement of disputes between masters and servants in a wide variety of trades and so on. Only gradually was this regimen dissolved, with inevitable implications for the nascent trade union movement whose relationship with government was in turn to cause further confounding of the state/society divide and indeed to continue so to do up to the present day.[13] However, what have been described as the immutable laws of capitalism seemed to make it necessary for regulation to be kept at a minimum, even though when occasion demanded the public and private streams mingled freely, as witness the injection of private capital into 'public' utilities with the state guaranteeing limited liability.[14] E. C. S. Wade noted the similar phenomenon of the interdependence of public and private interests in the railway companies of the nineteenth century, which made it extremely difficult to maintain the antithesis between the individual and the state.[15] At a more basic, if crucial, level there has been relatively little analysis of the role of the state in securing the enforcement of commercial agreements. Atiyah has pointed out, that with the exception of J. S. Mill, none of the classical economists even stopped to inquire what was involved in the enforcement of contracts, and why such enforcement was not itself a form of government intervention. There is, after all, arguably nothing 'natural' about laws for the enforcement of contracts.[16]

In fact it now seems perfectly clear that private power began to be increasingly indistinguishable from public power precisely at the moment, late in the nineteenth century, when large-scale concentration of capital became the norm. These very concentrations became to a major degree the cause of government intervention and, indirectly, a strong impetus to the emergence of the welfare state. Furthermore, as has often been remarked, the state has for much of this century imposed upon itself the task of solving market failures. According to this analysis its very legitimacy depends upon curbing abuses of the market while none the less continuing to guarantee the formal conditions for market behaviour.

This dual and precarious legitimacy of the modern welfare state leads to a dual role of the law; law still serves to organise markets in order to keep them running and efficient. It also takes over *purposive* functions by making markets instruments of fulfilling government-proclaimed rights. There is an inherent dualism in modern law which in the Weberian tradition was described as coexistence of formal and substantive law, or conditional and purposive programming, the latter always being at odds with and structurally weaker than the former.[17]

Another perspective on the compenetration of state and society is provided by analysing the public interest in terms of the results of interest-group pluralism. In this interpretation, legitimacy is afforded by some version of law as the provider of the conditions for a market version of the public interest, but with organized interest groups as the competitors and the political process as the market.[18] Although this has become heavily institutionalized in the United States it is 'networked' in the British political process in a largely informal way.[19] Whether interest groups can actively contribute to supplementing the formal conditions of democracy in the liberal welfare state is another matter.[20] Although institutional machinery for moderating competition between interests which seek to capture or privatize part of the state machinery is very underdeveloped in Britain, the phenomenon itself is not. The exploration of North Sea oil is a case in point, for it has been cogently argued that forces pushing for the co-option of offshore safety into the broader generic machinery of onshore safety administration found themselves in competition with the Department of Energy which was itself being pushed by national and international oil interests to give higher priority to the requirements of commercial production.[21]

The overall failure to examine the finer details of public/private intercourse is also in evidence in the general debate on regulation, which can and does occur in the public sector as in the private, while in both domains regulation, especially in Britain, can be formal or informal. The relationship of British Airways and the Civil Aviation Authority clearly illustrates the former point while the other commercial nationalized industries have been subject to only very occasional formal ministerial direction but to extreme pressure of the less formal variety. Ownership and regulation are conceptually distinct and at least four combinations are possible: *viz.* private ownership with or without regulation and public ownership with or without regulation. When 'delegalization' is discussed however, private ownership without regulation seems to be the model generally assumed. This is itself misleading, for various processes may link public and private decision-making even in the absence of formal regulatory mechanisms.[22] Furthermore, in so far as the state sees its role in part as being to create conditions for markets to flourish, it is thereby and immediately involved in private ordering. We know, for example, that conditions of a highly preferential kind may be offered by the public sector to the private, as well as by the public sector to another part of the public sector.

The contract state, corporatist and quasi-corporatist arrangements, and the networked society are all vital ingredients of an informed discussion of constitutionality, highlighting and identifying a distinctly ambiguous 'private' world. Few such matters receive their due attention in the orthodox constitutional texts. Furthermore, much of this decision and non-decision-making activity currently falls outside the supervision of Parliament, and certainly of courts of law.

Self-regulation or self-governance, for example, taking account as it often must, of general considerations of importance to the public, is in reality a delegation of public functions to private control. This is clearly true of important aspects of the work of the City of London, of trade unions and other commercial undertakings. It is forcefully spelled out for the Lloyds insurance market and the Stock Exchange by the Gower *Review of Investor Protection* to which our discussion will have cause to return more than once.[23] In fact the whole issue of self-regulation and the emergence of new legal forms of the 'soft' or 'reflexive' variety attests the importance of the compenetration of the public and private spheres. But the fusion of public and private is not, after all, either a new phenomenon or a particularly new observation:

voluntary groups and associations are a means by which some of the urgent business of society is performed. They are agencies of social control operating as arms of the state in the performance of some of the preferred activities of society. They may be considered to be the recipients of delegated power from the state.[24]

In speaking of the 'private governments' of the large corporations, Miller instanced the fusion of economic and political power which occurred because economic power centres are capable of bringing influence to bear upon governmental structures and because the corporate community itself is a political as well as an economic entity. Much officially announced public policy is an amalgam of the interactions of private bureaucracies and public officialdom with supercorporations which often enjoy the power to veto or at least substantially amend public policies. Very large corporations can behave, in effect, as the agencies of administration for government, particularly through huge programmes of contracting out, not least in the fields of research and development.[25] The specifically British manifestations of these trends we leave over to Chapter 6, but it is worth repeating that the delegated omnicompetence of British executive government makes the trends particularly worthy of study, especially in light of the general lack of mechanisms for accountability in these areas.

The phenomenon of state/society compenetration is a feature of all post-liberal polities and is by no means restricted to Britain and the United States. None the less the peculiar limitations of the still influential Dicean rule of law paradigm, exacerbate the problems within the traditions of a common law jurisprudence. There has been little notable success for example in shedding light on the intricacies of public/private relationships especially in relation to commercial dealings.

In several Western countries in the 1960's and 1970's the courts have enjoyed occasional successes in reasserting much-battered ideas of legality in the conduct of public business, but theirs is a rearguard action, limited in its scope by its primary reference to criminal laws. Nor is it plausible to expect an effective defense of the distinctiveness and autonomy of the societal realm to be mounted by economic and other organisations; on the contrary, most of them appear only too eager to 'colonize' the political realm, overtly or covertly appropriating public resources and usurping faculties of rule in order to place them at the service of sectional social interests (at best) or of the narrow oligarchies that run them (at worst).[26]

[Traditional interpretations of the rule of law in Britain have sought to distinguish public and private in a fairly sharp fashion. This has disguised political reality resulting in the emergence of a black-hole of constitutional unaccountability.] Yet, as Nevil Johnson has remarked, the dominant approach to the rule of law has been empirical and procedural so it should not prove impossible to alter methods and procedures of working to establish a new correspondence between ideals and reality: especially if more public and public/private conduct were to be seen in terms of the potential for using law as one factor in establishing and maintaining political authority.[27] Not least there must be a careful inquiry into certain decisions made privately that have constitutional consequences. Miller claimed that in terms of the American constitution, what is necessary is scrutiny and development of the total flow of decisions of a constitutional nature, wherever made, and not just those of the Supreme Court.[28] This is a yet more urgent necessity in Britain where the courts are disposed to deny that even their own judgments handed down according to regular law have any constitutional significance.[29]

At this point we have begun to touch upon our next theme which is the narrowness of the traditional concept of law: that used, albeit inarticulately, by the courts and by Dicey and his adherents. The inadequacy of this concept lies in its confinement of the 'legal' to only one institutional manifestation of public power – *viz.* the application of a limited set of approved rules by courts.

Autonomous law: a limited concept

In underwriting the form which Nonet and Selznick gave to the distinction between the legal and the political realms we have implicitly allied ourselves to a particular concept of law. In short we define law as legitimate public power and in particular its institutional manifestations. This broad claim needs to be substantiated, but it may be helpful to associate ourselves at the outset with the view that the special work of law is to identify claims and obligations that merit official legal validation and enforcement.[30]

In adopting this position Selznick drew on the work of Weber, who is normally associated *tout court* with the autonomous, *gesellschaft* concept of law which has so dominated Western, and particularly English, legal thought in the last century or so. He argued that in speaking of authority and legitimacy and in contrasting the charismatic, the traditional and the legal–rational, Weber thereby places law in a context of evolving forms of authority. Whether or not the evolutionary claims can be sustained, he surely has a point in claiming that when Weber speaks of the authoritative coercive nature of law the legal element is not the coercion itself but the authority. Selznick goes on to point out that rules of authoritative determination may take many forms and call upon many different resources. We should, he urges, see law as endemic in all institutions that rely for social control on formal authority and rule-making.[31] We would regard this statement as unduly narrow but it none the less evokes an acceptable flavour.

Most laymen and an uncomfortably large proportion of trained lawyers view the study of law in an exceedingly narrow way.[32] They tend to conceive of it only as our 'high rules of law' (what Habermas calls 'bourgeois formal law' and Unger 'rule of law' law)[33] thus identifying only what is in reality a highly localized and historically specific form of the genus 'law'. Contrast Eugen Ehrlich:

Though we know very little of the law of the early times of the peoples from whom the civilised nations of Europe have sprung, there can be no doubt that of what to-day is mostly, and sometimes even exclusively, called law, i.e. the fixed rule of law, formulated in words, which issues from a power superior to the individual, and which is imposed upon the latter from without, only a few negligible traces can be found among them.[34]

There is no evidence that previous legal forms were moving implacably towards their final flowering as bourgeois formal law, for it too was a transient phenomenon whose high summer has now clearly passed. Unger and Kamenka and Tay have shown that, at differing periods in world history, bureaucratic models and customary–interactive arrangements have provided the dominant forms of normative integration which law is usually thought to provide.[35] On the one hand, the concerns of a centralized state expressed through formal and informal rules, discretion, largesse, or whatever can constitute the main lines of legal activity, while on the other, looser voluntary associations depending upon shared cultural values and mutually accepted general standards can, at other times or in other aspects, perform the central functions of normative integration. The latter paradigm can be seen at work in most primitive communities,[36] in trade union organizations at certain stages of historical development, in the customary practices of merchant venturers and the like.

What this amounts to is that certain cohesive functions are performed in any given group or community by means of appropriate, historically-specific procedures and forms and that appearances are necessarily less significant than essences. Unfortunately, this matter is not always appreciated as readily as it might be, especially by scholars on the left of the political spectrum.

There is, in fact, much anti-law passion engendered in socialist literature[37] but at root this is little more than an objection to liberal–democratic, rights-based, private law: in short the *gesellschaft* form. This is plainly to confuse law as a transcendent phenomenon with one historically-located version, a confusion which is as clearly the fault of lawyers as of social scientists.

Parsons, for example, has argued that cohesion depends upon the integration of systems, upon goal-orientation and, *inter alia*, stable patterns of behaviour.[38] Habermas too claims that 'the fundamental function of world-maintaining interpretive systems is the avoidance of chaos, that is the overcoming of contingency'.[39] Unfortunately Parsons and many other distinguished social scientists have, until very recently at least, paid little regard to things legal in their analyses of compromise, equilibrium, institutionalized expectations and so on. What has been too frequently ignored is what

Savigny referred to as the totality seen from a specific viewpoint;[40] the social order examined from the point of view of legitimated procedures and their suitability for the advancing of that order's beliefs and values.

In a widely-admired article Kamenka and Tay have spoken to similar concerns to our own through the heuristic device of three broad-based ideal-types of law.[41] These types, categorized, after Tönnies, as *gesellschaft*, *gemeinschaft* and bureaucratic–administrative, are sufficiently well-known to have no need of detailed elaboration (though their ultimate theoretical status seems to us somewhat uncertain). The *gesellschaft* type is so very similar to the Dicean model of the rule of law that we can effectively collapse them into each other:

certain historical periods and certain countries do provide us with classical epochs in which a particular strain comes out with special clarity, comes to self-consciousness as it were, serves as a paradigm that illuminates in a new way our understanding of the past, and of the foreseeable future. Nineteenth-century bourgeois commercial society gives us such a paradigm for gesellschaft, a paradigm that has become even better understood as gesellschaft conceptions come under fire from gemeinschaft and bureaucratic-administrative quarters in both the nineteenth and twentieth centuries.[42]

In rejecting the Dicean notion of the rule of law we have already examined and exposed the inadequacy of such a model to supply sufficient explanation and justification for the operation of legitimate public power in contemporary conditions. In particular, one of the features of the *gesellschaft* model most commonly fastened upon as a cause for criticism is its formalism, its lack of concern with the imbalance of social and economic power relations in general and its abandonment of the search for substantive justice in particular. Marc Galanter, for example, has pointed out that the common law proceeds on the basis of equality before the law, while what he calls 'indigenous' dispute-settling (which approximates to *gemeinschaft* characteristics) finds it unthinkable to separate the parties from their statuses and relations. Common law decisions give a clear-cut all-or-nothing solution to isolated disputes, whereas indigenous processes seek a face-saving solution agreeable to all parties which takes into account the underlying social setting of the dispute.[43] Much of the contemporary debate over self-regulation and 're-flexive' law forms a variant on the *gemeinschaft* theme, emphasizing that certain sorts of legitimate public power may be exercised by quasi-autonomous bodies committed to publicly pronounced belief systems but operating within a framework of general directions imposed from the political centre.[44] In modern circumstances, however, 'self-regulation' partakes not only of *gemeinschaft* but of the bureaucratic–administrative form of law also. Let us speak to this matter briefly.

The development of the modern state has ensured that the bureaucratic legal form already rivals in importance liberal–democratic notions of law. An interventionist state renders purely private arrangements and private powers a diminishing part of the law's business, for the central problem of advanced industrial societies is no longer the problem of private property but that of administration and social control. Common lawyers historically have attempted to distinguish courts from tribunals, law from regulation and justice from administration, but these distinctions, while never theoretically coherent, have now become observably untenable. Determinants of policy in the fields of planning, the environment generally, broadcasting and welfare, for example, have replaced the pristine concern with clear rights and duties to the point where scholars can now speak openly of the dissolution of private law.[45]

In Britain, community workers have spoken of two legal systems: the traditional one and the administrative system which differs from the former in that its inequalities are exposed in a fashion which the traditional legal system long ago learnt to disguise.[46] Examples are legion. The homeless are housed under the Housing (Homeless Persons) Act 1977, too often according to the officially perceived 'merits' of the case, and accommodation is allocated accordingly: hostel, 'sink estates' or something more congenial. The administrative practices grafted upon immigration law are notoriously harmful to many individuals and families. The Housing Acts' contribution to urban renewal is grossly uneven in terms of the distribution of resources and so on. Let us borrow a summary:

contemporary legislation has largely lost those features of generality and abstractness that made 'classical' legislation into the instrument par excellence of parliamentary supremacy. Many laws are effectively *ad hoc* measures of an intrinsically administrative nature given the form of law in order to legalize the expenditures they involve and shield ministers and civil servants from having to take political or personal responsibility for them. In view of the enormous tasks of 'societal management' borne by contemporary governments, administrative action cannot be meaningfully programmed in the classical manner – that is by means of a law stating general conditions under which a given administrative action is to be taken. Instead, programs directing an agency, say, to increase the country's steel-making capacity by x per cent or to reduce industrial pollution in a given river by y per cent over z years, must leave the measures to be taken toward the target in question to administrative discretion, supposedly informed by the appropriate non-legal expertise.[47]

Typically then, legitimate public institutional power will be channelled into different forms for different purposes at different times. What has thus far been left unsaid relates to what should be seen as the quintessentially and transcendently legal. The law-jobs theory developed by Karl Llewellyn, while not unique, is the most systematic treatment of the necessary social function of law and the most coherent systemization of legal procedures readily available to constitutional lawyers.

The law-jobs theory posits that in every group, high or low, from a scout-troop to the United Nations, certain jobs need to be performed in the interests of social cohesion and stability. The law-jobs thus identify certain necessary features of social organization. The fundamental task of political and legal institutions ('law-and-government' in Llewellyn's terms) is that of becoming and remaining enough of a unity to be and remain recognizable as a group, a political entity or society.[48]

We are dealing then with *a priori* real or essential definitions. Real definitions purport to capture the essence of either the thing or the concept defined. They are not empirical generalizations though, of course, it is an empirical question whether the possible objects, of which they describe the essences, actually exist.[49] But, given that no one doubts the actuality of social organizations, the law-jobs are real, fundamental and enduring. Llewellyn subsumed the law-jobs under a number of discrete, though varying, headings or ideal types. We shall adopt a fourfold distinction and treat them at some length.

The law-jobs

The disposition of the trouble-case

This is the easiest of the law-jobs with which to identify. It comprises what Llewellyn called the garage-repair work of society: the redress of felt grievances. He discovered social institutions for performing this job among the Cheyenne Indians where others had failed to detect them and thereby made it clear that no particular machinery, no professional cadre or priesthood were required for a group to attend to this central line of business. If for current purposes we substitute for the culture of the Plains Indians public administration in welfare-capitalism, we can observe mechanisms for dispute resolution in public sector housing, the allocation practices of education authorities and the host of allowances available to the business community according to more or less discretionary criteria.[50] Such mechanisms indubitably exist and are 'legal'. The questions of how well they function, how publicly visible they are and whose interests they serve are of course the crucial issues of legitimacy. But unless we first *identify* such mechanisms as legal we have no initial purchase even to raise the question of legitimacy.

Preventive channelling

The second job (which again it must be remembered has to be performed in every group high or low) is that of 'producing and maintaining a going order instead of a disordered series of collisions'.[51] It involves the channelling of people's conduct preventively and arranging for participating in the scarce and the desirable. Procedures and institutions to effect this job may be customary (contracts, marriage ceremonies) or may be innovatory and concerned to re-channel, to change attitudes and forms. Legislation is the clearest example of the latter phenomenon but by no means the only one. A newly established local government subcommittee would serve as an example, as would the internal rules of a government department or other bureaucracy, or indeed a ministerial circular. Large areas of public life are concerned with facilitating or guiding activities – for example, planning the physical environment while leaving to private decision whether enterprise and innovation take place at all. Much lawyers' law emanating from the legislature is designed to provide facilities for private activity by individuals and corporations to regulate their own relations. All these matters are examples of the second law-job which is increasingly significant and evident in the processes of modern government. Providing processes for casting alternative votes, for institutionalizing a surrogate political process, for giving opportunities for wider constituencies to participate in policy-relevant learning processes – all these constitute the contemporary expression of concern for the legitimacy with which law-job two is performed.

The constitution of groups

The third job is necessarily presupposed by the others and concerns the establishment and allocation of the authority – what Llewellyn called 'the say' – required if they are to be performed. It is thus about the constitution of groups and the allocation of decision-making functions. Julias Stone refers to it as being concerned with 'tribunals, peacemakers, rulemakers',[52] but the significant point is that it is not limited to parliaments and courts nor is there any *conceptual* necessity for authority to imply hierarchy or indeed social differentiation. It is a central issue in administration and organized social life at large. Thus Llewellyn refers to this job when he speaks of the need to understand a public agency's organization, premises and policies, while Ehrlich had previously stumbled over it when referring to a rule which assigns to each and every member of voluntary associations their place within them.[53] In terms of public government we are also talking about 'finding your way around', a process assisted by, for example, adequate levels of public information and publicity and not least by grievance procedures.

Law-job three also highlights the problem of discretion and the convergence of law and government, which are never far apart. Bearing in mind that we are discussing the social totality seen from a specific viewpoint (a legitimate procedural one) this is not surprising. Llewellyn pinpointed the focus by investing government proper with a more idiosyncratic quality, while characterizing 'law-stuff' as that point on the spectrum where the effective character of the office reduced the effective influence of the office-holder,[54] a matter which begins to raise, though it does not exhaust, the question of legitimacy.[55]

Goal orientation

The fourth job is concerned with the 'whither' of the group at large: with goals, with objectives and therefore with policy. Llewellyn was clearly of the view that the legal can vitally affect energy-unleashing, co-ordination and community direction. The validity of his theory does not in any way depend upon this belief, but his claim that previous failures to meet social policy objectives have often resulted from defective technique constitutes a remarkable anticipation of current concern with learning processes and the expansion of policy-making constituencies. In any event he stressed that to observe the importance of this job was nothing new, but merely old insight forgotten because of laissez-faire ideology.[56] The focus makes us consider our substantive ideals of government and makes us consider that underneath policy judgements on little questions lie deeper policy judgements on large ones.

The significance of the extended concept of law for identifying the *location* of public power ought to be evident at this stage. It is, however, worth underlining that the law-jobs are so distributed in Western societies among 'legislative', 'judicial' and 'administrative' processes that, to encash the ideals underlying the concept of the rule of law, we need to be able to identify the decision-making processes of the state and provide institutionalization of our master ideals of openness and accountability.

A number of threads can now be drawn together. Given that the legal is constituted by a series of socially necessary tasks to be performed in any organizational framework, procedures for the resolution of grievances, for planning and monitoring, for describing the legitimate anatomy of groups are essential conditions of social being. Thus, to talk of 'more' or 'less' law in any given situation is to contradict oneself and to engage in riddles, whether the subject of discussion is contemporary processes of deregulation or nineteenth-century laissez-faire. 'More' or 'less' law only makes sense therefore in terms of changes in the balance between *gesellschaft, gemeinschaft* and bureaucratic elements. Given the force of this argument, the central constitutional question becomes one of legitimacy. Which procedures for performing these necessary tasks are collectively acceptable and which not? This is the problem of constitutionality which has too often been ignored by lawyers and political scientists alike. Because Britain has no foundation document, no 'ark of the covenant', the tendency is to identify the constitution with a descriptive account of a series of pragmatic working practices, ignoring the need to be concerned with organizational structures and discussion and decision mechanisms to produce legitimate outcomes.[57]

Once having established the base principles of the constitution, we should be concerned to produce *procedurally* legitimate outcomes which depend upon concrete social and political conditions and upon information and informed and rational debate involving a hard look at policy alternatives. We develop this theme in detail in Chapter 9. We argue in our chapter on parliamentary institutions that in Britain the traditional parliamentary claims for overall legitimation fail to carry any real weight or conviction and that, to borrow a phrase from an American source, the electorate 'buys representation in bulk-form'.[58] Traditional assumptions concerning cabinet government are no longer sustainable: the major locus of public power in Britain is focused around a federation of the great departments of state and their client groups. Since Britain has no federal constitution nor developed principles of public law, we are desperately short of mechanisms for producing legitimate outcomes through rational political choice and discourse.

The rule of law: a reconstitution

The authority of Parliament, of the rule of law and the constitutional conventions are, in one sense, all that we have in the way of fundamental constitutional tenets.[59] However, it does seem a little odd to label as 'fundamental' constitutional conventions, some of which seem to alter over time. On the other hand, although much store is laid upon the rule of law, there have been relatively few considered attempts in recent years to examine its essentials. In the century up to 1870 the whole machinery of government in Britain had to be overhauled and although change in Britain has tended to be slow, pragmatic and evolutionary the pace of administrative reform between 1800 and 1870 was really quite dramatic.[60] In terms of the exercise of political skills the extraordinary feature of the period was that such changes could occur without major political upheavals or bloodshed.[61]

None the less dramatic changes there were and they were achieved without any considered attempts at re-examination of constitutional premises and with relatively little alteration of our legal institutions or indeed of other institutions of accountability. The genius was comprised in the matter of stability through change: it was manifestly not evident in the matter of constitutional or legal architecture. The rule of law as the golden metwand continued to be waved in the face of radically different institutional political and administrative forms and yet the legal, the political and the moral were intertwined only in the rhetoric and not in relation to patterns of accountability. Indeed the overhaul of the machinery of government coincided to a remarkable degree with the dominance of legal positivism. As Atiyah has pointed out, in 1770 positivism had yet to appear as a legal philosophy, for 1776 was the year in which Bentham's *Fragment on Government* was published which was the source and the inspiration for much of John Austin's later work.[62] Marx, of course, had during the latter part of the nineteenth century accused Hegel of 'positivizing' natural law in his encomium of the Prussian Constitution. In the same way, though with less philosophical sophistication, Austin and Dicey seem to have 'positivized' the rule of law. As we remarked at p. 20 above, positivistic accounts fail to appreciate that institutions and systems come into being through human agency. Bentham's purpose in insisting upon a strict separation of facts and values was, of course, to make precisely this point.[63] Yet in the hands of an Austin or a Dicey positivist analysis itself become an engine of mystification concealing the dramatic nature of changes in the system.

It was not until well after Bagehot's death that British political life was transformed by the effective transfer of power from the floor of the Commons to the great party machines and the Whitehall bureaucracies in some sort of concert.[64] The narrow basis of party programmes and the personalization of electoral politics around party leaders are to a considerable extent responsible for weakening political contributions to policy analysis and prescription at executive levels. Within this context ministers tend to adopt a bureaucratic style which reflects dependence upon their department, rather than to develop an interest in, or mastery of, policy problems.[65]

The development of a centralized state apparatus, with para-state concentrations of power linked to it through clienteles and the new feudalism of corporate power has occurred, while lip-service continues to be paid to a concept of the rule of law which is largely silent about the true anatomy of public power. If the central weakness of Dicey, even at the time he wrote, was a concentration upon formalistic judicial power to the exclusion of the growth of bureaucratic power, how much weaker is the claim of the orthodoxy to continued relevance in a massively altered framework? Britain is little different from other welfare states in terms of the types of issues with which it is confronted, but the problems here are in many ways more acute because reconciling demands and performance takes place in a more restricted arena. It is the informality of the political system, a major advantage in accommodating political change in the nineteenth century, that now facilitates the extension of executive powers in unforeseen ways, and insulates policy-making from its environment.[66] This seems to us to amount to a negation of democratic values which coalesces with concerns about rationality to lead us to believe that our constitution is in fact discourse inefficient.

In bureaucratic, if not in democratic, terms a centralized rule-based system of law may be acceptable when dealing with routine and repetitive conditions. However, this is hardly appropriate when societies are faced with the formidable elaboration of the agendas of government tending towards 'rationality crises', the severe diffi-culty of tracing causality in policy terms and the equivalent prob-lems of monitoring outcomes. Where it is important to organize people and systems for carrying out activities which are novel and where future conditions are unstable, it makes far less sense to prescribe from the centre the concrete actions that ought to be taken to accomplish these various tasks. Democratic concerns and the need for learning processes to ensure the efficiency of the policy process lead ineluctably to the view that some form of participatory decision-making is required as a source of knowledge, a vehicle of information and a foundation for consent.[67] The urgent task for constitutional lawyers then becomes to reconstitute the rule of law in terms of its institutional expressions, retaining commitment to the underlying principles which espouse non-arbitrariness, the containment of unaccountable discretion and the perhaps newer commitment to a decision-making process which is rational. This latter desideratum is simply another way of expressing the belief that a public learning process is required for the resolution of many problems facing an increasingly complex national and international community and that institutions directed to advancing that process are a necessity. The rule of law, as we have argued, is a master ideal and a legitimating sentiment which needs to be constantly related to modern concerns and periodically updated in institutional settings.

Although autonomous, formal, Dicean law remains a vital con-dition for the establishment of basic human rights (not that our own system provides any strong guarantees of this sort) the primary focus of a modern rule of law should be the institutional conditions for furthering rational public choices. Where older versions of law of a *gesellschaft* kind are concerned to provide frameworks for private ordering without much regard for the relationships thereby constructed or the choices made within them, a revised and reconstituted rule of law has at its heart systems-building for the better achievement of collective choices within a framework of open accountability and rationality:

the achievement of legality is seen as the refinement of basic principles, their application in depth, and their extension to new social settings. As this evolution takes place however, the line between the legal and the political is blurred. . . . The latest historical outcome – the renewing synthesis – is the absorption of legal ideals into the political order and, at the same time, the creation of supportive institutions, values and modes of thought. Law *aufgehoben* is polity achieved.[68]

The epistemological warrant for evolutionary claims aside, we are convinced that Selznick has here reaffirmed the essentials of the rule of law in its modern context and in so doing has rekindled the medieval associations between law, politics and collective expectations – in short constitutionality. The rule of law is not the description of a set of working practices espoused by Dicey. It is a belief in the governance of the nation through order, choice and free expression. In the conditions of the late twentieth century, in Britain in particular, the rule of law is much more of a rallying cry than an institutional reality. To bring the expectations and the reality into closer harmony the institutional expression of the doctrine needs to be updated and revised. We turn to these matters in Part Three of this essay. We hope we have done enough here to convince our readers that an immanent critique of constitutional belief is both necessary and timely. Before concluding this section on our constitutional heritage however, we would like to recommend the following observations as a timely summary of much of the preceding argument:

Whereas in the nineteenth century there was argument about who should vote, in the twentieth century there is argument about what is properly subject to voting. Thus a trade union official must be seen to be elected, but not the chairman of a nationalised industry, not the manager of a factory, not the proprietor of a newspaper. This qualified and selective democracy is an inevitable liberal position while it is tied to economic individualism and private property in the means of production. It is on strong ground in the means of opposing bureaucratic collectivism, but on very weak ground in the matter of any serious general democracy.[69]

Leaving aside Williams's choice of examples, we believe he has accurately pinpointed the major contemporary constitutional dilemma: *viz.* how to realize open and accountable government through the development of consistent constitutional patterns. The rest of this essay is an attempt to justify the general assertions which we have been making so far and to outline in a highly programmatic fashion what is required for the relegalization of the British state and for the re-emergence of the ideals which inform the spirit of the rule of law.

Summary

In Part Two of the book, which we have entitled 'The business of governing', we examine the traditional constitutional and political institutions and their role in the conduct of the nation's business, together with the other means of conducting that business which Dicean analyses tend to obscure. Our aim in this section will be to provide what we termed in Chapter 1 a model for producing an anatomy of legitimate public power – a cast of constitutional actors and roles. In drawing upon our preceding remarks we hope not only to map out the true extent of legitimate public power but to show just how different that reality is from orthodox constitutional formulations. This will allow us to move forward in Part Three to develop an argument for a revised institutional response to this state of affairs which could reinvigorate debate about the rule of law and invest it with renewed meaning and vigour.

Having argued for a concept of law whose true essence is legitimate institutional power we hope to identify its existence and promote its presence, in places and by procedures which differ from those of conventional legal analysis and prescription. In so doing we ought to be able to show that the values which underlie the legal system *simpliciter* should logically be extended to other areas of legitimate institutional procedures. These, after all, are our larger constitutional principles so that revising our constitutional anatomy is the natural preliminary to reconstitutionalization through a revised contemporary rule of law.

References

1   Nevil Johnson, *In Search of the Constitution* (Methuen 1977), p. 149.
2   M. Horwitz, 'The history of the public/private distinction' *University of Pennsylvania Law Review*, **130** (1982), pp. 1423–8.
3   See generally P. Nonet and P. Selznick, *Law and Society in Transition:*

Toward Responsive Law (New York: Harper and Row 1978), and esp. at 57, 59, 78.

4   F. W. Maitland, *The Constitutional History of England* (Cambridge University Press 1955), p. 155. See also Christopher Hill, *Intellectual Origins of the English Revolution* (OUP 1965), esp. p. 256.

5   This theme is developed and applied in I. Harden and N. Lewis, *De-Legalization in Britain in the 1980s*, Working Paper no. 84/125 (European University Institute, Florence 1984).

6   *Toward Responsive Law*, p. 112.

7   R. Parker, 'The past of constitutional theory – and its future', *Ohio State Law Journal*, **42** (1981), at pp. 22–3.

8   Alan Gewirth, *Reason and Morality* (University of Chicago Press 1978), p. 54 and *passim*.

9   ibid., esp. at 32, 247, 270–89, 307–8.

10   For a highly sophisticated defence of an irreducible moral 'constitutional' core see D. Beyleveld and R. Brownsword 'Law as a moral judgment vs law as the rules of the powerful', *American Journal of Jurisprudence, 23* (1983), p. 79.

11   R. Austin, 'The problem of legitimacy in the welfare state', *Pennsylvania Law Review*, **130** (1982), p. 1517 and see also J. Habermas *Communication and the Evolution of Society* (Heinemann 1979), esp. ch. 5.

12   See e.g. M. Horwitz, 'The history of the public/private distinction', and P. S. Atiyah, *The Rise and Fall of Freedom of Contract* (Clarendon 1979).

13   Sir William Holdsworth, *A History of English Law*, vol. xi (Methuen/Sweet and Maxwell 1938) p. 518.

14   See K. Davies, *Local Government Law* (Butterworths 1983), p. 33; and M. Horwitz, *The Transformation of American Law 1780–1860* (Harvard University Press 1977), pp. 110–14.

15   Introduction to A. V. Dicey, *The Law of the Constitution*, 9th edn (Macmillan 1939) p. lxxxviii.

16   Atiyah, p. 330–1.

17   Norbert Reich, 'The regulatory crisis: does it exist and can it be solved?' *Government and Policy* vol. 2 (Pion 1984) pp. 177–97.

18   Horwitz (1982); Richard Stewart, 'The reformation of American administrative law', *Harvard Law Review*, **88** (1975), pp. 1667–813.

19   N. Lewis and I. Harden, 'Sir Douglas Wass and the constitution: an end to orthodox fairy tales?', *Northern Ireland Legal Quarterly, 35* (1984), pp. 213–30.

20   See e.g. R. A. Dahl, and C. E. Lindblom, *Politics, Economics and Welfare* 2nd edn (Chicago: University of Chicago Press 1976).

21   W. G. Carson, *The Other Price of Britain's Oil* (Martin Robertson 1982) p. 297. See also Lewis and Harden, 'De-Legalisation in Britain in the 1980's'.

22   N. Lewis and I. Harden, 'Privatisation, de-regulation and constitutionality: some Anglo-American comparisons', *Northern Ireland Legal Quarterly*, **34** (1983), pp. 207–29.

23   L. C. B. Gower, *Review of Investor Protection, Report Part 1* Cmnd. 9125 (1984).

24   A. S. Miller, *The Modern Corporate State, Private Governments and the American Constitution* (Greenwood Press 1976) p. 28.

25   ibid., pp. 29, 129–30. See also B. L. R. Smith and D. C. Hague (eds.), *The Dilemma of Accountability in Modern Government: Independence vs Control* (Macmillan 1971).

26   G. Poggi, *The Development of the Modern State* (Hutchinson 1978), pp. 144–5.

27   Johnson, *In Search of the Constitution*, p. 149.

28   Miller, p. 18.

29   The *locus classicus* of this position is *Duncan v Jones* [1936] 1 KB 218. See also *British Airways Board v Laker Airways* [1984] 3 WLR 413.

30   *Law, Society and Industrial Justice* (New York: Russell Sage 1969), p. 5.

31   ibid., pp. 6–7.

32   Much of what follows is extracted from N. Lewis, 'Towards a sociology of lawyering in public administration', *Northern Ireland Legal Quarterly*, **32** (1981), pp. 89–105.

33   J. Habermas, *Legitimation Crisis* (Heinemann 1976), p. 86.

34   *Fundamental Principles of the Sociology of Law* (Harvard University Press 1936) (trans. Moll), p. 28 but see also pp. 34, 163 and 118–19.

35   *Law in Modern Society*; E. Kamenka and A. Ehr-Soon Tay, 'Beyond bourgeois individualism, the contemporary crisis in law and legal ideology', in E. Kamenka and R. Neale (eds.), *Feudalism, Capitalism and Beyond* (Edward Arnold 1975).

36   See e.g. B. Malinowski, *Crime and Custom in Savage Society* (RKP 1926); K. Llewellyn and E. Hoebel, *The Cheyenne Way* (University of Oklahoma Press 1941). The point is also tellingly made by Selznick, *Law, Society and Industrial Justice*, pp. 4–17.

37   E. Kamenka, 'Socialism, anarchism and the law', in E. Kamenka (ed), *Law and Society* (Edward Arnold 1978). For an example of such anti-law passion see Z. Bankowski, 'Anarchism, Marxism and the critique of law', in D. Sugarman (ed.), *Legality, Ideology and the State* (Academic Press 1983).

38   T. Parsons, *The Social System* (RKP 1951).

39   *Legitimation Crisis*, p. 118.

40   Quoted by Julius Stone, *Social Dimensions of Law and Justice* (Stevens 1966) p. 30.

41   Kamenka and Tay, 'Beyond bourgeois individualism'.

42   ibid., pp. 142–3.

43 *Hindu Law and the Development of the Modern Indian Legal System*, quoted in Selznick *Law, Society and Industrial Justice*, p. 14.
44 Harden and Lewis, 'De-legalisation in Britain'. See also: Gower, Teubner, Reich.
45 Kamenka and Tay, 'Beyond bourgeois individualism'.
46 See e.g. Community Development Project, *The Limits of The Law* (1977).
47 Poggi, pp. 143–4.
48 K. Llewellyn 'Law and the social sciences especially sociology' *Harvard Law Review*, **62** (1949), p. 1291. The law-jobs theory is treated at various places by Llewellyn but the most rigorous exposition is to be found in 'The normative, the legal and the law-jobs', *Yale Law Journal*, **49** (1940), p. 1355.
49 For real definitions see, Martin Hollis, *Models of Man* (CUP 1977), esp. at 59, 62.
50 Valerie Hannon, 'The Education Act 1981: New rights and duties in special education', *Journal of Social Welfare Law* (1982), pp. 275–84. See also P. Birkinshaw, *Grievances, Remedies and the State* (Sweet and Maxwell 1985).
51 Llewellyn, 'The normative, the legal and the law-jobs', at p. 1376.
52 *Social Dimensions of Law and Justice*, p. 650.
53 K. Llewellyn, 'The place of skills in legal education', *Columbia Law Review*, **45** (1945), pp. 345–91.
54 'The normative, the legal and the law-jobs', at p. 1384.
55 Poggi, p. 107.
56 'The normative, the legal and the law-jobs', at p. 1388.
57 See Habermas, *Communication and the Evolution of Society*.
58 G. Marshall and G. C. Moodie, *Some Problems of the Constitution*, 5th edn (Hutchinson 1971).
59 See H. Parris, *Constitutional Bureaucracy* (Allen and Unwin 1969).
60 See e.g. Atiyah, pp. 238–9.
61 ibid., p. 151.
62 H. L. A. Hart, 'Bentham and the demystification of the law', *Modern Law Review*, **36** (1973), pp. 2–17.
63 Crossman, introduction to Bagehot, p. 37.
64 See e.g. P. Self, *Administrative Theories and Politics* (Allen and Unwin 1972).
65 D. Ashford, *Policy and Politics in Britain* (Blackwell 1981), p. 266.
66 Gewirth, p. 100.
67 Selznick, *Law, Society and Industrial Justice*, p. 28.
68 Raymond Williams, book review in the *Guardian*, 10 October 1984.
69 H. W. Arthurs, 'Rethinking administrative law: a slightly Dicey business', *Osgoode Hall Law Journal*, **17** (1979), pp. 1–45 at p. 43.

Part Two

The Business of Governing

PART TWO

The Functions of Governing

The task of this section of the book is twofold. In the first place we shall attempt to give an account of the processes of government in modern Britain – an account that will be at the level of a conceptual map with only sufficient empirical detail to illustrate and support our main contentions. Second, we assess the extent to which the key institutions of our constitutional heritage, Parliament and the courts, currently fulfil the implicit promise of accountability for the exercise of public powers. These twin aims dictate what at first sight may appear to be an eccentric ordering of the material. To consider Parliament first in an account of the process of making the decisions of government might seem perverse in view of the marginal role rightly ascribed to it in the political science materials. Similarly, to deal with central government departments before what we have called the institutions of disintegrated government and the structures and processes of various policy communities may seem to be putting the cart before the horse. The intention behind this way of proceeding, however, is to pursue the logic of immanent critique by moving outwards from what is in *constitutional* terms the centre of gravity of the polity. That this entails moving from the periphery inwards in terms of effect on policy output is one of the major points that we are seeking to emphasize.

Finally in Chapter 7 we examine the courts and consider in particular how far their development of principles requiring that discretionary powers be exercised 'reasonably' and 'fairly' constitutes an adequate constitutional response to current processes of government. The conclusion that they do not will perhaps come as no surprise, but the purpose of Chapter 7 goes beyond description of the inadequacies of judicial review. Adjudication is itself partly a form of immanent critique and the courts are thus, in one aspect, the constitution's institutionalization of the performance of that activity.* We shall seek to draw two conclusions from Chapter 7: first, that the courts have, *by their own criteria*, failed to do as much as they should have done to ensure and promote legitimate government; second, that in any event what is necessary to achieve that end is beyond the reach of the courts alone.

---

* See especially, Ronald Dworkin, *Taking Rights Seriously* (Duckworth 1977); M. Unger, 'The critical legal studies movement', *Harvard Law Review*, **96** (1983), pp. 561–675.

4 Parliament

Two propositions must form the starting point for any analysis of the role of Parliament in modern Britain. The first is that Parliament does not govern. The second, for which we have already argued at length in Part One, is that *authority* to govern flows *through* Parliament.

No one who devotes more than a moment's thought to the matter can suppose that Parliament 'governs' Britain. Important members of the government, the Prime Minister, cabinet and non-cabinet ministers and others are indeed members of Parliament – or peers – and this organic link between Parliament and the executive is of fundamental importance. However, even if we restrict our attention for the moment to the relatively well charted and publicly visible institutions of central government it is clear that more of the business of government is carried on in Whitehall than in the Palace of Westminster. This much is surely uncontroversial. It is perhaps worth restating the truisms which make Parliament essential to the business of governing. The leader of a party which has a majority of seats in the Commons usually becomes Prime Minister and forms a government. Whether or not there is a party with a majority, it is a necessary condition of a government's survival that it can win votes of confidence in the Commons. Governments need to be able to enact legislation and sometimes they incur defeats. The need to win majorities in both Houses conditions to some extent the content of legislative proposals and the limited availability of parliamentary time imposes the need for prioritization and compromise in the government's legislative programme.

All this does not mean however, that Parliament controls the government: rather it is the government which, in the normal course of events, exercises control over Parliament through the medium of party discipline. But this is perhaps to go too far too soon. We shall explore in detail later the ramifications of party dominance of the parliamentary forum. Before doing so we must look more closely at the nature of the authority to govern which Parliament provides.

The legislative supremacy of Parliament

The omnicompetent authority of Parliament finds its traditional constitutional expression in the idea of its legislative supremacy.

Parliament has under the English constitution, the right to make or unmake any law whatsoever ... no person or body is recognised by the law of England as having a right to override or set aside legislation of Parliament.[1]

In a crude and highly provisional way we might think of Parliament as one point of a triangle of which the other points are, broadly, 'government' and 'the governed'. In its modern form the legislative supremacy of Parliament asserts authority over the governed; there is in Britain no entrenched protection of human rights, no judicial or other review of primary legislation. Legislative supremacy was, however, originally formulated as a *restriction* on the authority of the executive over the governed: the Crown could make new laws only through and with the consent of Parliament.[2] In seeking to reinstate that aspect of legislative supremacy which constitutes a restriction of the authority of government, it is tempting, but mistaken, to discover immanent in the seventeenth-century concept the later continental European theory of the *rechtstaat*.[3] As we have already indicated, there are features of the Dicean conception of the rule of law, such as the exclusion of arbitrary or discretionary action by public officials, that are similar to the ideals of the *rechtstaat*. The Dicean formula, however, emphasizes *common law* declared by the courts, rather than *legislation* made by Parliament.

Indeed, constitutional law defines an Act of Parliament merely in terms of the completion of various stages in the Lords and Commons and the giving of the royal assent: procedural formalities which offer no promise that the resulting product will have the characteristics of generality and abstractness required by the liberal conception of law. Instructive also is the contrast between the discussion of delegated legislative and 'judicial' or 'quasi-judicial' authority in the inter-war examination by the Donoughmore Committee of the powers conferred by statute on government ministers.[4]

Delegated legislation was approached largely in terms of the need for delegation if governments were to be able to obtain the quantity and quality of legislation they required, while the issue of principle was seen as being the need for improved parliamentary scrutiny of such legislation.

In relation to the 'judicial' powers of ministers, however, the Committee perceived a crucial constitutional issue which it cast in Dicean terms: the threat to individual rights from undermining the traditional role of the courts.

It is not surprising that the Donoughmore Committee, orthodox in its approach, should have failed to recognize that the issues with which it was called upon to deal required abandonment of the formalistic categorization of governmental powers, rather than an attempt to deal with an imbalance within it. It was not, after all, until the 1960s that 'discretion' was discovered as a general problem. In fact, we come closer to an understanding of the logic of the triangular relationship between Parliament, government and the governed which our constitutional heritage embodies by considering not the *formal* aspect of the legislative supremacy of Parliament but its *substance*.

Historically, the purpose of the requirement that the Crown should use legislation rather than prerogative powers to levy taxes was to ensure that it could interfere with property only with the consent of the representatives of the property owners.[5] A similar pattern can be discerned in the requirement that legislation must authorize expenditure: if Parliament denies the government 'supply' it has no lawful alternative to resignation.[6] The general proposition which emerges is clear: the process of government shall be carried on only with the consent of the governed as expressed through their parliamentary representatives.

Ministerial responsibility

More than any other single factor, the presence of the 'political' part of the executive within Parliament itself has conditioned the latter's role. Although attempts were made in the late seventeenth century to exclude holders of Crown appointments from Parliament in order to avoid the obvious danger of royal subversion of its independence through the use of patronage,[7] the advantage of having present in Parliament to be questioned and called to account those responsible for the exercise of governmental power eventually proved decisive in constitutional development. It is *ministerial responsibility* which has become the key constitutional doctrine concerning the relationship of Parliament to government. In the first half of the nineteenth century, the growth of administrative activity under statutory powers was frequently embodied in public boards, headed by appointed officials, such as the Poor Law Commissioners.[8] Only in the latter half of the century did the central government department, headed by a minister sitting in and answerable to Parliament, come to be accepted as the standard formula. Departures from that formula then needed justification.

As we shall see, the responsibility of ministers for the conduct of business in their departments is largely fictional and increasingly irrelevant as the boundaries of public and private become blurred in institutions and activities at one or more remove from central departments. Ministerial responsibility remains, however, fundamental to the claims of legitimacy of executive power in Britain and is the starting point for an immanent critique of the role of Parliament. The nineteenth-century model of the constitution sought to accommodate the existence of discretionary public power (which Dicey had largely ignored) through the device of individual ministerial responsibility. This complemented harmoniously, without altering in essence, the Dicean concept of the rule of law. While the courts policed the boundaries of ministerial powers by reference to the common law rights of individuals, Parliament scrutinized the actions of ministers within those boundaries. The extension of a traditional 'over-life-size' role for ministers[9] thus compensated for, at the same time as it justified, the failure of the courts to develop canons of administrative legality.[10]

Collective responsibility

The idea of the collective responsibility of ministers to Parliament is, in one sense, no more than a natural concomitant of individual responsibility. When ministers make decisions jointly then they are all responsible for what is done. At the extreme this means that, if the government as a whole cannot retain the confidence of the House of Commons, it must resign. As originally formulated the doctrine related to the business of the cabinet:

For all that passes in the Cabinet every member of it who does not resign is absolutely and irretrievably responsible . . . . It is only on the principle that absolute responsibility is undertaken by every member of the Cabinet, who, after a decision is arrived at, remains a member of it, that the joint responsibility of Ministers to Parliament can be upheld and one of the most essential principles of Parliamentary responsibility established.[11]

But within this formulation, which at first sight appears to be concerned with ensuring the effectiveness of parliamentary censure, can already be seen the shadow of the censor. What is being said, in effect, is that certain people are not permitted publicly to criticize government policy. Today not only cabinet ministers but whips, even parliamentary private secretaries, are liable to be sacked by the Prime Minister if they criticize government policy or reveal matters pertaining to its formulation, whether or not they were personally involved in, or even knew of, the decisions concerned.[12]

Parliament and party

Our attempt to describe the constitutional role of Parliament has proceeded so far by reference to the triangular model of Parliament, government and the governed, in which it is implicitly assumed that Parliament has a corporate identity separate from government. Much constitutional debate is conducted in the same terms. Here for example, is the House of Commons Select Committee on Procedure:

the balance of advantage between Parliament and Government in the day-to-day working of the Constitution is now weighted in favour of the Government to a degree which arouses widespread anxiety and is inimical to the proper working of our parliamentary democracy.[13]

Cutting across this contrast between Parliament and government is the domination of Parliament by political parties. The resulting institutional dynamic makes the fundamental division that between government and opposition *within* Parliament.

This disjuncture between the constitutional role of Parliament as a corporate actor *vis-à-vis* government, and the reality of government dominance of Parliament through party is a complex phenomenon. A constitution is a framework, not a substitute, for the conduct of democratic politics and party organization is a legitimate and necessary element of the latter. However, as we shall seek to demonstrate, the omnipresence of party is a powerful, though by no means the only, constraint on the ability of Parliament adequately to scrutinize the activity and inactivity of government.

Historically, the emergence of mass political parties is associated with the extension of the franchise and the acceptance of democracy as a legitimating principle. Party, in the sense of factions and of the representation of particular interests – even of differing conceptions of the public interest – antedates the democratic franchise, as does the concept of a loyal opposition.[14] Organization of Parliament is essential in order to enable a body composed of several hundred persons to function at all and it is, as Bagehot pointed out, party which fulfils this role.[15] The constitutional problem is not party as such, but the relationship between party conflict and the ability of Parliament adequately to scrutinize the activities of government. As we have already shown in Chapter 2, it is an essential requirement of the concept of representation, and thus of democratic representation, that the function given to Parliament by the British constitution of ensuring full and open scrutiny of government should be performed. We shall argue in due course that the processes of making and implementing public decisions in modern Britain are now so diffuse and complex that, just as Parliament does not and cannot govern, neither should it seek to perform the activity of scrutiny directly. Rather, it should ensure that scrutiny takes place.

The strength of the parliamentary tradition in Britain is such that despite the increasing prevalence of appeals to 'mandate' it is rare for claims to governing authority to be presented in terms which exclude Parliament altogether. It is rather that the logic of electoral competition leads to the confrontation between government and opposition parties being treated as if it, *in itself*, constituted the mechanism of Parliament's scrutiny of the executive. Hence the extended notion of 'collective responsibility' and other manifestations of party discipline are invested with a dubious constitutional significance and elevated above the principle of accountability which lies behind the concept of individual ministerial responsibility to Parliament – the accountability of government.

Accountability to Parliament

The evolution of parliamentary processes over time has involved the creation of new procedures and the modification of old ones as well as changes in their purpose and significance as a result of other political and institutional developments. Consequently there is frequently a degree of mismatch between the *form* of a procedure, which is largely the result of its history, and its contemporary perceived function. We shall follow tradition by organizing our discussion along the lines of the formal divisions: distinguishing, for example, parliamentary questions from the work of select committees and from the procedures attendant on the passage of legislation. We shall be seeking to explain what we describe in terms of the contribution made by the various procedures to accountability through adequate and effective scrutiny. Let us begin to establish the necessary criteria by considering a much-quoted passage from J. S. Mill's *Representative Government*:

There is a radical distinction between controlling the business of government and actually doing it. The same person or body may be able to control everything, but cannot possibly do everything; and in many cases its control over everything will be more perfect, the less it personally attempts to do .... It is one question, therefore, what a popular assembly should control, another what it should itself do. It should ... control all the operations of government.[16]

The word 'control' is liable to be seriously misleading in this context, however the notion is elaborated. At the risk of labouring points already covered in detail it is worth repeating why this is so. One connotation which might be attached to 'control' is the *gesellschaft* concept of legislation, establishing general rules which are then applied in an uncontroversial way to particular circumstances. Another is the (in many ways correlative) concept of administrative policy-making which envisages the identification of all possible alternatives, their evaluation and the choice of one course of action which is then implemented. Neither analysis captures the mode of operation of the modern state: *a fortiori*, neither applies to the relationship between Parliament and government. On the other hand, to equate 'control' merely with *contrôle*, the *ex post facto* scrutiny of administrative action, is too limiting.

In reality the possible relation of Parliament to decision-making can be explored under three overlapping and interlocking heads:

1 obtaining information;
2 requiring reasoned explanation of action and inaction, past and proposed;
3 debate, i.e. the testing of information and reasoned explanations in an open forum.

We shall now consider how far parliamentary procedures can deliver these desiderata. First of all, let us examine the most obvious route by which to obtain information: the parliamentary question.

Parliamentary questions[17]

The parliamentary question (PQ) became popular in the second half of the nineteenth century, naturally enough since question time, regarded as 'pre-eminently a device for emphasising the individual responsibility of ministers',[18] was developed in that period. Modern procedures impose severe restrictions on questions tabled for oral as opposed to written answer and as a result question time has largely ceased to be used as a mechanism for extracting information from ministers.[19] It is the 'glamour and publicity', a chance to trip up a minister on a supplementary, which make it popular with MPs and naturally this engages considerations of party.[20] For ministers to put up a creditable performance is a way of strengthening claims upon office and boosting party morale. Failure, on the other hand, is one of parliamentary performance rather than of conduct of the minister's department. Increasingly, therefore, questions for oral answer are vague or conventional, the real point being the supplementary. The answers likewise are not intended to be informative so much as to sidestep the questioner's real point.[21]

On the other hand, the question which receives a written answer in *Hansard* is used as a means of obtaining information and is effective within a limited compass.[22] Considerable civil service effort is put into replies to PQs since inadequate or demonstrably false answers can cause political damage to the minister.[23] Correspondingly the best civil service ingenuity is put into ensuring that ministers are not embarrassed by too much information being given and so the adversarial pattern which makes question time largely a set-piece ritual carries over into written answers also:

The central point is that the MP is often seen by civil servants preparing answers to PQs as an actual or potential adversary, to be helped as *little* as possible – whereas departmental ministers need to be buttressed with as *much* help as possible.[24]

In practice this approach to the answering of PQs means that MPs are often faced with a version of the chicken-and-egg problem: in order to extract information they must already know enough to ask the right question. The significance of party therefore is not only that it is fundamental to the relationship between ministers and Parliament but that it provides motive and justification for the all-pervading confidentiality in which the activities of government are cloaked. Ministerial responsibility in other words operates to deny in practice what it claims to provide in constitutional theory: accountability. This charge is strengthened if we examine other aspects of the PQ and the restrictions imposed upon it.

Questions to ministers 'should relate to the public affairs with which they are officially connected, to proceedings pending in Parliament, or to matters of administration for which they are responsible'.[25] This is interpreted to mean that questions may be asked about the non-exercise as well as the exercise of a power – that accountability for the exercise of public power should embrace 'non-decision-making'. It is also interpreted to mean that if a minister does not possess a specific power in relation to some matter then questions about that matter cannot be put. The rationale of this limitation is said to be to prevent MPs putting pressure on ministers to interfere in matters when they have no right to do so.[26] The corollary, however, is that when ministers do so interfere they can deflect questions about what they have done by denying that they have authority to do it – which may be precisely the critical premise of the question. In fact the language of 'interference' is wholly inadequate to encompass the networks of relationships that characterize the operations of the modern state. The private nature of such contacts, fundamental to their current operation, is preserved by denying that they are subject, even in principle, to parliamentary scrutiny.

There are, in addition, numerous subjects on which answers are refused even within the admitted areas of ministerial responsibility. It is important to realize that 'an answer cannot be insisted upon, if the answer be refused by a Minister'.[27] The only sanction which can be brought to bear is a vote of censure on a minister, so that in effect the ambit of the PQ is restricted to what the government thinks it should be. The list of prohibited topics is lengthy and covers not only 'security' matters, such as telephone tapping or accident rates for military aircraft, but also, for example, matters of commercial confidence in relation to the nationalized industries, forecasts of inflation and the system of cabinet committees. The most important limitation on the PQ is the general convention that policy advice given to ministers by civil servants is confidential. The anonymity of the civil service is sometimes presented as if it were a kind of self-denying ordinance necessary to ensure that Parliament can perform its proper function of excoriating guilty ministers.[28]

The supposed sanction of ministerial resignation for departmental errors has shown little signs of life for thirty years, since the departure of Sir Thomas Dugdale over the Crichel Down affair, and was moribund for many years before that.[29] It is also claimed that the efficient functioning of the public service depends on secrecy. Whatever the worth of these arguments, their effect is to deny to Parliament the information necessary for it to be able to scrutinize policy-making effectively. Not only is the work of civil servants *within* departments shielded from Parliament's gaze, but so also is the network of interdepartmental committees and contacts between civil servants and people and institutions outside central government. Discussions at ministerial level, in cabinet and its committees, are of course subjects on which PQs will be refused because of 'collective responsibility'.

In general, then, the PQ is hedged around by restrictions and limitations on its effectiveness as a means of obtaining information: indeed it is probably as much an assistance to government as a check on its activities, since the 'planted' question provides a regular and useful mechanism for making ministerial announcements as well as being a weapon in the party battle. Sustained campaigns of questions by individual MPs (such as Tam Dalyell over the Belgrano affair) have had some impact, particularly in forcing matters on to the political agenda. The effect on policy-making in general, though, is marginal and indirect.

The PQ is only one of the procedures that we need to examine in order to gauge the effectiveness of Parliament. Historically it was through its control of taxation and expenditure that Parliament asserted its power over the executive. The contemporary importance of budgetary processes – 'expenditure is policy; policy is expenditure'[30] – points in the same direction as the historical link: to the financial procedures of Parliament as a vital element in its scrutiny of government.

Financial procedures in Parliament[31]

The financial procedures of Parliament are complex and our discussion will be limited to matters bearing on our central themes: the subordination of Parliament to the executive in control over taxation and expenditure, and the limited scope of the procedures to ensure provision of information and the opportunity for critical appraisal and debate.

A basic constitutional rule is that payments out of the consolidated fund or the national loans fund and the levying of taxation require statutory authorization.[32] While this rule is usually stated in terms which embrace both spending and taxes, such a formulation is liable to be seriously misleading. The historical rationale for requiring parliamentary sanction for taxation is different from that for spending and has a different legal status.[33] Thus the declaration in the Bill of Rights of 1689 'that the levying money for or to the use of the Crown by pretence of prerogative without grant of Parliament ... is illegal' states a principle enforceable in the courts by individuals. The Dicean version of the rule of law is implicated in the need for legislation to impose taxes.[34]

On the other hand, the requirement of legislative authorization of spending is merely 'based on ancient constitutional usage'.[35] Procedures that originated when money was reluctantly and intermittently granted by Parliament to a monarch who could no longer 'live of his own' have not been developed to ensure an adequate constitutional framework for public expenditure in the era of big government and state responsibility for economic policy. The idea that judicial protection of individual rights can ensure constitutionality makes sense only if attention is focused exclusively on revenue, and questions of spending (and borrowing) are ignored. In fact, the Dicean view is in danger of being outflanked even on its own terms. Nationalized industry pricing policy under a regime of negative external finance limits, for example, has in effect been used to tax consumers without legislation and it seems unlikely that any judicial remedy would be available.[36] In the absence of involvement of the courts in enforcing control over spending, no other body, and most certainly not Parliament, has been able to place limits on the growth of executive discretion.

One of the basic rules of financial procedure, deriving from the era when extra resources were only granted by Parliament to the Crown sporadically and for specific purposes, is that the initiative in financial matters rests with the executive. The ramifications of this principle are of considerable importance. It is procedurally impossible for Parliament to increase, or extend the objects and purposes of, a department's estimate or to propose a higher rate or altered incidence of taxation. Even in relation to the financial resolutions accompanying ordinary legislation, the financial initiative of the Crown can be, and is, used to restrict the scope of possible amendment.[37] In the case of the estimates, even reductions, while procedurally permissible, are treated by government as an issue of confidence.[38] In effect, therefore, the opportunity for Parliament to amend government financial proposals is limited to proposing reductions in taxation.

The financial initiative of the executive clearly encapsulates the subordination of Parliament in control over the formation of policy. But more significantly, given the constitutional expectations which attach to Parliament, it has encouraged the neglect of financial procedures from the point of view of scrutiny and debate. Traditionally, Parliament has not received, nor would it have been capable of evaluating, assessments of policy alternatives either from government itself or from other sources. For all that the United States Congress plays a very different constitutional role from Parliament (and one with characteristic defects in terms of the encouragement of incrementalism and clientelism) the contrast between the degree of information received by Parliament and by Congress is stark.[39]

The most obvious, and to foreign observers the most perplexing,[40] defect of budgetary processes in Parliament is the absence of any formal link between proposals for spending and taxation. In sharp contrast with the ritual importance attached to budget day, debate of the estimates (perhaps unsurprisingly in view of what has already been said) is perfunctory. Indeed, 'supply days' were traditionally used for debating subjects chosen by the opposition, which rarely selected matters directly connected to the estimates. In 1982 a new standing order provided for nineteen 'opposition' days and three estimates days to replace the former supply days.[41] It remains the case, however, that the four days of debate on the budget are separate from the estimates days: the latter in any event including the time available not only for examining the main estimates but also supplementary ones.[42]

The separation of the estimates from the budget proposals is only one aspect of the antiquated and defective nature of the financial procedures of Parliament. Despite improvements in the amount, timing and presentation of information to Parliament it still receives merely the conclusions of the key decision-making processes. The framework of scrutiny is still wedded to the concepts of its last major overhaul: that of the nineteenth century. The annual financial cycle, in which every year is treated as a closed period, and the Gladstonian concern with financial regularity checked through audit have not been supplemented or amended to cope with the fundamental changes that have occurred in central government finance. Nor has Parliament been more than a bemused observer of more recent changes which have increased central government control over borrowing and expenditure by the public sector as a whole. Thus, supply procedure gives Parliament no direct means of examining either the amount of government borrowing or its sources, although statutory maxima are provided for government lending to the various public corporations.[43]

The absence of any mechanism for parliamentary authorization of borrowing is not the only lacuna in the financial procedures. As regards spending, only some 60–70 per cent of total public expenditure (as defined by the public expenditure white paper) is voted by Parliament in the estimates.[44] Public expenditure which does not appear in estimates, and which is not funded through the consolidated fund, includes national insurance benefits, local authority spending and certain categories of expenditure by the public corporations. In addition, other items such as net payments to the European Communities are, by statute, charged directly on to the consolidated fund and do not require to be voted annually. The significance of this disjuncture between the estimates and the concept of public expenditure used by government is that it is partly a consequence of, but also reinforces, the exclusion of Parliament from the effective machinery for planning spending: the Public Expenditure Survey Committee (PESC). Furthermore, Parliament has had no part to play in the establishment of what has become the principal control mechanism over public spending, the setting in various forms of cash limits.[45] The latest move in this direction has been actually to plan in cash terms, a development which has led to some important information no longer being presented to Parliament and the public.[46] The consequence is that Parliament can tell little or nothing from the information presented in the estimates and the public expenditure white paper about policy changes, nor about the effectiveness and efficiency of spending.

The presentation of the estimates in cash-planning terms exacerbates other weaknesses of Parliament's financial procedures, from the point of view of scrutiny of the policy represented by spending, as well as the effectiveness and efficiency with which the policy is being pursued. The estimates are divided into individual votes (185 in 1983–4) and votes are further subdivided between functional programmes, subheads and sometimes individual items. None of these subdivisions can be increased by amendment, even if corresponding reductions in other items within the same vote are proposed.[47] This enables parliamentary control to be outflanked on two sides. On the one hand, the unit of appropriation for the purposes of the Appropriation Acts is the vote, not the individual items. This provides the executive with a degree of discretion, exercised by the Treasury, to sanction transfers between items within a vote without further parliamentary approval.[48] On the other hand, the degree of detail given in the estimates is often insufficient to enable Parliament to examine proposed expenditure on particular programmes. For example the Treasury and Civil Service Committee complained in 1982 that the Trident submarine programme did not appear in a single exclusive vote.[49]

Finally in our consideration of the gaps in present supply procedure, mention needs to be made of the contingencies fund. This fund represents an important exception to the general principle that expenditure must receive prior parliamentary approval. In principle, sums drawn from the fund are replaced when *ex post* parliamentary approval for the expenditure is voted, the maximum drawings being limited to 2 per cent of the previous year's authorized supply expenditure.[50] The use made of the fund appears to have increased considerably in recent years: advances in 1981–2, for example, amounted to £2616 million.[51] In the case of advances made near the beginning of a financial year, up to two years may elapse before Parliament receives notification. The Treasury usually requires that Parliament be informed in advance (sometimes through a planted question) of expenditure on services for which no legislative authority yet exists.[52] Uses made of the fund include, in particular, preparations in advance of legislation such as the setting up of the parliamentary ombudsman's office in 1966 and the National Enterprise Board in 1976–7. The fund was also used to finance the manufacture of the first British atomic bomb.[53]

Doubts exist about the legality of the contingencies fund, though it seems evident that the matter is not one which could ever be brought before the courts.[54] The significance of the fund and especially its uncertain legal status lies in what it reveals of the relationship between Parliament and the executive. In fact, the fund is now used not merely to cover unanticipated needs, but to conceal certain expenditures from Parliament and to facilitate the ordinary administrative activity attendant upon the setting up of new services and institutions. That government bills will in due course be enacted is taken for granted and the process of administration no longer waits upon parliamentary approval. The financing of the process is none the less still governed by rules and principles but these are established and monitored by the Treasury: the executive polices itself and the role of Parliament is one of *ex post* comment on what has been done.

So far in our discussion of financial procedures, we have focused on what is, in constitutional theory, the apparatus of parliamentary *control* over the financial arrangements of government. It is perhaps worth re-emphasizing that the point is not that the inadequacy of that apparatus prevents Parliament from actually controlling the key policies – Parliament does not and cannot govern. Rather, it is that the gaps in the need to obtain parliamentary *authority* for what is done restrict the provision of information and the scope for adequate scrutiny and debate.

We turn now to consider more directly the provision of information to Parliament about the government's spending and taxation plans in the light of its overall economic policy. There have been a number of changes made in recent years which have improved the flow of information to a limited extent and have enabled select committees, in particular the Treasury and Civil Service Committee, to engage in regular appraisal of government policy. Although these developments have facilitated the monitoring of changes in policy and the comparison of stated intentions and forecasts with performance, the processes of policy-making and consideration of options remain hidden from view.

The autumn statement by the Chancellor contains discussion of the current monetary and fiscal position, and projections of revenue and likely spending in the year ahead, and the short-term forecast for the economy required by the Industry Act 1975. There is also a preliminary announcement of the external finance limits (in effect cash limits on borrowing) for the nationalized industries.

The public expenditure white paper is the next major financial document to be published, giving details of spending plans for the next three years. Criticisms of the form of the white paper were detailed in evidence to the Treasury and Civil Service Committee in its examination of the 1983 version:

public expenditure plans are presented almost entirely bereft of any explanation or justification as to why the figures should be as they are and not higher or lower. They are not related to any projection of the path of the economy over the medium term, to any forecast of available revenue or to any statement of intended budgetary policy . . . a proper assessment of the plans contained in it has to await the publication of the Budget documents.[55]

While public, and indeed parliamentary, attention still tends to focus on the tax proposals in the budget statement made in the spring a good deal of other information accompanies the publication of the formal budget resolutions which form the basis of the Finance Bill. The supply estimates are published at this time, as is the financial statement and budget report (FSBR) which includes the government's medium term financial strategy (MTFS). The MTFS brings together projections of expenditure, tax and borrowing for the next four years and it is this information which is referred to in the extract above as being necessary for adequate assessment of the public expenditure plans in the white paper. There appears to be something of a dilemma here: delaying the white paper until budget day and the publication of the FSBR leaves insufficient time for Parliament to consider the plans before the Finance Bill and supply estimates have to be approved. Earlier publication, however, means that scrutiny is conducted on the basis of inadequate information. But the problem is of the government's own creation, stemming from its refusal to publish draft papers on its revenue proposals.

Reform – obstacles and implications

Proposals for reforming parliamentary financial procedures have been discussed increasingly over the last decade or so, but the potential of reforms to effect change, and the significance that such changes would have, can be easily misunderstood. A number of different factors need to be taken into account.

As we have already indicated, the executive cannot be considered as a unitary body in so far as the planning of expenditure, revenue and economic policy is concerned. There is a complex structure of power and influence within central government (as witness the virtual exclusion of the cabinet from taxation decisions) to say nothing of other parts of the state such as local government and the public corporations, or of quasi-government and private bodies. Proposals for increasing the possibility of parliamentary scrutiny and debate face severe obstacles in so far as they threaten to disrupt existing relationships – hence the fate of the Armstrong Committee's proposal for a 'green budget'.[56] But there is more to it than that. Put crudely, such changes as have taken place in parliamentary financial procedures have historically been more about the Treasury's desire to ensure its own control over central government departments, than about facilitating open scrutiny and debate. The Treasury, for example, was a strong advocate of the establishment of the Public Accounts Committee (PAC) in 1861:

The very capable permanent Treasury chiefs had given the matter much thought and had come to the same conclusions as eventually had the Parliamentary investigating committee. The Public Accounts Committee looked like strengthening the Treasury's already strong hand.[57]

The PAC examines the accounts of government departments and of a range of quasi-government bodies, focusing on questions of propriety, efficiency and effectiveness of spending. While the PAC is respected, indeed feared, in Whitehall, its work can be seen fundamentally as an adjunct to the financial control over government exercised by the Treasury.

Just over a century later the same assumption that parliamentary authority could be usefully employed to buttress the Treasury's concern for economy lay behind the introduction, at the Chancellor's suggestion, of a debate on the annual public expenditure white paper. The government was careful however to ensure that parliamentary involvement should come only at the stage when the PESC review had been completed and agreed by cabinet, rather than while decisions remained to be made. It is important to make clear that we are not arguing either that Treasury control is a bad thing or that the Public Accounts Committee and the debate on the public expenditure white paper are valueless in terms of accountability. Rather, the implication of the historical record is that the effective impetus for change has not been the desire to increase the accountability of government to Parliament, but to use parliamentary scrutiny to enhance the effectiveness of control within government. Consequently, the changes made have taken a form which ensures, so far as is possible, that the secrecy and lack of open debate which characterize policy-making are not disrupted.

As an illustration, let us anticipate somewhat the discussion of select committees. While the Public Accounts Committee in its work of *ex post* scrutiny of the economy, efficiency and effectiveness of spending has been serviced by the Comptroller and Auditor-General's department (now the National Audit Office) other select committees have very limited investigatory resources available to them. Proposals to combine the work of the PAC and its resources with that of committees examining the *policy* behind spending proposals have consistently been rejected by government.[58] Unlike most of the work of the PAC, examination of the policy represented by spending proposals threatens to impinge on the closed nature of governmental decision-making processes.[59] Such scrutiny is permitted through parliamentary select committees, but is constrained, *inter alia*, by lack of resources. Without a continuous supply of information and analysis by a regular staff, it is perhaps not surprising and not unwelcome to government that departmental select committees have in general shown less interest in the scrutiny of the estimates than was the general intention of Parliament when setting them up.

Financial procedures – conclusion

The information supplied to Parliament and the machinery available to make use of that information are inadequate to ensure that there is scrutiny and debate of the real choices available to government over spending and revenue. In constitutional terms the 'power of the purse' is very limited. The necessity for parliamentary authority in order to ensure the legality of what is done by the executive is partial and incomplete – the machinery of estimates, appropriation and audit, and on the revenue side the budget, do not in practice reach to the heart of the policy-making process.

The process of legislation

Legislation is first and foremost *government* legislation. Of the public bills enacted by Parliament, the overwhelming majority are introduced by ministers. Private members' bills (i.e. public bills introduced by backbenchers) reach the statute book comparatively rarely and it has even been suggested that private members' bills should arguably 'be regarded as a peculiar species of government bill'.[60] Such bills can be very useful to government, particularly where controversial social issues are concerned: one constituency can be satisfied without government having to take the blame for antagonizing their opponents. The private member's bill does create a limited exception to the otherwise exclusive government initiative in proposing legislation, but government opposition is usually fatal, and in practice the provision of government time is necessary to enable any opposed bill to reach the statute book. Even where a government would rather not have had legislation on a particular topic, but feels constrained by the bill's support from killing it, the government will try, through negotiations, to ensure that the resulting legislation is at least harmless from its point of view.[61]

There are three central features of the legislative process which interlock and which are essential to an understanding of Parliament's role *vis-à-vis* government in the production of legislation.

First, in the intention of government at any rate, the introduction of legislation into Parliament marks the completion not the beginning of the policy-making process. Changes are often made during the progress of a bill, but these represent defeats, unavoidable compromises, or very rarely second thoughts as the result of persuasive argument. It remains true that, as in other aspects of government, the fulcrum of policy-making is the department and its client groups together with the processes of cabinet decision-making. It is extremely rare for legislation, once presented to Parliament, to be withdrawn or defeated altogether and even substantial amendment involves 'persuading the Government to admit publicly that it has had second thoughts'.[62]

The second aspect of the legislative process concerns time. Something like half of the parliamentary timetable is taken up with one or other aspect of the business of legislation, but governments inevitably find that they have to prioritize among bills and this indeed is one of the key jobs of the cabinet Legislation Committee.[63] All bills have to go through much the same stages (limited short cuts do exist) and controversial legislation close to the heart of a government's political programme has to compete with less controversial, though often administratively essential, bills which originate in departmental policy rather than manifesto promises.[64]

The third factor that needs to be mentioned before we examine the details of the legislative process, is that Parliament operates in a mode which is overwhelmingly consensual. It is the 'usual channels', informal contacts between government and opposition parties, which provide the context for the workings of the House of

Commons and its publicly visible adversary forms. The conventions which underlie the usual channels are stabilized by a number of factors. In the final analysis a government which retained the loyalty of its party could, in effect, suspend parliamentary government. It would thereby forfeit legitimacy and probably would not be able to command the necessary parliamentary votes unless its action were justified by the opposition having abandoned the conventions of the usual channels.[65] For the opposition, however, there would be nothing to gain by so doing: it would forfeit the opportunities which existing procedures give it to conduct the party battle and, especially given the constraints of time which force government to bargain, even to modify legislation. At the same time, however, the opportunities for the opposition to win significant changes in proposals are very limited and, in making concessions, government is constrained by the bargains already struck with outside interests in the prelegislative period.[66]

Public bill procedure[67]

Public bill procedure falls into a number of distinct stages, beginning with the formal first reading after which the text of the bill is officially printed. At second reading the bill's sponsor – a minister from the relevant department in the case of government bills – introduces it and there is then opportunity for debate. This is usually the first stage at which the general principles of the proposed legislation receive discussion in Parliament, though it is possible that white paper proposals, or a ministerial announcement of the bill, will have been debated previously. A vote may take place if the motion to read the bill a second time is opposed. Second reading is followed by the committee stage, giving the opportunity for detailed amendment of the clauses of the bill, which is then reported back as amended. Further amendment is usually possible on report: after which comes the third reading, usually without, or with only a very short, debate.

This brief description assumes that a bill has been initially introduced in the Commons and this is indeed the case for most legislation of political importance.[68] Once a bill has completed its third reading, it goes through similar stages in the Lords where further amendment, often initiated by the government, may take place. Once the bill is agreed in the same form by both Houses (disagreements are considered below) it receives the royal assent and becomes law.

How far do the procedures just described ensure that legislative proposals receive adequate scrutiny and debate? It might be supposed that the second reading is of crucial importance, since it is at this stage that the principles of the legislation are discussed, often for the first time in a public forum. In practice, however, only a relatively small number of second reading motions are pressed to a division and reasoned amendments are rarely selected for debate unless proposed by the opposition front bench.[69] This reflects the fact that by the stage of second reading – indeed by the first reading – the policy-making process is so far advanced that it is difficult for parliamentary debate to have any significant effect on the principles underlying the bill. The main value of second reading debates from the point of view of actual impact on the legislation is to provide an occasion on which MPs can urge the minister to accept changes which may be proposed later in committee.[70]

Committee stage procedure

Committee stage is taken either in a Committee of the Whole House or in a standing committee consisting of sixteen to fifty MPs appointed to reflect party strengths in the House. In practice, urgent, very minor and very important legislation goes to a Committee of the Whole House and the 'usual channels' normally provide agreement on the allocation of particular bills, as well as the size and composition of standing committees.[71] MPs likely to prove a nuisance to either front bench have been frequently excluded from standing committees.[72] The procedures of standing committees will not detain us here. Suffice it to say that they possess very shadowy identities. Their membership is reconstituted for each bill, the chairperson is a neutral figure and the form of proceedings is adversary, structured around clause-by-clause examination of the bill. Not surprisingly, therefore, standing committees tend to be dominated by government and by the rituals of party conflict in the same way as the House itself. As far as controversial legislation is concerned the opposition seeks to reject it totally or alter its basic principles. Such amendments are of course resisted and since everyone knows that they have no chance of being accepted on their merits, the issue becomes tactical: a matter of delaying the committee's progress until the point where government resorts to compromise or a timetable motion. In either event, but especially the latter, many clauses of the bill may receive no real consideration at all.[73]

In general then, the committee stage is not a distinct contribution to the process of legislation at all. In so far as amendments are made, or promises are given to look again at a clause or introduce a government amendment at a later stage, these represent the indicia of action taking place elsewhere: in party meetings, in cabinet, or in departmental discussions with pressure groups. The only other real function of standing committees is to make drafting changes or amendments of a technical kind which are often necessary as the result of inadequate or hurried preparation of legislation.[74]

They were devised in the 1880s as a species of *select* committee and were originally expected to function in an investigative and deliberative mode.[75] As the initiative in proposing legislation shifted from Parliament to the executive, standing committee proceedings also changed, developing their present form in which the committee is really no more than a device to save government time on the floor of the House.

Report and third reading

At the report stage further amendment of a bill is possible but in practice only government amendments, often in fulfilment of promises made in committee, stand any real chance of success. The opportunities for the opposition or backbenchers to propose amendments are limited by the Speaker's power of selection which is used particularly to avoid repetition of discussion which has taken place in committee. Standing orders provide that when a bill has been considered by a Committee of the Whole House and is reported unamended, it is not then considered further before third reading. The effect of this is to make the government even more reluctant to accept amendments in committee. Not to do so at least saves time on report and may, where controversial legislation is concerned, avoid political embarrassment attaching to further debate in the House.[76] Once the third reading has been completed the bill is introduced into the Lords.

The House of Lords

The role of the Lords in the legislative process has been the subject of a considerable amount of political and academic comment, perhaps more than is justified by its real importance. As a result of the Parliament Acts 1911–49 the Lords can obstruct the will of the government by delaying 'money' bills for a month and other public bills for no more than a year.[77]

The Parliament Acts have not often been invoked, for in cases of conflict a compromise is usually reached (as with the Trade Union and Labour Relations Act 1976) or the Lords concede. In practice, proceedings in the Lords provide an opportunity for making amendments, usually of a drafting kind, in cases where committee stage discussion in the Commons has been guillotined or otherwise truncated. Many such amendments are proposed by the government, which also finds it useful to introduce certain bills in the Lords to save time in the Commons.

The useful work done by the Lords in 'tidying up' legislation is generally not disputed, but their powers are also sometimes used to amend or reject controversial government legislation. In recent times the basis for the claim that the Lords have legitimate authority to obstruct government (whether or not to the maximum extent permitted by the Parliament Acts) has often been confused and contradictory. Two main strands however seem to emerge: first, that it is good that government should be made to 'think again' about legislation, even if ultimately it gets its own way; and second, that in certain cases, the Lords may constitute the only bulwark against 'unconstitutional' legislation. But in general the Lords are in no position to remedy the deficiencies we have outlined, their proceedings being even further removed from the policy-making processes that generate legislation.

In relation to the second proposition the eccentricities of the method of composition of the House of Lords (a mixture of heredity and patronage), the fact that many of its members profess party allegiance, a majority to the Conservatives, and the absence of any statement of principles explaining the constitutional guarantees that the Lords intend to enforce make it a somewhat implausible candidate for the role of *Conseil Constitutionel*.[78] There are occasions on which the Lords do make real and important changes to legislation and there is evidence that ministers are in general more prepared to accept amendments in the Lords than in the lower House.[79] But all this is really only to underline the weakness and deficiencies of the Commons rather than any intrinsic virtue of the Lords. For all its charms, both quaint and quirky, the Upper House is ineffectual in the face of executive power as the Commons.

While reform (as well as abolition) of the Lords appears occasionally on the political agenda, most of those who have sought ways of strengthening Parliament against the executive have looked to changes in the Commons. In particular, select committees have seemed to offer the promise of escaping the rituals of party conflict and the reality of executive dominance of the floor of the House.

Select committees

Despite early setbacks, two decades of select committee reform have finally resulted in a system that is working surprisingly well albeit at the margins of the policy process.

Departmental select committees on education and science, agriculture, and Scottish affairs functioned briefly in the late 1960s and early 1970s, but were then wound up by government. In the case of agriculture, the reason was clearly that the committee had demonstrated too much independence, embarrassing the government by examining the contentious issue of the effects on British farming of entry to the EEC.[80] 'Specialist' select committees on science and technology, race relations and immigration and (a survivor from the 1950s) nationalized industries continued to exist but their work was confined to very limited areas of public policy.

The Expenditure Committee (established in 1971 to replace the former Estimates Committee) was given wider terms of reference than its predecessor, covering investigation of spending proposals in the public expenditure white paper rather than being confined to the formal estimates. Operating through three subcommittees, the Expenditure Committee had, by the time it was wound up in 1979, achieved a considerable degree of success in establishing that a select committee could, despite the pressures of party, examine live and politically controversial issues and criticize government policy. The general purposes subcommittee managed with the assistance of specialist advisers to become a sort of alternative Treasury,[81] reporting, for example, that the out-turn of public expenditure in 1974–5 had been £5 billion more in real terms than was planned in the 1971 white paper and that the bulk of the increase could not be accounted for by announced policy changes.[82]

The Expenditure Committee was constrained by a number of factors which also weighed upon the other committees. Government rarely made time for reports to be debated in the House and departments were often extremely slow in issuing replies, with the consequence that the issues involved became stale. Thus for the Expenditure Committee, the average length of time taken by departments to respond to reports made between 1971–5 was four to five months and by June 1977 only sixteen of the Committee's seventy-six reports had been debated. Other committees generally fared worse on both counts.[83] The independence of select committees was also limited by the fact that selection of MPs to serve on them was in the hands of the whips. More crucially perhaps, the committees constituted an unprofitable backwater, offering no hope of real political power or preferment. Against this background of very limited success at establishing select committees as instruments for the scrutiny of government policy, fourteen departmentally-related select committees were set up in 1979.[84]

The committees were given broad terms of reference: to examine the expenditure, administration and policy of government departments and their associated public bodies. There seems to be general agreement that they have on the whole been surprisingly effective in the range of their investigations, the quality of the reports that have been produced and in the capacity which they have demonstrated to operate independently and on a bipartisan basis.

The work of the committees can be broadly classified into three types: (1) the short investigation of a particular 'issue' with the intention of providing information or contributing to current controversy; (2) 'watchdog' investigations, the monitoring on a regular basis of the work of departments; (3) longer-term, 'Royal Commission' style investigations of policy in a particular area.

Various factors contributed to the degree of independence which the committees have enjoyed. Their establishment by standing order for the duration of a Parliament, rather than on a year-by-year basis, together with support for the new system among MPs created a situation in which, by contrast with the late 1960s, 'no-one in government, minister or official, can expect a committee to be engineered out of existence'.[85] Selection of MPs to sit on committees was entrusted not to the whole House – which would mean in effect to the whips – but to the Committee of Selection, whose members are likewise appointed for the duration of a Parliament. These changes have had some of their intended effect in lessening the degree of control exercised by the 'usual channels' over the initial selection of members.[86]

It is easy, however, to exaggerate the significance of the select committee system in general and the 1979 reorganization in particular. Given the almost complete failure of other aspects of Parliament and its procedures to deliver any real scrutiny of government policy, even minor success by the committees was bound to appear an enormous step forward, although certain specific weaknesses of the select committees were neither dealt with by the 1979 reforms, nor subsequently. These are but pointers to the fact that the change in the relationship between Parliament and the executive which select committees have been able to effect has been marginal not fundamental and that the obstacles in the way of fundamental change remain as strong as ever.

Information and resources

There is little doubt that a great deal of factual information which would not otherwise have been published has come into the public domain as a result of the committees' work. The Liaison Committee, which consists mainly of chairpersons of the departmental committees, drew attention in particular to the Chancellor's autumn statement 'instituted in part-response to pressure from a select committee'.[87]

Part of the problem for the committees is that they are almost entirely dependent on the willingness of the executive to supply information and have little chance of challenging a refusal. They are empowered to 'send for persons, papers and records', but subject to two important limitations. MPs, including ministers, cannot be required to attend a committee except by an order of the whole House and such an order is also needed to require ministers holding the office of secretary of state to produce papers.[88] In practice this means that whereas a refusal by a private body or individual to give evidence or produce documents can be reported to the House as a breach of privilege, a committee must go in the first instance to the House in order to require attendance by ministers or production of documents by a secretary of state. The difference is highly significant in that use of the government's whipped majority to refuse to punish a *prima facie* breach of privilege is a more politically contentious matter than to use it to deny a committee authority which it is in the discretion of the House to give or to withhold. Furthermore, the government's dominance of the business of the House presents severe procedural obstacles to a committee even getting a relevant motion debated. The government has given assurances on these matters:

There need be no fear that departmental ministers will refuse to attend committees ... or that they will not make every effort to ensure that the fullest possible information is made available to them. . . . [W]here there is evidence of widespread general concern in the House regarding an alleged ministerial refusal to disclose information to a select committee, I shall seek to provide time to enable the House to express its views.[89]

While the Liaison Committee was satisfied in 1982 that the first undertaking had been honoured satisfactorily, so that the second had not had to be invoked, the fact remains that select committees are in a much weaker position than they would be if they had specific powers to require attendance and documents from ministers. Where potential disputes arise, committees must proceed in the knowledge that all the procedural advantages rest with the government and that strong appeals to party loyalty are likely to be made.

Most of the witnesses who appear before select committees are civil servants who are limited in the evidence they can give by a Civil Service *Memorandum of Guidance for Officials Appearing before Select Committees*. Forbidden topics include advice given to ministers; interdepartmental discussions; cabinet committees; private affairs of individuals supplied to a department in confidence; 'questions of public controversy' and sensitive information of a commercial or economic nature.[90] It is clear from this catalogue that the official view is that select committees should not only work within the conventions of individual and collective ministerial responsibility but also within the general framework of closed government.

The capacity of committees to undertake a sufficiently broad range of investigations is severely hampered if they cannot establish subcommittees which are themselves entitled to exercise the powers to send for persons, papers and records and to make reports. Only the Foreign Affairs, Home Affairs, and Treasury and Civil Service Committees have this facility, however, and a number of others have found their lack of subcommittees to be a severe constraint. The government has consistently refused to support the extension of the power to set up subcommittees, principally on grounds of economy – both in departments and House of Commons staffing.[91] Despite this limitation the committees have produced a large number of reports, but as was the case prior to 1979, very few have been specifically debated in the House. With the permission of the whips (which is sometimes refused) an indication may be placed on the order paper when a committee report is relevant to an item on the day's business, but the government has refused to allocate time specifically for debating select committee reports.

Ultimately the ability of the government to sustain the procedural barriers which limit the information and resources available to select committees derives from party unity in the House. While select committees have produced a number of bipartisan reports on politically controversial subjects – the 'sus' law, monetary policy and the Ministry of Defence's disinformation campaign during the Falklands conflict, to take three prominent examples – party has impinged upon the committees from the inside as well as externally.[92]

Select committees: conclusion

Given the general ineffectiveness of our parliamentary institutions and the pervading cloak of secrecy which protects the workings of government from scrutiny, the performance of the select committee system since 1979 has been a remarkable achievement. Ministers are now subject to frequent examination, a large amount of information has been placed in the public domain, reports critical of government policy and methods of policy-making have been produced and have contributed to debate. Furthermore, the existence of the select committees has had effects within departments in encouraging greater rigour in policy formulation and justification.[93]

It none the less remains true that the work of select committees is largely insulated from the main institutional dynamics of Parliament. On the one hand the committees can function effectively only as bipartisan and therefore as *backbench* bodies. But it is the conflict between government and opposition front benches which remains central to the political role of Parliament. Interlocking harmoniously with the front-bench party battle is the design of procedures to ensure the speedy dispatch of government business. The result is a general failure to debate committee reports and the exclusion of the committees from any institutional role in relation to legislative procedures.

With the exception of the Public Accounts and Treasury and Civil Service Committees, the select committees remain similarly un-linked to the financial procedures of the House. The Treasury Committee has managed to establish for itself a regular pattern of reporting on the autumn statement, public expenditure white paper and the budget. The PAC reports are linked to the audit of expenditure carried out by the National Audit Office as the last stage of the financial cycle that begins with the estimates. The other committees however, have no such regular access to the parliamentary agenda.

This marginality of select committees to parliamentary processes serves to disguise the inadequacy of their resources to carry out the work of scrutiny which comes within their formal remit. It is not surprising that their work has been criticized for superficiality and has been sporadic and incomplete in its coverage. There is no systematic monitoring of departmental estimates and examination of departments' 'associated bodies' has been very patchy.[94] Nor has the 'prelegislative' activity, which the Procedure Committee felt could usefully be undertaken, been much in evidence. It is hard to envisage government agreeing to sanction any substantial, or even modest, increase in the resources available to select committees. Whether in these circumstances the committees will be able to retain the degree of interest and goodwill from MPs that they have enjoyed remains to be seen.

Parliament: conclusions

The tempting simplicity of Bagehot's distinction between 'dignified' and 'efficient' elements of the constitution – with Parliament now largely consigned to the former category – is inadequate for the purposes of immanent critique. It is inadequate, that is to say, when the constitution is considered to be not only a machine for delivering a flow of decisions but also as a set of promises about those decisions and how they shall be made. Parliament does not govern, but more importantly neither does it fulfil the constitutional promise of accountability implicit in the notion that authority to govern flows through Parliament. It does not ensure that sufficient information is made public, it does not scrutinize the work of government effectively and it does not ensure adequate debate about policy and choices.

We have looked at a number of the key parliamentary processes – questions, legislation and financial procedures – and have seen that, while not totally ineffective, they are severely limited by government control of the business of Parliament, grounded in party dominance, and by the exclusion of Parliament from all but the final stages of policy-making.

There are other aspects of the subordination of the procedures of the House to the speedy dispatch of government business which we have not mentioned: the difficulty in obtaining emergency debates of matters of current importance; the possibility of suspension of standing orders; the almost complete absence of even formal opportunities for the consideration of delegated legislation.[95] It is perhaps worth saying a little more about the latter topic, since, in terms of sheer bulk at least, delegated legislation vastly outweighs primary legislation. Parliament is unable to amend proposed delegated legislation: it can only approve or reject it as it stands, and it cannot even discuss different ways of achieving the objectives of a proposed statutory instrument (SI).[96] While the government must find time for debating a limited category of SIs (those which require an affirmative resolution before finally becoming law) the large number of instruments subject only to the negative resolution procedure (i.e. which become law unless the House resolves otherwise) are rarely discussed. In practice, it is difficult for MPs to get a 'prayer' against an SI debated and reforms effected in 1973 to enable standing committees to debate SIs have resulted mainly in a saving of government time and not in increased opportunities for discussing the merits of proposed delegated legislation.[97]

The almost complete absence of parliamentary scrutiny and debate contrasts with the high degree of consultation, mostly non-statutory, which departments engage in with affected interests in the making of delegated legislation. Parliament can play a limited role in relation to primary legislation by way of revision of drafting; providing an opportunity for interests excluded from – or aggrieved by – the informal consultation to make their views known; and injecting some wider notions of public interest into the results of private deals. Even this is absent in the case of delegated legislation.[98]

References

1   A. V. Dicey, *Introduction to the Law of the Constitution*, 9th edn, with an introduction by E. C. S. Wade (Macmillan 1939).

2   *Case of Proclamations* 1661 12 Co. Rep. 74. After 1688 the doctrine took the form expressed by Dicey.

3   See esp. K. Dyson, *The State Tradition in Western Europe* (Martin Robertson 1980), and G. Poggi, *The Development of the Modern State* (Hutchinson 1978).

4   Report of the Committee on Ministers' Powers. Cmd. 4060 (1932).

5   C. B. MacPherson, *The Political Theory of Possessive Individualism: Hobbes to Locke* (Oxford University Press 1962).

6   See E. C. S. Wade and G. Phillips, *Constitutional and Administrative Law*, 9th edn, A. W. Bradley (Longman 1977), p. 187.

7   House of Commons Disqualification Act 1975, Wade and Phillips, pp. 153–4.

8   F. M. G. Willson, *Public Administration* **33** (1955), p. 43; H. Parris, *Constitutional Bureaucracy* (Allen and Unwin 1969); A. Davies, *What's Wrong with Quangos?* (Outer Circle Policy Unit 1979).

9   Dyson, p. 41.

10 M. J. Vile, *Constitutionalism and the Separation of Powers* (Clarendon 1967), p. 231.

11 Lord Salisbury, 1878, quoted in G. P. Wilson, *Cases and Materials on Constitutional and Administrative Law*, 2nd edn (CUP 1976), p. 57.

12 B. Sedgemore, *The Secret Constitution* (Hodder and Stoughton 1980); R. S. Goldston, 'Patronage in British Government', *Parliamentary Affairs* **30** (1977), p. 80; see also, Edmund Dell, *Collective Responsibility: Fact, Fiction or Facade?* (RIPA 1980).

13 First Report of the Select Committee on Procedure, HC 588, Session 1977/8 para. 1.5.

14 S. H. Beer, *Modern British Politics*, 2nd edn (Faber and Faber 1982).

15 W. Bagehot, *The English Constitution*, introduction by R. H. S. Crossman (Fontana 1963).

16 J. S. Mill, *Utilitarianism, on Liberty and Considerations on Representative Government* ed. H. B. Acton (Dent 1972), pp. 229–30. Originally published 1861.

17 See generally, N. Chester and N. Bowring, *Questions in Parliament*, (Clarendon 1962); N. Chester, 'Questions in the House', in S. A. Walkland and M. Ryle (eds.), *The Commons Today* (Fontana 1981); Charles Medawar, *Parliamentary Questions – and Answers* (Social Audit 1980).

18 Chester and Bowring, p. 287.

19 The 'usual channels' arrange the order in which PQs to four or five ministers will be taken each day. The effect of this rota, combined with the limited amount of time available for oral answers and the maximum period of notice for a PQ mean that perseverance and luck are needed to ensure an oral answer, particularly on current matters. Chester, pp. 178–83.

20 Chester, p. 185.

21 See R. H. S. Crossman, *The Diaries of a Cabinet Minister*, 3 vols. (Hamish Hamilton and Jonathan Cape 1975–7), vol. 1, pp. 146–7; Medawar, pp. 2–4.

22 The possibility of a PQ also gives MPs a degree of leverage in ordinary correspondence with ministers: Crossman indeed appears to have confused the two (see *Diaries*, vol. 1, pp. 628–9).

23 P. Kellner and Lord Crowther-Hunt, *The Civil Servants* (Macdonald Futura 1980), pp. 163, 243.

24 ibid., p. 164 (emphasis in original).

25 Erskine May, *Parliamentary Practice (The Law, Privileges, Proceedings and Usage of Parliament)*, 20th edn by Sir C. Gordon (Butterworths 1983), p. 336.

26   Chester, p. 187.

27   Erskine May, p. 342.

28   See e.g. the statement of Foreign Secretary George Brown, *Hansard*, 5 February 1968, col. 112.

29   See e.g. S. E. Finer, *Public Administration*, **34** (1956), p. 377.

30   H. Heclo and A. Wildavsky, *The Private Government of Public Money*, 2nd edn (Macmillan 1981), p. 345. The following section deals with parliamentary processes, the mechanism of planning public expenditure is considered further in Chapter 5 below.

31   See Erskine May, chs. 27–30; First Report of the Select Committee on Procedure (Supply) 1980–1 HC 118; Sixth Report of the Treasury and Civil Service Committee, *Budgetary Reform*, Session 1981–2 HC 137; First Report of the Select Committee on Procedure (Finance) Session 1982–3 HC 24–I, Second, Seventh and Tenth Reports of the Treasury and Civil Service Committee, Session 1984–5 HC 110, 323, 544. (These Reports are cited hereafter by session and number.)

32   These are the two major accounts through which central government finance operates. Broadly speaking, the consolidated fund receives tax revenues while borrowing, including that for on-lending to the nationalized industries and local authorities passes through the national loans fund (NLF). See Sir Leo Pliatzky, *Getting and Spending* (Blackwell 1982), pp. 24–7. Total government drawing from the NLF in any year is not, however, subject to parliamentary approval.

33   T. Daintith, 'The executive power today', in J. Jowell and D. Oliver (eds.), *The Changing Constitution* (Oxford University Press 1985).

34   *Bowles v Bank of England* [1913] 1 ch. 57; *Congreve v Home Office* [1976] QB 629. cf. on delegated legislation *A-G v Wilts. United Dairies Ltd* [1921] 37 TLR 884.

35   Erskine May, p. 767. The processes involve the presentation to Parliament of estimates which are approved by resolution and followed by the enactment of Consolidated Fund and Appropriation Acts; 'Supply' procedure.

36   See First Report of the Select Committee on Energy, *Electricity and Gas Prices*, Session 1983–4 HC 276.

37   Erskine May, pp. 766–7, 771, 769, 818.

38   Ann Robinson, 'The House of Commons and Public Expenditure', in Walkland and Ryle (eds.), *The Commons Today*.

39   The Congressional Budget and Impoundment Control Act 1974 created a Congressional Budget Office and separate staffs for budget committees. See, Dennis S. Ippolito, *Congressional Spending*, (Cornell University Press 1981), p. 130.

40   1981/2 HC 137 makes international comparisons in Annex 2.

41   SO 19 introduced following HC 118, 1980–1.

42   i.e. Additional estimates to cover expenditure unforeseen at the time the main estimates were voted.

43 See Report of the Select Committee on Procedure HC 118, 1980–1, p. xi.

44 The Treasury and Civil Service Committee gives the figure of 60 per cent: HC 137 1981–2, p. xxi. The higher figure appears in HC 24–1 1982–3, p. xv. Comparisons are complicated by the fact that about 40 per cent of supply does not rank as public expenditure – including e.g. sums transferred to local authorities and public corporations. (HC 118–111, 1980–1 Appendix S, background note by the Treasury.)

45 See, Pliatzky, pp. 135–47, 195–200; HC 137 1981–2.

46 HC 137 1981–2, p. xxiv. A survey of non-government users of the published statistics showed virtual unanimity that cash planning has made the figures less useful: Andrew Likierman and Peter Vass, *Structure and Form of Government Expenditure Reports: Proposals for Reform* (Certified Accountant Publications 1984).

47 Erskine May, pp. 776–8.

48 ibid., p. 777. A procedure known as 'virement'. Such changes will eventually be reported to Parliament *ex post* through the audit procedures. The Treasury sometimes requires a supplementary estimate to be used rather than virement. This is a matter for the Treasury's sense of propriety (monitored by the Public Accounts Committee) and perhaps also the Treasury's wish to discipline departments.

49 HC 137 1981–2, p. xv.

50 Contingencies Fund Act 1974. (The 2 per cent figure relates to *outstanding* drawings.)

51 HC 24–1 1982–3, p. xliii.

52 ibid., p. xliv.

53 HC 137 1981–2 Appendix 20 (Memorandum of Professor J. S. Read, p. 176).

54 HC 137 1981–2 Appendix 20.

55 Third Report of the Treasury and Civil Service Committee 1982–3, HC 204 Appendix 1 (Memorandum by Terry Ward).

56 Armstrong Committee, *Budgetary Reform in the UK* (Oxford University Press 1980). See also, Treasury and Civil Service Committee, *Budgetary Reform* 6th Report 1981–2 HC 137.

57 Chubb, *The Control of Public Expenditure* (Clarendon 1952), p. 33. See also H. Roseveare, *The Treasury* (Allen Lane 1969), p. 141.

58 Likierman and Vass, p. 32.

59 The National Audit Act 1983, which *inter alia* provides statutory authority for 'value-for-money' audits by the Comptroller and Auditor-General specifically excludes him from questioning, 'the merits of the policy objectives of any department, authority or body in respect of which an examination is carried out'. (s6(2)); cf. the terms of reference of the Ombudsman: Parliamentary Commissioner Act 1967 s12(3). The work of the National Audit Office has, however, had real impact

in exposing inadequate policy-making structures. See e.g. *Monitoring and Control of Investment by the Nationalised Industries in Fixed Assets*, HC 284 Session 1984–5.

60   Gavin Drewry, 'Legislation', in Walkland and Ryle, at p. 94.

61   e.g. the transformation of St John Stevas's Parliamentary Control of Expenditure (Reform) Bill into the National Audit Act 1983.

62   Wade and Phillips, p. 771.

63   See Crossman, vol. 1, pp. 59, 497–8.

64   ibid. See also Ivor Burton and Gavin Drewry, *Legislation and Public Policy* (Macmillan 1981), for an analysis of the legislation of the 1970–4 Parliament in terms of 'policy' and 'administration' bills.

65   In fact standing orders already provide a number of powers vested in the Speaker, which can be used to counter overt obstructionism. See S. A. Walkland (ed.), *The House of Commons in the Twentieth Century* (Oxford University Press 1979), pp. 161–6.

66   See e.g. 9th Report of the Select Committee on Energy, HC 636 Session 1977–8, para. 70.

67   The following is a very simplified account. For more detailed treatment see Erskine May, ch. 2; Wade and Phillips, ch. 11A. *Private* bills (i.e. those which affect only particular bodies, localities or individuals) and hybrid bills are subject to a different, quasi-judicial procedure.

68   See Burton and Drewry, p. 112.

69   J. A. G. Griffith, *Parliamentary Scrutiny of Government Bills* (Allen and Unwin 1974), ch. 2.

70   ibid., p. 30.

71   ibid., p. 48.

72   See Sedgemore, p. 195.

73   Griffith, pp. 21–2, and see Crossman, vol. 1, p. 629.

74   See the Report of the Renton Committee, *The Preparation of Legislation*, Cmnd. 6053 (1975). In France the detailed consideration of government legislation from a drafting point of view is one of the functions of the Conseil d'Etat, carried out *before* a *project de loi* is presented to parliament. See Bernard Ducamin, 'The Role of the Conseil d'Etat in Drafting Legislation', *International and Comparative Law Quarterly,* **30** (1981), p. 882.

75   S. A. Walkland, 'Committees in the British House of Commons', in J. Lees and M. Shaw (eds.), *Committees in Legislatures: A Comparative Analysis* (Martin Robertson 1979).

76   Griffith, p. 145. Griffith refers to the European Communities Bill in 1971–2 as a possible instance.

77   The exact period of delay is uncertain because of the statutory method of calculation. The definition of a 'money' bill is complex and narrow. See Wade and Phillips, pp. 182–4. Bills to extend the life of a Parliament, private bills and delegated legislation are outside the scope of the Parliament Acts procedure.

78 For the French *Conseil Constitutionel*, which has jurisdiction to ex-
    amine the constitutionality of legislation before its promulgation, see
    L. Neville Brown and J. F. Garner, *French Administrative Law*, 3rd
    edn (Butterworths 1983), pp. 9–14. *The Conseil d'Etat*, in addition to
    its role in examining the drafting of government legislation before it is
    presented to parliament, advises on its constitutionality; see Ducamin
    (note 74 above).
79 Griffith, p. 231.
80 Anne Davies, *Reformed Select Committees: The First Year* (Outer
    Circle Policy Unit 1980), p. 5.
81 S. A. Walkland, 'Whither the Commons?', in Walkland and Ryle, p.
    289.
82 See Pliatzky, pp. 135–7.
83 Session 1977/8, HC 588–1, paras. 6.3 and 6.15–17.
84 Covering agriculture, defence, education, science and the arts, em-
    ployment, energy, environment, foreign affairs, home affairs, trade
    and industry, Scottish affairs, social services, transport, Treasury and
    civil service and Welsh affairs.
85 Davies, p. 5.
86 ibid., pp. 16–17.
87 HC 92 Session 1982–3, para. 10.
88 Erskine May, p. 698.
89 Statements by the Leader of the House, *Hansard*, 25 June 1979, col.
    45, and 16 January 1981, col. 1312.
90 Quoted in Davies, p. 34.
91 HC 92 Session 1982–3, paras. 36, 38; HC 363 Session 1984–5 para. 28
    written answer, *Hansard*, 12 May 1983.
92 See also Third Report of the Foreign Affairs Committee, Session 1984/
    5.
93 Sir Douglas Wass, *Government and the Governed* (RKP 1984),
    pp. 69–70.
94 Likierman and Vass, p. 33; HC 92 Session 1982/3 para. 26. The Liaison
    Committee's claim in 1985 that ' . . . for the first time in at least half a
    century, the House is carrying out its historic function of examining
    and debating details of government expenditure on a systematic basis'
    represents a gross overstatement. See HC 363 Session 1984–5 para. 13.
95 On emergency debates see R. L. Borthwick, 'The Floor of the House',
    in Walkland and Ryle (eds.), pp. 73–4. On suspension of standing
    orders see e.g. Wade and Phillips, p. 181. On delegated legislation see
    Wade and Phillips, ch. 33 and HC 588–1 1977–8.
96 Erskine May, p. 619.
97 HC 588–111 1977–8, Appendix 1, p. 12.
98 On inadequacies of drafting, partly as a result of inadequate consul-
    tation in the case of supplementary benefit regulations see Tony
    Prosser, *Test Cases for the Poor* (Child Poverty Action Group 1982).

5 Central government, politicians and the departments of state

Ministerial responsibility to Parliament fails as an interpretation of the constitutional promise of accountability for the exercise of public power because a Parliament dominated by the executive cannot effectively call ministers to account. In this chapter we develop further our critique of ministerial responsibility by arguing that orthodox constitutional theory implies false claims not only about the role of Parliament *vis-à-vis* the 'delegated omnicompetence' of the executive but also about the nature of the executive itself.

The authority which flows from Parliament is concentrated in the 'over-life-size' figures of ministers who, individually in relation to their departments and collectively in the form of the cabinet, constitute Parliament's primary agents for the exercise of public power. For an agent to be accountable in the way that the concept of ministerial responsibility implies, it is not necessary that the agent should directly exercise the power that has been conferred. However, if power is to be delegated further, Parliament or its primary agents must design and implement systems of decision-making which themselves ensure adequate accountability for the exercise of the power which is subdelegated. Systems of this kind are largely absent from British constitutional arrangements at central government level (except, to a limited extent, in respect of financial accountability). The constitutional claim to accountability thus rests almost exclusively upon the direct responsibility of ministers to Parliament with the implication that most of the power conferred by the authority of Parliament is exercised by, or at the direct behest of, ministers themselves. The dominance of Parliament by party, furthermore, implies the pre-eminent importance of *collective* responsibility. It is thus to the cabinet that we should look in the first instance for strategic direction of the policies of the government as a whole.

'Ministers are Kings in this country':[1] but not all kings are equal and in particular not all ministers are members of the cabinet. Since the time of Bagehot's *The English Constitution* the cabinet has been regarded as the pre-eminent institutional embodiment of the efficient secret of the constitution: 'the nearly complete fusion of the executive and legislative powers'.[2] Bagehot's claim, that the cabinet is 'a board of control chosen by the legislature, out of those whom it trusts and knows'[3] now has a hollow ring given the degree of executive dominance of Parliament. That dominance, the unitary nature of the state, the absence of limits on legislative authority and of a developed administrative law system, all combine to produce a massive concentration of political authority at the centre of government. Political authority does not in and of itself enable ministers and cabinet to exercise the degree and type of control over the processes of government implied by exclusive reliance on the notion of ministerial responsibility as the mechanism of accountability. In other words, the role of cabinet, and of ministers in relation to their departments, is partly a matter of constitutional myth.

It is a trite wisdom of political science that the relationship between ministers and civil servants is not one of simple command: policy is not 'made' by ministers and 'implemented' by civil servants. Ministers have great power and influence over central government policy-making but they are not the only policy-makers, nor given the size and complexity of modern government is it remotely conceivable that they could be. The functions of the modern state make it impossible for the executive as a whole to be a mere transmission belt for implementing the will of Parliament as declared in legislation.[4] Likewise, within the executive, the process of government cannot be a mere transmission belt for implementing the individual or collective political will of ministers. In fact, the exclusion of opposition and backbench government supporters from decision-making in Britain means that compared with other democratic systems a 'remarkably thin layer of politicians' oversees the policy process.[5]

In addition to the *de facto* delegation of authority from ministers within central government there are institutions and networks of public policy-making outside the central government arena altogether. In Chapter 6 we shall examine the institutions and processes of fragmented government: non-departmental public bodies, quasi-government and quasi-non-government, self-regulatory and 'corporatist' structures. In this chapter we explore policy-making within the central government apparatus. From a perspective which focuses primarily on the policy process and its outcomes, such a division is inherently artificial since disintegrated government consists in part of a framework for the relationship between central departments and their clienteles. For a constitutional critique, however, the division is a necessary one. We must begin by establishing that the implicit claim of the doctrine of ministerial responsibility that all policy is the handiwork of the 'thin layer of politicians' is false and that it cannot therefore provide the basis for genuine accountability for the exercise of public power.

There is a further implication of our analysis which bears directly on the substance of the policies emerging from the system we describe. Much of what we say in this chapter will concern the lack of rational policy-making mechanisms. In our discussion we shall seek above all to demonstrate that the model of decision-making implied by exclusive reliance on ministerial responsibility as an accountability mechanism simply fails to describe the real world. The consequences of an absence of rational planning, however, go beyond the issue of accountability to bear upon the effectiveness of policy-making: the capacity of our governing institutions to identify public objectives and formulate policies to achieve them. A consequence of pretending that we do actually possess constitutional accountability is to preclude institutional and procedural developments that could promote more effective as well as more accountable decision-making. That efficiency and accountability cannot be sharply distinguished and the contribution that a revised rule of law could make to promoting both will be principal themes of Part Three.

The cabinet

As is well known to constitutional lawyers, the emergence of the cabinet in the struggle for power between the Crown and Parliament and the subsequent development of the cabinet system of government took place outside the framework of statute and common law. Traditional constitutional thinking has employed the Dicean concept of 'convention' to describe the working practices of cabinet government but it is Bagehot's specific description of the nature of cabinet government that has continued to dominate the thinking of constitutional lawyers. Bagehot's method of inquiry which involved the criticism of received ideas on the basis of empirical investigation, has thus been neglected and 'the book in which he achieved such an exact separation of political myth from political reality became part of the dignified facade behind which a new "efficient secret" could operate'.[6] Discovering the nature of the efficient secret of government's contemporary functioning is a matter of complex conceptual and empirical inquiry of a kind which constitutional lawyers have signally failed to undertake.

Once the cabinet had developed into 'an informal but permanent caucus of the parliamentary chiefs of the party in power'[7] the existing institutional framework of government meant that the promises of the rule of law were cashable only through the party political processes of representative democracy, and hence through collective ministerial responsibility. However if collective responsibility to Parliament is to ensure such accountability, then it must be the case that cabinet formulates and imposes a coherent political judgement on all questions of the exercise of public power. In fact, the cabinet does not and cannot systematically review and discuss all the policies of the government as a whole. Departments have the pre-eminent role in formulating policy for particular areas of government activity, and cabinet only rarely discusses issues which fall exclusively within a particular departmental field of responsibility. The extent to which the work of any one department impinges upon others or raises party political issues which require the attention of the 'informal caucus' of party chiefs varies considerably. It is only the Treasury with its primary responsibility for economic management and public spending whose policies continually bear upon the departmental interests of other ministers and the political standing of the government as a whole.

The full cabinet normally meets only once or twice a week for a few hours. Much cabinet business is now done in committees, the existence of which has not usually been publicly acknowledged in order to preserve the myth of collective responsibility of the cabinet as a whole and to prevent questions of the terms of reference, composition and chairing of such committees becoming matters of public debate.[8] The transaction of cabinet business through committees was an inevitable consequence of the increasing scale of government activity and the growth of areas of policy requiring interdepartmental co-ordination. War-time conditions gave considerable impetus to such developments and after the Second World War (unlike the first) there was no return to the classical model of cabinet government in which decisions were for the most part taken by the cabinet as a whole. 'The point of decision, which in the 1930s still rested inside the Cabinet, was now permanently transferred either downwards to these powerful Cabinet committees, or upwards to the Prime Minister.'[9]

Like the cabinet, the office of Prime Minister is not a creation of public law and most of the effective powers which attach to it are not legally defined. Appointment and dismissal of ministers, the creation and composition of cabinet committees, membership of the cabinet, its agenda, procedure and the minutes recording its discussions and decisions are all matters over which the only effective limitations on the power of the Prime Minister are political.[10] There can be little doubt that the low public visibility of cabinet committees lessens the political constraints on the Prime Minister in deciding their composition and the areas of public policy with which they shall deal. Perhaps especially in a cabinet in which different strands of opinion within the governing party are represented, the committee system offers effective opportunities for the private outmanoeuvring of internal opposition to policies which have the Prime Minister's support.[11]

It is undeniable that prime ministerial authority is considerable and that the scope of that authority – partly because of the cabinet committee system – now embraces matters which previously were treated as exclusively departmental. However, it is no more plausible to regard the office of Prime Minister as the *locus* of various levels of constitutional expectation than it is to so regard the cabinet. In the first place we have seen that existing parliamentary mechanisms of accountability are geared towards the individual and collective responsibility of a plurality of ministers and not towards a presidential style of authority. More significant given the focus of this chapter is that, despite the importance of prime ministerial power and the massive 'political clout' that results from its commitment to a particular policy, it is far from being the case that the Prime Minister can exercise the kind of rational control over the policies of government that orthodox constitutional theory ascribes to the cabinet.

There is, of course, no 'Prime Minister's department', although there is the cabinet office and a private office which contains a number of senior officials and supporting staff. The cabinet office, while in a sense serving the cabinet as a whole, is in effect responsible to the Prime Minister and the relationship between the permanent secretary to the cabinet office and the Prime Minister is a very close one. The cabinet office prepares agendas and minutes of

cabinet and committee meetings and also plays a crucially important co-ordinating role in facilitating and suggesting possible compromises where conflicts exist. The close relationship between the
Prime Minister and the cabinet office therefore provides the former
with considerable leverage over the machinery of government.
Setting agendas and preparing the minutes of cabinet meetings is a
crucial operation since the minutes in particular are circulated
within Whitehall the day after the meeting and constitute a defini-
tive basis for the activity of departmental civil servants. The co-
ordinating role of the cabinet office is moreover a confidential one.
Suggested resolutions of conflict within committees are available
only to the committee chairperson and not to the cabinet or the
committee as a whole[12] though they will, of course, have received
prime ministerial endorsement if the matter is of sufficient political
importance.

In general, the power and influence of the Prime Minister has to
be exercised *through*, and is therefore conditioned by, the departmental structure of government. The Prime Minister can steer
cabinet in a particular direction by manipulating agendas, minutes
and the committee structure. He or she can by-pass cabinet to deal
directly with particular ministers and even to a limited extent pre-
empt them by dealing with departments directly. If, however, we
are seeking what the idea of ministerial responsibility to Parliament
enjoins us to discover – rational co-ordination and direction of the
policies of the government as a whole – then none of the mechanisms or institutional resources we have discussed so far can even
begin to provide it. The cabinet system does not provide a decision-
making forum which can critically evaluate policy alternatives and
plan strategically in an informed way.

Cabinet and committee discussions of policy issues take place
largely on the basis of departmental briefs provided to ministers.
While ministers have an interest as party politicians in the success of
the government as a whole, the institutional role of departmental
ministers, and also their personal political reputation, is primarily
dependent on the successful defence of the interests and policies of
the department itself – in Parliament, the media and also in cabinet:

the essence of any collective Cabinet discussion is that it takes place on the
basis of statements by interested parties . . . . Where the proposals are contested by a colleague whose departmental interests are adversely affected,
the discussion assumes an adversarial character and the Cabinet acts in

what amounts to a judicial role. But where as so often happens, there's no adversary, the Cabinet simply hears the case which the Minister concerned presents, and this case is inevitably put in terms which suit the Minister himself.[13]

If the full cabinet does not function in a collective mode, cabinet committees do not fill the gap. Some such committees exist on a more or less permanent basis to co-ordinate areas of policy which impinge on a number of departments while others are set up on an *ad hoc* basis to review and report on particular policies. What such committees do not achieve, however, is any overall strategic planning of government policy.[14] Nor can they succeed in correcting the departmental bias of policy-making: the information which they receive and the alternatives available for choice still bear the departmental imprint, albeit filtered through processes of discussion, compromise and brokerage in the interdepartmental committees of officials which shadow cabinet committees.

The problems of creating procedures and institutions for rational policy planning embracing prioritization and co-ordination are not ones which have been ignored in British central government. Several attempts have been made to effect procedural and institutional changes that would enable the cabinet to perform the role ascribed to it by orthodox constitutional theory. The initiatives which have been taken, however, have either failed to live up to the original intentions of their promoters, as was the case with the Public Expenditure Survey Committee (PESC), or have proved short-lived, as with the Central Policy Review Staff (CPRS) and Programme Analysis and Review (PAR). PESC was introduced a decade before the CPRS and PAR and, with modifications, has endured to become of key importance in government decision-making. However, before we discuss expenditure – which is at the heart of much of the policy process and thus of the relationships between Treasury, cabinet and spending departments – it is instructive to examine the innovations which failed to survive: CPRS and PAR.

The Central Policy Review Staff[15]

Both PAR and the CPRS, introduced by the 1970 Conservative government, were in part the fruits of studies conducted while in opposition which had drawn lessons from approaches to policy analysis and budgeting that were then popular in the US and from the methods of private business. The original idea was to create a 'central capability unit' to embrace functions that were currently institutionally separated and thus enable government to reap the benefits which corporate planning supposedly gave to business. This was to involve combining the cabinet office, the public expenditure side of the Treasury and the management functions of the Civil Service Department. This ambitious suggestion was never implemented and in the event the CPRS emerged as a small independent unit within the cabinet office. The white paper which defined its role did not do so in a way consonant with its limited resources and isolated institutional position. Its functions were defined as being to assist ministers to work out the implications of their basic strategy in terms of policies in specific areas; to establish relative priorities to be given to different sectors of their programme as a whole; to identify those areas of policy in which new choices could be exercised, and to ensure that the underlying implications of alternative courses of action were fully analysed and considered.[16] Quite how a small staff of fifteen to twenty people was supposed to seize the strategic heights of the policy process in this way was not clear and the first head of CPRS, Lord Rothschild, put its purpose rather differently as being to 'sabotage the over-smooth functioning of the machinery of government'.[17] In the event CPRS was able to act neither as an agent of, nor as a catalyst for, strategic planning by government.

There were two central problems facing CPRS, both related to its institutional setting. In the first place, once the rhetoric of strategic co-ordination had been operationalized into the actual workings of an administrative process, it turned out to be the case that almost everything the CPRS could do was in competition with the activities of the cabinet office, Treasury or departments. Second, in practice CPRS lacked the institutional clout to compete effectively over a sustained period in the way necessary to have any real impact.

The intended role of the CPRS represented a challenge to the cabinet office because, as Lord Rothschild's 'sabotage' dictum made clear, it implied disruption of the consensual, bargained and accommodative style of conflict resolution that the cabinet office employs.[18] The principle of operation of CPRS, a focus on comprehensive analysis of the substance of policy, was incompatible with the skilful manipulation of the administrative *politics* of policy-making which is the mode of operation of the cabinet office and of Whitehall networks generally. Whereas CPRS needed to sharpen issues, define choices more precisely, highlight differences and specify criteria, the requirements of consensual accommodative bargaining are almost precisely the opposite.

The contrast between the work of the cabinet office and the intended role of the CPRS was made even more acute by the fact that, whereas the former operates exclusively within the closed world of Whitehall networks, CPRS was able to draw on external contacts. Partly composed of 'outsiders', non-civil servants from a variety of backgrounds, the CPRS could make contact with industry, the City and other interests whose views would normally be channelled into the central government policy process via departments. Thus CPRS not only threatened to disrupt the closed world of interdepartmental consultation and bargaining but, from a departmental point of view, its activities risked upsetting established relationships with client groups, by altering the terms of access to policy-making. Furthermore, whenever the CPRS trespassed into the territory of any particular department, as increasingly it came to do, its analysis was vulnerable to accusations that it was not doing its intended job, that it was inadequately staffed and resourced to duplicate the work of departments and that, not having any executive functions, it failed to understand the real constraints on policy in areas of departmental responsibility.

The relationship between the Treasury and the CPRS was perhaps the most complex of all: unsurprisingly given the central importance of the Treasury and its financial network in the Whitehall system. In so far as policy-making at departmental level is subjected to critical appraisal and external stimulus to self-appraisal, it is the Treasury which is the institution responsible. We shall examine in more detail later the scope of the Treasury's overseeing role, but the point here is that to have any real impact on government strategy CPRS needed to be able to speak independently and authoritatively to issues of resource allocation in the context of overall economic policy. However, in practice it was unable to compete effectively with the Treasury.[19] In addition to having in its expenditure divisions four times as many people involved in 'marking' departments as there were in the CPRS,[20] the Treasury has guaranteed and regular access to departments on all aspects of policy that involve expenditure. CPRS, on the other hand, had to make special arrangements with departments each time a study in which it engaged overlapped a department's field of responsibility. 'Its activities were episodic, a foray here and a foray there. And not being continuously involved, as the Treasury has to be, it was unable to comment authoritatively on the whole.'[21]

To a limited extent CPRS was useful to the Treasury as an ally in its dealings with departments. Its broad remit meant that it could examine areas of policy which had no financial implications, something which the Treasury itself was unable to do. This was of some significance at a time when the Treasury was seeking, particularly through PAR, to encourage departments to undertake strategic policy analysis.[22] Finding an occasional niche for itself as an ally of the Treasury was, however, a far cry from the original aspirations for CPRS. Intended to serve the cabinet as a whole, CPRS foundered on an institutional version of Catch 22. For it to function effectively the cabinet had already to be the kind of body which the perceived need for CPRS implied it was not: one that was capable of acting collectively. Let us pursue this theme further by considering PAR.

Programme Analysis and Review

PAR was intended to complement in terms of *process* the institutional development of a central capability unit within government. As with CPRS the original concept was never fully implemented and within a relatively short span of time what had been done was largely tamed and absorbed by the village life of Whitehall.[23] It had been suggested that the annual PESC exercise should be preceded by a comprehensive analysis of the various components of each department's programmes showing how they related. Cabinet should then choose particular policies for more intensive study – Programme Analysis and Review – requiring departments to justify existing programmes before the final decisions on public expenditure were taken. These ideas, developed by the Conservative Party in opposition, coincided with concerns that had emerged within the civil service itself and which focused on the deficiencies of PESC. PESC provided machinery for estimating the future cost of maintaining existing policies and programmes. What it did not do was ensure analysis of individual programme goals and effectiveness. Neither did it co-ordinate the objectives of government as a whole. It had failed to overcome the tendency for rational prioritization to be subordinated to interdepartmental bargaining. Furthermore, policies which had no, or more significantly only indirect, effects on public expenditure were not subject to PESC analysis.

It was the Treasury, at the forefront of the movement to define PAR as the logical counterpart of PESC, which eventually took the central role in its implementation rather than CPRS or the Civil Service Department. If PAR was to function at all it was probably essential that the Treasury should be the organizer since only it had the existing network of relationships to departments and the institutional authority necessary to ensure that anything of substance was done. The Treasury did not attempt to introduce the more ambitious idea of comprehensive programme structures for departments as a framework for specific PARs. Instead it proceeded through traditional kinds of channel, establishing an interdepartmental PAR committee and seeking to develop PAR gradually with the co-operation of departments. In the event, however, the attempt to incorporate PAR into the existing framework of Whitehall culture and assumptions proved a failure, as was perhaps inevitable since 'the political system in its widest sense discourages analysis'.[24] Explaining why this is so through an examination of the failure of PAR takes us some way towards understanding the real nature of ministerial responsibility for policy.

The selection of topics, the procedural ground rules for conducting reviews and most crucially the point of contact between a completed review and the decision-making process were the key issues on which PAR succumbed to the federal nature of central government.[25] Departments tended to avoid offering, as candidates for PAR, programmes that were politically sensitive or where client groups might be offended. The Treasury, like departments themselves, had little interest in interdepartmental PARs and the CPRS had scant success in encouraging them. Two factors were of crucial importance in how the reviews were actually carried out. First, the consensus among departmental officials was that ministers should be excluded from the conduct of reviews. While this made PAR more 'manageable' it contributed also to the subsequent lack of political interest in its results which was undoubtedly a feature in its demise.[26] A necessary corollary of the lack of ministerial involvement, given the myth of ministerial responsibility, was that PARs should be kept confidential; the membership of the PAR committee was secret and even completed PARs were not made available to Parliament.

The overwhelming reason for the failure of PAR was that it lacked sufficiently strong institutional support within the process of government. It can be debated whether this was the result of having no client or too many clients to give it any sense of direction[27] but one thing is abundantly clear: cabinet neither used PAR effectively nor provided any political impetus to support it.[28] Ministerial support for PARs at cabinet level was not forthcoming because there is no institutional dynamic corresponding to the rhetoric of collective responsibility. Cabinet involves shifting coalitions of ministers who are first and foremost heads of individual departments. There is a basic tradition that ministers do not intervene in each other's departmental business: to do so wins no friends and is a sure way of making enemies. In so far as the results of a PAR could be used to justify claims for additional resources for a department, they were simply one more weapon to be used within the existing framework, but PARs which received no or only lukewarm support from their departmental minister were not promoted by other ministers. PAR only survived as something which Whitehall took seriously for as long as it did because of the then Prime Minister's personal commitment. They could not, however, make up at cabinet level for the absence of any real principle of collective responsibility. Ministers did not find PAR useful in making the kinds of decision or the kinds of political judgement that the workings of cabinet demand. As civil service products PAR reports had little immediate party political relevance, and as departmental products they were absorbed into, or more usually submerged by, the insular and adversary processes of cabinet discussion of departmental issues.

Both CPRS and PAR were finally wound up by the Thatcher government. In the case of PAR at least, terminated in 1979, this was merely a formal recognition of what had taken place *de facto* several years before. When it became clear that ministers generally were not interested in PAR, departments began the process of reducing commitment to the exercise until it became a matter of merely going through the motions. CPRS on the other hand survived as more than a mere shell by becoming, 'less and less a troublesome critic of general policy directions and more a well-adjusted member of the community surrounding it'.[29] By the time it was finally abolished in 1983 there was no sense that any distinctive contribution to the process of government was being lost as the result of its demise.[30]

The Public Expenditure Survey Committee

Policy-making for public expenditure is dominated by the Treasury, central government spending departments and the rather shadowy presence of the Bank of England. Public spending decisions are made in the overall context of macroeconomic policy and, together with revenue decisions, also constitute the fundamental elements of such policy. We cannot here undertake any detailed analysis of economic policy-making in general, but it is important in understanding the general expenditure process to put it against the background of the relationship between spending and macroeconomic policy and the institutional context of that relationship.[31]

The Bank of England performs a number of tasks which are of major importance to the conduct of macroeconomic policy: managing the foreign currency reserves, the exchange rate and the financing of the government's borrowing requirement, and hence, through its operations in financial markets and influence on banking liquidity, affecting interest rates. The Bank's relationship with City financial institutions forms part of the complex web of quasi-government discussed in Chapter 6. The Bank is also 'plugged in at many levels to the Whitehall interdepartmental committee network' and there is a close and regular working relationship between Treasury and Bank officials as well as frequent meetings between the Governor of the Bank, the Chancellor and the Prime Minister.[32] The elevation of monetary policy from its subordinate role as handmaiden to Keynesian demand management to a place of pre-eminent importance in macroeconomic policy has undoubtedly increased the importance of the Bank in the economic policy process.[33] In monetarist as in Keynesian theories, however, the significant variables of macroeconomic policy depend to a large extent on government spending and revenue, and the size and method of dealing with the difference between them.[34] Thus, despite the importance of the Bank, financial markets and other influences on economic policy-making, it is the Treasury that remains at the heart of the key budgetary decision-making processes. The Chancellor of the Exchequer not only has responsibility for taxation but exercises that responsibility with little or no opportunity for input from the cabinet. As far as expenditure decisions are concerned the Treasury is the lynchpin of the decision-making process. Its expenditure divisions continually monitor and negotiate on a bilateral basis with departments and it is the Treasury which has control of the PESC exercise.

Broadly speaking, expenditure decisions can be divided into two categories: those concerning total public spending and those which allocate the total within and between different programmes. Concern for expenditure totals has always been the Treasury's central focus: this was so in the days of Gladstonian finance when the balance between the annual estimates and revenue was crucial, and remains so today when the Treasury's primary task is that of macroeconomic management, for the reasons we have already given. How the aggregate public expenditure figures translate into individual programmes is only of limited significance from a macro-economic standpoint. The importance of public expenditure, how-ever, does not reside exclusively in its macroeconomic impact. To a very large extent public policies on such matters as housing, edu-cation, defence – indeed towards the responsibilities of any of the spending departments – *consist of* expenditure decisions. Macro-economic factors may be relevant at this level, as well as to decisions on aggregate spending, but other considerations are also of funda-mental importance: in particular prioritization between and within programmes and programme goals and effectiveness. It is primarily to the departments that we should look to find analysis of the appropriate kind (though of course analysis at this level cannot encompass prioritization between the programmes of *different* departments).

The nature of the bilateral relationship between departments and the Treasury and the quality of analysis which the latter is able to demand and perform itself in relation to the allocation of spending seems to have changed little over several decades.[35] Writing in 1950 the then permanent secretary to the Treasury defined the 'Treasury man's business' as being 'to form a layman's judgement on whether the case presented for more expenditure, however admirable it may appear from a particular point of view, is out of scale with what can be allowed on a common-sense judgement of things when other demands are taken into account.' In the 1980s essentially the same view was expressed by a senior Treasury official: the Treasury's objective 'is not to get immersed too much in the merits of any particular policy, but first to look at whether what is being proposed is compatible with the department's agreed public expenditure pro-gramme and with the policy of the government as a whole on these matters'.[36] The 'agreed public expenditure programme' mentioned in the second quotation refers to the PESC system which was designed to produce more informed choices by ministers about public expenditure.

The Public Expenditure Survey Committee is an interdepartmental group composed of officials from the Treasury and departmental finance officers. The annual PESC report aims to show the future cost of existing government policies, if these remain unchanged, over a period of years (originally five, later four, then three). The central idea behind the system was to find a more rational way of planning public expenditure than the year-by-year process of adding up the estimates recording the results of bilateral Treasury/departmental negotiations to discover, a couple of months before the budget, the likely balance between revenue and expenditure in the following year.[37] PESC was not supposed itself to be a decision-making mechanism, rather it was to provide information to enable public expenditure to be planned by ministers for a number of years ahead. This, it was hoped, would avoid the disruption to departmental programmes caused by short-term cuts and enable ministers both to decide the proportion of real national economic resources to be devoted to the public sector and to prioritize between different competing claims for the available resources.[38] Not only was it difficult to compare the actual performance of departments with earlier plans, but, in relation to the planning of total public expenditure and prioritization between competing claims, PESC failed to live up to the expectations of its founders. The PESC exercise rapidly became a further area for bilateral negotiation between the Treasury and departments: over what, for example, constituted an existing policy which should be included in PESC and what was a new policy or policy change. Furthermore, PESC did not enable the Treasury to force departments to compete with each other: new policies were still decided sequentially through bilateral bargaining or cabinet level decision rather than simultaneously and competitively.[39]

The PESC survey itself is not published. The Public Expenditure White Paper reports decisions made on the basis of PESC, not the results of the survey itself. It was (and still is)[40] extremely difficult to compare government's stated intentions with eventual spending. At the level of total public spending this made it easier for ministers to avoid what in a harsh economic climate was the politically inconvenient logic of PESC: that government should relate total spending to available resources.[41]

After the crisis in public expenditure of the mid 1970s the PESC system was supplemented from 1976 onwards by the imposition, over wide areas of public spending, of limits in actual cash terms to expenditure in the forthcoming years.[42] Futhermore, the guidelines for the conduct of PESC were changed to prevent automatic recosting of existing policies and a new rule was promulgated to the effect that Treasury ministers could not be overruled in cabinet committees except by appeal to the full cabinet.[43] From 1981 the PESC exercise itself has been calculated in cash terms. Programmes for the forthcoming year are expressed in current cash prices and figures for the subsequent years are based on an estimate of what the general rate of inflation and the rate of public sector pay increases will be.[44]

Not only have these developments increased Treasury control of aggregate public expenditure, but more importantly cash planning has also made less feasible any attempt to plan individual programmes or to prioritize in a systematic way within and between programmes.

Information provided by Treasury techniques of economic forecasting goes 'a long way towards giving Ministers collectively enough material to make a rational choice about the division of resources between the public and private sectors'.[45] The fact that the Treasury is able to produce information of this kind does not, however, mean that decisions on economic policy, revenue and expenditure are in fact taken by the cabinet collectively. The PESC report is not even presented to the cabinet as a whole (although ministers can see the copies which their officials possess). What goes to cabinet is a report by Treasury ministers on the findings of the survey and recommendations on future total public expenditure.[46] These recommendations are based on an underlying revenue strategy in the context of broader economic policy, but these are matters which are primarily the departmental responsibility of Treasury ministers. The cabinet has no access to the advice which they receive and which underpins the recommendations made. Nor does the cabinet have any independent source of counteranalysis to challenge the Treasury view. Inevitably, therefore, whatever difficulties there may be in getting cabinet to agree first a figure for aggregate public expenditure and then, in the light of that figure, the implications for particular departmental programmes, it is the Treasury's assumptions which condition the exercise.

After cabinet has agreed a provisional figure for total public spending the process of official and ministerial bargaining about the programmes of individual departments begins. Again this is conducted on a bilateral basis between departments and the Treasury. From time to time cabinet committees have been given jurisdiction over disagreements that cannot be resolved at this stage but the fundamental dynamic of the exercise remains that of the cabinet system generally: political push and pull, bluff and coalition-building rather than any attempt rationally to plan a set of *governmental* priorities.[47]

The new managerialism

Before concluding that the planning of public expenditure is now simply a matter of short-term budgeting we must assess the impact of the efforts to improve 'management' and 'efficiency' within the public sector which have been undertaken by the present government: in particular the Rayner scrutinies and the Financial Management Initiative (FMI).[48] The main focus of both the scrutinies and the FMI has been efficient use of resources rather than, as in the case of PAR, effective policy planning.[49] The aim of the Rayner scrutinies was to have an exemplary function in encouraging efforts: (1) to improve value for money by reducing costs, streamlining administration and establishing clear management responsibility; and (2) to identify and tackle underlying obstacles to good management and thus to eliminate waste resulting from 'over-complicated and cluttered systems'.[50] The desirability of removing waste and inefficiency from the public service cannot of course be seriously questioned. However, despite the fact that the scrutinies are said to take nothing for granted and to 'question all aspects of the work under scrutiny to the point of challenging its very existence'[51] it is evident that the kind of information provided and analysis conducted is very different and much more limited that anything which PAR envisaged.

The objective of the FMI is also to promote the efficient use of resources through improving departmental management in ways that 'support the control and management of expenditure policy at all levels', from cabinet downwards. The intention is that managers should have not only 'well-defined responsibility for making the best use of their resources, including a critical scrutiny of output and value-for-money' but that this should be based upon 'a clear view of their objectives; and means to assess, and wherever possible measure, outputs or performances in relation to those objectives'.[52]

Once again, despite the reference to clear objectives, the central focus of the FMI is *management control*. Measurement of output through performance indicators to gauge the efficiency and effectiveness with which a department carries out its programmes logically presupposes specification of the policy objectives which the programme is designed to achieve.[53] The FMI itself, however, cannot provide such objectives, unless economy, the reduction of expenditure *per se* is the overriding goal. This may indeed be so, but does nothing to clarify the purposes of such spending as continues to take place.

Some commentators have detected in the managerial emphasis of the Rayner scrutinies and FMI re-emergence of the old distinction between policy and administration in a new form.[54] This is little more than a revival of technicist, 'end-of-ideology', ideology which we have spoken to consistently. Furthermore, the belief that there can be any clear divide between policy and administration ignores the necessity for learning processes, a matter to which we shall pay more attention in Part Three.[55]

Public spending priorities and effectiveness: a summary

What we have said in this chapter so far supports the conclusions reached by the Treasury and Civil Service Committee in its report on the 1984 autumn statement:

The evidence we have received does not convince us that there are adequate machinery and procedures to enable Cabinet to take an overall view of the relative merits of departmental programmes.

Secondly, there seems to be very little discussion by the Cabinet as a whole of which priorities are appropriate within each department.[56]

However, we wish to go beyond the conclusion that in relation to the setting of priorities the cabinet is, in Bagehot's terms, a 'dignified' rather than an 'efficient' institution. If our argument has been convincing thus far its implication is that in relation to strategic control of government policy as a whole (with the exception of the planning of *total* public expenditure) the dignified role of cabinet does not mask an 'efficient secret' at all. British constitutional arrangements lack an 'efficient' mechanism for rational prioritization and strategic planning: this is the real secret which the myth of collective ministerial responsibility serves to conceal.

Within traditional constitutional thinking such a problem would undoubtedly be identified as 'political'. The definition of 'political' might be broad or narrow but would exclude the perception of the issue as being also one of constitutional *law*. We have argued in Chapter 3 that the concept of law used in conventional constitutional discourse is unduly restricted and that the job of setting collective goals and of designing processes and institutions for that purpose, should be understood as appertaining to the legal. In Chapter 9 we make this conception more precise by defining the legal task as being to ensure that a hard look is taken at decisions and non-decisions in the policy-making process: something which present arrangements for collective cabinet decision-making manifestly fail to secure.

The weakness of strategic planning and monitoring in central government makes it even more important to emphasize that 'the effective level of policy-making in the British political system is the department'.[57] It is to the role played by ministers in their individual departments that we now turn.

Ministers and departments

Departments are headed by ministers who are said to be 'constitutionally' individually accountable to Parliament for what is done by and in the department. Statutory powers are usually conferred upon ministers and not upon departments but in practice the exercise of many such powers may never involve the personal attention of the minister.[58] In the formulation of policy, there is a wide range of variation in the degree of ministerial initiation of and involvement in the decision-making process. It is the minister, however, who speaks for the department and defends its policies, its decisions and the manner in which powers have been exercised. The minister fights for the department in cabinet and committee and, in the case of spending ministers, in bilateral negotiations with the Treasury. The role of the minister as publicist, representative and defender of the department in a variety of forums is of key importance in the current functioning of our political institutions, but it tells us little or nothing, about the role of the minister *within* the department.

Bagehot first clearly enunciated the function of ministers in preventing 'the incessant tyranny of Parliament over the public offices' and in 'standing between the department and the busybodies and the crotchet-makers of the House and country'. He also saw them as fulfilling another purpose: that of bringing a 'representative of outside sense and outside animation in contact with the inside world'.[59] The idea that ministers bring to bureaucratic administration a leaven of common sense together with an injection of energy and that otherwise the task of administration is best left undisturbed by external criticism or involvement depends upon a number of presuppositions which seem to us to be insupportable in modern circumstances. First, there is the idea that administration can be separated from the determination of objectives and policies and can therefore be judged by unproblematic criteria of efficiency.

Bagehot's ideas also assume the nineteenth-century conception of the limited role and functions of the state in which the formulation of public policy is of sufficiently narrow compass to be performed by parliamentary institutions. In other words Bagehot's view of the function of government departments, and hence of the individual minister's role, assumes both that collective responsibility is a reality and that departments are not 'the effective level of policy-making in the British political system'. In modern circumstances departments do play a central role in the policy-making process: they do not merely administer the implementation of policies decided collectively by ministers. The corollary is that the constitutional promise of accountable government is not now realizable to any extent through individual ministerial responsibility. Bagehot's description of the part played by ministers in protecting departments from publicly visible external criticism and pressure is entirely realistic. The result, however, is not, as Bagehot thought, the immunity from irrational and sectional pressures of a rational and efficient administration serving public goals formulated by cabinet and debated in the forum of the nation, Parliament. Rather, ministerial responsibility conceals a highly secretive mode of policy-making in which the formulation of public objectives and policies to achieve them is a largely unaccountable process which is neither rational and effective nor immune from sectional pressures.

Ministers and civil servants

Discussion of this topic has to a large extent failed to free itself from the incubus of orthodox constitutional assumptions. It is true that serious commentators do not seek to maintain the view that ministers decide policy which civil servants then implement. None the less, the assumption remains that the traditional notion of ministerial responsibility is not merely one mechanism – which has perhaps outlived its usefulness – for ensuring constitutional accountability, but the only possible such mechanism in the British context. This attitude makes assumptions even less realistic than those that underpin the myth of collective responsibility. It is not only cabinet and ministers, with all the resources of the central government machine at their disposal, who are supposed to make coherent and rational policy choices which can then be implemented to ensure achievement of the objectives the policies reflect – this same feat is supposed to be achievable even by parties in opposition. Consider for example the following extracts from a parliamentary select committee report:

many who have been, or who are, ministers . . . say that they find on their coming into office that some departments have firmly held policy views and that it is very difficult to change these views. When they are changed, the department will often try and reinstate its own policies through the passage of time and the erosion of ministers' political will. . . . In considering these allegations it is necessary to make two points which to some extent justify these practices to the extent that they may exist. First the workload of most departments is so great that all decisions cannot be taken by ministers. It is natural that ministers would want to delegate some matters to the civil service . . . . Secondly, the civil service has a duty to preserve the overall consistency of Government policy when a minister embarks on a course of action conflicting with that of a minister in another department.[60]

Now, except in relation to certain narrow classes of statutory duty or power, the relationship between ministers and civil servants is rarely one of *express* delegation.[61] In a constitutional sense all those who exercise public power are delegates of Parliament but this is merely to state the problem of accountability not to solve it. The policy-making role of the civil service is not in general something which is a matter of choice by ministers: it is a necessary structural feature of modern government. Nor is the problem of accountability which results any longer, even if it ever was, one which could be solved by arguing that civil servants should be accountable to ministers who in turn are responsible to Parliament.

This means that the 'problem' of civil service power cannot usefully be approached in terms of a conflict between ministers and civil servants in which the question is 'who wins?'. This is not to deny that such conflicts occur or the possibility that civil servants may sometimes act in ways that are improper. However, for the most part and for most of the time public power is exercised by ministers and civil servants acting in a co-operative, even symbiotic, mode. Our earlier discussion of public expenditure should have demonstrated that the size of modern government and the complexity of the tasks that it undertakes mean that public policies and decisions are not in reality made by ministers rather than by civil servants. Nor can civil servants be made hierarchically accountable to ministers for all the work that they do through mechanisms of express delegation and *ex post* or *ex ante* monitoring of defined delegated tasks. This is not because civil servants have usurped power which does not belong to them and which should properly be returned to ministers, although the continuing dominance of the idea of ministerial responsibility encourages this illusion. '[I]n the real world Ministers and civil servants are inextricably mixed up with each other'[62] and the constitutional problem is how to make the resulting system of government accountable for the use and non-use of public power.

In practical terms the policy process involves many more civil servants than ministers: there are 100 or so ministers and political advisers in central government but 3000 or so senior civil servants 'operating every day in the field of public policy: working closely with Ministers, advising on delicate political matters and identifying initiatives to be examined and followed'.[63] Governments come into office committed to certain political objectives which they may reformulate, alter or supplement while in office. The detailed work of policy-making – forecasting the likely impact of policies, assessing what is possible, at what cost, and under what sets of possible external environmental changes – is something for which ministers must rely on relationships of trust and confidence with the civil service.[64] A powerful and energetic minister or Prime Minister can have considerable personal impact on the policy-making process. Likewise the broad political aspirations of the party in power and the nature of the party political battle all make a difference to the exercise and non-exercise of public power.[65] It is the civil service, however, which drafts the papers that ministers see, which filters the information reaching ministers to reduce it to manageable form and which thereby in many cases and for much of the time plays the crucial role in defining problems and possible solutions.

Thus, for all their political neutrality, the actual work of civil servants is scarcely devoid of political content: on the contrary the higher one goes in the civil service the more vital political sensitivity and judgement become. Sir Douglas Wass makes the point very well:

I myself had to take a number of quite political decisions in 1976 when I represented the government at the meeting of the International Monetary Fund . . . . Of course I reported back to my political chiefs on what I was doing. . . . But the execution was mine and the objective I aimed at was to say what I thought Mr Healey would have said, had he been able to attend the conference. On other occasions I have had to act for my Minister when I was far from clear what position he would have taken. At such moments I have had to do what I thought was right and rely on the confidence that I felt my Minister had in me.[66]

The old constitutional paradigm of relationships between civil servants and ministers has continued to dominate official thinking and pervaded the numerous inquiries that have been held into the workings of the civil service. Between 1850 and 1968 there were fourteen major studies of the service, including the Fulton Report, but none, including Fulton, came to grips with the inadequacy of the traditional constitutional understandings.[67] All were focused too narrowly on the internal structure of the civil service rather than on what governments do and so neglected the constitutional challenge posed by the growth of the state and change in its structure and functions.[68] More generally the 'institutionitis' of the Wilson and Heath years, the almost obsessive tinkering with the machinery of government and the structure of departments, similarly neglected the constitutional dimension, as have later changes such as the abolition of the Civil Service Department.[69]

In many ways the Thatcher government's managerialist emphasis on efficiency is a return to one of the underlying themes of the Fulton Report: improved efficiency through creating 'accountable' management structures with a clear allocation of personal responsibility and authority. More controversially perhaps, even the current creeping politicization of the civil service, through emphasis on 'loyalty' to government policy and objectives as a precondition for promotion and the employment of non-career civil servants to fill certain senior posts, can be seen as a logical development of Fulton's other main emphasis which was on the characteristics of civil service personnel.

Fulton's main recommendations were all important: clearer lines of managerial responsibility, the creation of a Civil Service Department separate from the Treasury, a more fluid career structure for civil servants emphasizing the role of 'specialists' as opposed to 'generalists' and consequent changes in recruitment policies. There is little reason, however, to dissent from Ashford's assessment that:

the most naive part of the report was the conviction that if different kinds of people, presumably more socially representative and more professional, were put in the upper ranks of the civil service, then the policy-making process would be simultaneously more 'democratic' and more efficient.[70]

From our perspective, one of the most interesting of Fulton's specific recommendations was that each department should have a planning unit to be responsible for long-term planning and research and to ensure that the department's day-to-day policy decisions were consistent with long-term strategies. The units, it was suggested, should be staffed mainly by specialists and headed by a 'specialist' senior policy adviser who would have direct access to the minister without having to go through the permanent secretary. It was hoped that this would break the grip of civil service 'generalists' on the policy-making process.[71] The ways in which the Fulton proposals were modified or even neutralized by the civil service itself provide a fascinating case study of the civil service in operation and the resistance of the Whitehall machine to fundamental change.[72] The general civil service view seemed to be that departments already had adequate planning capacity of the kind Fulton was proposing although, for example, the planning organization of the Department of Education and Science was heavily criticized by the Organization for Economic Co-operation and Development on Fulton-type grounds in 1975.[73] The OECD criticism highlights only one example of the failure of government departments to engage in adequate long-term planning. Parliamentary select committees have pointed to many other cases.[74]

Despite the accuracy of Fulton's diagnosis of the problem and the clear implication in Kellner and Crowther-Hunt's account that the civil service deliberately sabotaged Fulton's recommendation, there is a strong case for arguing that the planning unit proposal for departments was bound to fail to achieve Fulton's objectives for reasons similar to those which account for the failure of CPRS and PAR at cabinet level. To introduce rational policy planning mechanisms into central government requires that attention be paid to 'the critical interface between political and administrative actors'.[75] The resistance to change of Whitehall structures is not simply a question of bloody-minded conservatism by civil servants. The structures have evolved in response to and to accommodate the political demands which appear in constitutional terms as the exclusive reliance on ministerial responsibility to a Parliament dominated by the party system. As has been well remarked, there are good historical justifications for civil servants' scepticism about administrative reform: typically reform efforts have been short-lived and have failed to achieve significant lasting change. Thus a reactive, short-term and incremental style of decision-making has continued to predominate. For example, the OECD report on the DES mentioned earlier concluded that 'there is no attempt at a new identification and formulation of educational goals in a world where the traditional canons of knowledge, values, attitudes and skills are continually questioned'.[76] 'Incrementalism' – the focus on marginal adjustments to existing policies, the bases of which are not subjected to overall critical analysis – is the deeply entrenched policy style of British government.[77]

Let us briefly summarize our view as to why both the 'rationalist' and the 'managerial' responses are inadequate as solutions to the constitutional problems of the modern state.

The managerial focus has accepted rather than questioned the policy/administration distinction and consequently has failed to address the issue of how objectives and goals can be determined and modified in complex environments.[78] In the case of the FMI and the Rayner scrutinies the overwhelming emphasis on economy has led to financial planning becoming a substitute for, rather than a mechanism of, policy planning.

Cash limits can be implemented and lower spending rates achieved at the same time as the overall analytic capabilities of government decline. To say the policy is 'the number' opens the way for all sorts of ignorance and irrationality in the policy process – ignorance about what is being achieved by the numbers, irrationality that hits spending targets but misses policy objectives.[79]

The 'rationalist' reforms on the other hand have sought to introduce analysis of policy in terms of objectives and effectiveness and thus have tackled the issue that the managerial response ignores. As we have seen, however, the institutional pressures generated by the dominance of party political considerations within the processes of government marginalized PAR and CPRS and led to their demise. These institutional pressures take *constitutional* form as the doctrines of collective and individual ministerial responsibility: ideas which are premised on a clear distinction between processes of policy-making and implementation, between policy and administration. What may appear paradoxical is that the structures created or proposed for PAR, CPRS and Fulton-style planning units were also premised on those distinctions. All neglected what we have called the 'learning' dimension. The seeming paradox is resolved, however, once we recognize that the constitutional doctrine of ministerial responsibility is mythical in two senses. It does not describe the actual world in which ministers and civil servants are 'inextricably mixed up with each other' but nor, in modern conditions, does it describe a possible world. It does, however, function as a powerful ideological consideration. Attempts at reform must be consistent with preservation of the myth and thus must not challenge the distinction between policy and administration. This of course guarantees that the reforms could not succeed in the real world: something which those inside the Whitehall machine know full well.

Secrecy: the cement of the constitution

We have tried to show that the concept of ministerial responsibility to Parliament implies a picture of executive decision-making that is false, but that the ideological importance of the concept has very real effects in structuring and stabilizing the way in which government works. Crudely, ministers do not engage in effective planning, and ministerial responsibility helps ensure that government as a whole does not do so either. On the other hand, in the incremental and reactive system that actually exists the policy that results is the work of both civil servants and ministers rather than the latter alone. The effort to conceal this state of affairs – in order to preserve the fiction of accountability – helps ensure its continuation.

Ministerial responsibility to Parliament could not continue to appear to satisfy the constitutional promise of accountability were it not for the secrecy which protects the workings of government from public view. That the British is one of the most secretive of democratically elected governments is now widely recognized. There is little point in our rehearsing in detail the factors which make for lack of openness in Britain since numerous accounts are already available[80] and we discuss freedom of information in more detail in Chapter 9. There are, of course, matters which government seeks to keep completely secret, documents concerning which may not be released for thirty or even 100 years,[81] but official secrecy is less about the complete suppression of all reference to particular matters than about information and opinion *management*. As Kellner and Crowther-Hunt put it, our political traditions have produced a subtle but deep-rooted system of information-rationing.[82]

As is well-known the 'catch-all' provisions of section 2 of the Official Secrets Act apply, *inter alia*, to all Crown servants including ministers and civil servants, and to all information whether or not it is given an internal Whitehall security classification. The section 2 offence is committed by someone who communicates official information, 'to any person, other than a person to whom he is authorised to communicate it, or a person to whom it is in the interest of the state his duty to communicate it'.

As was made clear in the Official Secrets Act trial of Clive Ponting, there is no coherent public law theory of the interests of the state as conceptually distinct from whatever the policies of the government happen to be:

Interest of the State . . . means the policies of the State . . . the policies laid down for it by the recognised organs of Government and authority.

We have General Elections in this country. The majority party in the House of Commons forms the Government. If it loses majority support it ceases to do so, but for the time being, it *is* the Government, and its policies are those of the State.[83]

Despite the fact that civil servants are heavily involved in formulating policy they have no independent duty to provide Parliament with information. Ministerial responsibility implies the right of ministers to define the interests of the state, including what information it is in the interests of the state to disclose and to whom. Excluded thereby is any conception that the ability of Parliament to hold government accountable is itself an interest of the state which might impose duties of disclosure on civil servants. To put the matter another way, ministers have the right to decide how much and what kind of information to disclose, even to Parliament, for as long as they can command a majority. The concept of accountability through ministerial responsibility is thus made incoherent even in its own terms.

In general, policy on information disclosure is no more exclusively a matter for ministers than any other area of policy. 'Authorization' for the purposes of section 2 is rarely a formal or express granting of permission, instead reliance is placed on

implied authorisation, flowing from the nature of each Crown servant's job . . . . Ministers are, in effect, self-authorising. They decide for themselves what to reveal. Senior civil servants exercise a considerable degree of personal judgement in deciding what disclosures of official information they may properly make and to whom.[84]

Growing pressure for more open government led to a reformulation of official policy on disclosure in a letter from Sir Douglas Allen, later Lord Croham, Head of the Home Civil Service, sent to permanent secretaries in 1977.[85] The major emphasis of the Croham Directive was on factual and analytical material, 'background material relating to policy studies and reports' to be released in the form of 'deliberate presentations in the later stages of discussion and development of policy'. Typically perhaps the Directive was itself not published but was leaked to the press.

While the change of policy marked by the Directive was perhaps mainly governed by the hope of deflecting pressure for a more comprehensive approach to FOI it has had some real impact in encouraging disclosure and is still, formally, government policy.[86] Disclosure of information remains discretionary, however, in relation both to its extent and timing. It is also important to emphasize that most 'disclosure' or 'communication' of information does not take place within the framework of the Croham Directive at all. The Directive is concerned with placing information on the public record in the sense that it is made generally available. However, the other vital aspect of official secrecy, besides its role in maintaining the fiction of ministerial responsibility, is to enable government to use the selective and partial disclosure of information as a positive instrument of policy. Access to official information thus becomes a privilege for which a price must be paid, one element of which is frequently the maintenance of a greater or lesser degree of confidentiality in respect of the information that is received. One facet of this is the system of self-censorship operated by the press and other media. The lobby system, which benefits both journalists and government, depends on preserving the 'unattributable' nature of briefings by ministers and civil servants.[87] Briefings, of course, can develop into leaks: in this context the only criterion which distinguishes the authorized from the unauthorized – and therefore the legal from the illegal – disclosure of information is the political interests of the government.

Just as important to the working of modern British government as the management of release of information to the media is the access to official information given to selected groups as part of the ordinary every-day functioning of the policy process.

Departments and clienteles

So far in our consideration of central government the major theme that we have been pursuing is that policy is not made exclusively by politicians in the way that reliance on ministerial responsibility to Parliament as the sole mechanism for the constitutional accountability of government would imply. We have shown that civil servants are necessarily deeply involved in the policy-making process and that the capacity of government to plan, to formulate clear objectives and to pursue them effectively is highly problematic. None of this is new, none of it would surprise practitioners of government or political scientists. However, the perception of these realities by the 'political nation' is rarely if ever translated into constitutional debate. To some extent this is the result of a failure by constitutional scholars to re-examine the concepts that underlie the legitimation claims of the British state, but there are other, interlocking, factors at work also. Official secrecy and information management help to prevent the inadequacies of traditional constitutional claims from becoming a matter of general knowledge. Futhermore, the widespread acceptance among both practitioners and observers of government of a situation in which the 'dignified' parts of the constitution conceal the 'efficient' parts from public scrutiny is underpinned by the belief, first clearly formulated by Bagehot, that this is an essential aspect of good government.

The unspoken heart of the argument for closed government is that private debate amongst civil servants and ministers produces more *rational* policies, freed from public pressure, which is assumed to be irrational. Wise men, cogitating quietly on the nation's problems, will produce 'right' answers, if they are shielded from the hubbub of the political marketplace. But once exposed to pressure groups and vested interests and newspapers that will get it all wrong, who knows what absurdities will result.[88]

Of the various assumptions on which this argument depends we wish, at this point to challenge only one. We have not brought our argument thus far merely to substitute for the constitutional fiction that policy is made by ministers and implemented by civil servants an equally fictional picture of government in which policy is made by ministers and civil servants acting jointly in an hermetically sealed box called 'government'. British government is closed in the sense that its workings are concealed beneath a cloak of secrecy. It is not, however, closed in the sense that public servants, ministers and officials are insulated from sectional pressures and interests. On the contrary, the doctrine of implied authorization to reveal official information reflects the fact that the policy process involves continuous contact between public officials and private or sectional interests. In the real world not only ministers and civil servants but also a wide range of client groups, vested and sectional interests are all 'inextricably mixed up with each other'. Far from shielding government from the hubbub of the political market-place secrecy conceals the fact that to a large extent the executive has *become* the political market-place.

In Britain there is no *a priori* reason to exclude the possibility of capture or colonization of parts of the central government apparatus by private interests.[89] That departments 'mark' pressure groups and special interests and that 'political decisions at every level of government are reached with a view, in part at least to satisfying these pressure groups and interests'[90] is not *per se* evidence of the confusion of public and private in the policy process. However it does appear to be the case that some of the groups and clienteles affected by the policies and programmes of government have a special status in relation to the departments concerned which makes 'capture' a distinct possibility. The position of the National Farmers Union in relation to the Ministry of Agriculture, and of oil companies in relation to the Department of Energy are documented examples of contemporary importance.[91]

More generally, there are a number of factors resulting from the federal nature of central government, which encourage, if not capture, at least a high degree of identification with interests of client groups on the part of departments or sections of departments. The incremental style of Whitehall administration makes it easy to accommodate pressure from clients since the evolution of policy within departments is subject to little external review and departments themselves have more to gain than to lose by such accommodation. Satisfied clients will not seek to embarrass ministers and there is anyway a natural tendency for departments to seek to maintain and enhance their programme spending since this is the mark of a successful department. In some cases orchestrated 'pressure' from clients can be a useful weapon in battles with the Treasury or other departments.[92]

Given the central role that departments play in policy formation and the weakness of mechanisms for strategic planning and control the constitutional importance of the relationships between departments and client groups should be clear. In the absence of mechanisms of accountability which are capable of embracing every stage of, and all the participants in, the policy process, the separation of public and private and the formation of a coherent view of the public interest transcending sectional interests are merely articles of faith.

References

1 N. Johnson, *In Search of the Constitution* (Methuen 1977), p. 84.
2 W. Bagehot, *The English Constitution*, introduction by R. H. S. Crossman (Fontana 1963), p. 65.
3 ibid., p. 67.
4 The 'transmission belt' analogy is taken from R. Stewart, 'The reformation of American administrative law', *Harvard Law Review*, **88** 1667–1813 at 1675. cf. *Rechtstaat* theory; see e.g., F. Hayek, *The Road to Serfdom* (George Routledge 1944), p. 54.
5 D. E. Ashford, *Policy and Politics in Britain* (Blackwell 1981), p. 39.
6 Bagehot, p. 37.
7 A. L. Lowell, *The Government of England* (New York: Macmillan 1908), p. 56.
8 See the minute of February 1978 from James Callaghan to ministers reproduced in P. Kellner and Lord Crowther-Hunt, *The Civil Servant* (MacDonald Futura 1980), pp. 273–4.
9 Crossman, introduction to Bagehot, p. 49.
10 See G. W. Jones, 'The Prime Minister's power', 1965, *Parliamentary Affairs*, **18**, 167–85; A. King (ed.), *The British Prime Minister*, 2nd edn (Macmillan 1985).
11 See R. H. S. Crossman, *The Diaries of a Cabinet Minister*, 3 vols. (Jonathan Cape 1975–7) for accounts of many examples from the 1964–70 Labour administration.
12 Sir Douglas Wass, *Government and the Governed* (RKP 1984), p. 35.
13 ibid., pp. 10–11.
14 ibid., p. 31.
15 See esp. H. Heclo and A. Wildavsky, *The Private Government of Public Money*, 2nd end (Macmillan 1981) ch. 7; W. Plowden, 'The British CPRS', in P. R. Baehr and B. Whittrock (eds.), *Policy Analysis and Policy Innovation* (Sage 1981).
16 *The Re-organisation of Central Government* Cmnd. 4506 (HMSO 1970), paras. 44–8.
17 Quoted in Ashford, pp. 31–2.
18 See Heclo and Wildavsky, esp. pp. 311–12.
19 ibid., p. 330.
20 Wass, p. 38.
21 ibid.
22 Andrew Gray and Bill Jenkins, 'Policy analysis in British central government: the experience of PAR', *Public Administration*, **60** (1982), pp. 429–50 at p. 441.
23 See Heclo and Wildavsky, ch. 6; Gray and Jenkins (1982).
24 Gray and Jenkins (1982), p. 447.
25 Ashford, p. 33, Heclo and Wildavsky, p. lxv. See also Central Policy Review Staff, *Relations Between Central Government and Local Authorities* (HMSO 1977).

26 Gray and Jenkins (1982), pp. 437–8.
27 See Heclo and Wildavsky, p. xliii; Gray and Jenkins (1982), p. 445.
28 Gray and Jenkins (1982), p. 442.
29 Heclo and Wildavsky, p. xlvi.
30 Wass, p. 38.
31 See generally, Ashford, ch. 3, W. Keegan and R. Pennant-Rea, *Who Runs the Economy?* (Maurice Temple Smith 1979); W. Grant and S. Nath, *The Politics of Economic Policymaking* (Blackwell 1984); Paul Mosley, *The Making of Economic Policy* (Harvester 1984).
32 Keegan and Pennant-Rea (1979), pp. 98–9.
33 M. Moran, 'Monetary policy and the machinery of government', *Public Administration*, **59**, pp. 47–61; *idem* 'Power, policy and the City of London', in R. King (ed.), *Capital and Politics* (RKP 1983); Keegan and Pennant-Rea, pp. 96–104. On monetary policy in the heyday of Keynesianism see the Radcliffe report, *Report of the Committee on the Working of the Monetary System*, Cmnd. 827 (HMSO 1959). On monetary policy after 1979 see, Treasury and Civil Service Committee, *Monetary Policy*, 3rd Report Session 1980–1, HC 163–I.
34 For the relationship between the concepts of money supply and government borrowing see HC 163–I, Session 1980–1, ch. 6 and appendix 3.
35 The classic analysis is that of Heclo and Wildavsky. See esp. ch. 3.
36 Sir Edward Bridges, *Treasury Control* (Athlone Press 1950), p. 28; H. Young and A. Sloman, *But, Chancellor* (BBC 1984), p. 43. See also H. Roseveare, *The Treasury* (Allen Lane 1969), pp. 294–6.
37 The pre-PESC system is described in Otto Clarke, *Public Expenditure, Management and Control* (Macmillan 1968). See also Sir Leo Pliatzky, *Getting and Spending* (Blackwell 1982), pp. 33–5.
38 The PESC system was introduced following the Plowden report, an edited version of which was published as Cmnd. 1432 (HMSO 1961). See esp. para. 7.
39 See Heclo and Wildavsky, esp. p. 227.
40 See 3rd Report of the Treasury and Civil Service Committee, *The Government's Expenditure Plans 1983–84 to 1985–86* HC 204 1982/3 Appendix 1.
41 See Heclo and Wildavsky, p. xix.
42 *Cash Limits on Public Expenditure* Cmnd. 6440 (HMSO 1976).
43 Pliatzky (1982), pp. 140, 145.
44 See Pliatzky (1982), pp. 195–200; *idem* 'Have volumes gone underground? An interim report on cash planning', *Public Administration*, **61** (1983), pp. 323–6, T. Ward, 'Cash planning', *Public Administration*, **61** (1983), pp. 87–90; *idem* 'PESC in crisis', *Policy and Politics*, **11** (1983), pp. 167–76.
45 Wass, p. 13. See also Keegan and Pennant-Rea, pp. 80–96, and *Report*

of the Committee on Policy Optimisation (the Ball Committee) Cmnd. 7148 (HMSO 1978).

46   Pliatzky (1982), p. 54.

47   See e.g. First Report of the Treasury and Civil Service Committee, Session 1984/5 HC 44. *The Government's Economic Policy: Autumn Statement*, paras. 10–11. See also S. Jenkins, 'The "Star Chamber"', PESC and the cabinet', *Political Quarterly*, **56** (1985), pp. 113–21; Joel Barnett, *Inside the Treasury* (André Deutsch 1982), esp. p. 103.

48   I. B. Beesley, 'The Rayner scrutinies', in A. G. Gray and W. I. Jenkins (eds.), *Policy Analysis and Evaluation in British Government*, N. Warner, 'Raynerism in practice: anatomy of a Rayner scrutiny', *Public Administration*, **62** (1984), pp. 7–22; *Efficiency and Effectiveness in the Civil Service*, Cmnd. 8616 (HMSO 1982); *Financial Management in Government Departments*, Cmnd. 9058 (HMSO 1983); L. Metcalfe and S. Richards, 'The Impact of the Efficiency Strategy: political clout or cultural change?', *Public Administration*, **62** (1983), pp. 439–54; A. G. Gray and W. I. Jenkins, 'Lasting reforms in Civil Service management?', *Political Quarterly*, **55** (1984), pp. 418–27, M. Minogue, 'Theory and Practice in public administration', *Policy and Politics*, **11** (1983), pp. 63–85.

49   Gray and Jenkins (1984).

50   Beesley, p. 31.

51   ibid., p. 33.

52   Cmnd. 9085 paras. 1–4.

53   i.e. 'corporate management' presupposes 'corporate planning'. See further below on corporate planning Chapter 8.

54   Metcalfe and Richards (1983), p. 440. See also M. Hill, 'The policy–implementation distinction: a quest for rational control?', in S. Barrett and C. Fudge, (eds.) *Policy and Action* (Methuen 1981).

55   See e.g. M. Landau and R. Stout Jr, 'To manage is not to control: or the folly of type II errors', *Public Administration Review*, **39** (1979), pp. 148–56 at 149.

56   HC 44 Session 1984/5, paras. 10–11.

57   Ashford, p. 33.

58   The '*Carltona*' doctrine (see *Carltona Ltd v Commissioners of Works* [1943] 2 All ER 560) means that the courts will not seek to penetrate the veil of ministerial responsibility, the decision of the official being regarded as the decision of the minister himself.

59   Bagehot, pp. 165–6, 178.

60   Eleventh Report from the Expenditure Committee, Session 1976/7 HC 535–I paras. 137–42.

61   As we have already explained (footnote 58 above) the courts do not treat the matter as one of delegation at all.

62   Wass, p. 46.

63   ibid., p. 11.

64 Kellner and Crowther-Hunt, pp. 233–8; Heclo and Wildavsky, pp. 130–1; Wass, lecture 3.
65 cf. Richard Rose, *Do Parties Make a Difference?* (Macmillan 1980).
66 Wass, pp. 48–9.
67 See J. B. Bourn, 'The main reports on the British civil service since the Northcote–Trevelyan Report', *The Civil Service* (The Fulton Report) Cmnd. 3638, vol. 3(2), pp. 423–65 (HMSO 1968). On the development of the modern civil service see H. Parris, *Constitutional Bureaucracy* (George Allen and Unwin 1969).
68 Ashford, p. 69.
69 ibid., pp. 72–3.
70 The post-Fulton reforms are discussed briefly below. See also Cmnd. 4506 (HMSO 1970) *The Re-organisation of Central Government* and generally Ashford, pp. 75–6.
71 *The Civil Service*, vol. 1, pp. 57–9.
72 See Kellner and Crowther-Hunt, pt 1.
73 Kellner and Crowther-Hunt, pp. 206–8.
74 See *The Government's White Paper on Public Expenditure: The Social Services*, 3rd Report of the Social Services Committee, 1979/80 HC 702–I; *Efficiency and Effectiveness in the Civil Service*, Report of the Treasury and Civil Service Committee 1981/2 HC 236.
75 Ashford, p. 73.
76 Quoted in Kellner and Crowther-Hunt, p. 279.
77 On incrementalism in expenditure decisions see generally Heclo and Wildavsky. See also J. J. Richardson and A. G. Jordan, *Governing Under Pressure* (Martin Robertson 1979).
78 See esp. Metcalfe and Richards.
79 Heclo and Wildavsky, pp. xxxix–xl.
80 Comparative material is available in I. Galnor (ed.), *Government. Secrecy in Democracies* (New York: Harper and Row 1977); Civil Service Department, *Disclosure of Official Information: A Report on Overseas Practice* (HMSO 1979); D. C. Rowat (ed.), *Administrative Secrecy in Developed Countries* (Macmillan 1979). For accounts of secrecy in Britain see e.g. D. Leigh, *The Frontiers of Secrecy* (Junction Books 1980), Kellner and Crowther-Hunt, ch. 11, R. Delbridge and M. Smith, *Consuming Secrets* (Burnett Books 1982).
81 Public Records Act 1958.
82 pp. 281–2. For the growth of a 'formal system of opinion management' in Britain see K. Middlemas, *Politics in Industrial Society* (Andre Deutsch 1979), pp. 350–70.
83 *R. v Ponting* [1985] *Criminal Law Review*, 318. The relevant part of the judgment of McCowan J. is quoted in C. Ponting, *The Right to Know* (Sphere 1985), pp. 190–1.
84 The Franks Report, vol. 1 *Report of the Committee*, Cmnd. 5104 (HMSO 1972), para. 18.

85   See Kellner and Crowther-Hunt, appendix 4; Ponting, pp. 53–7; Outer Circle Policy Unit, *A Consumer's Guide to Open Government* (OCPU 1980), pp. 19–21.

86   See OCPU *A Consumer's Guide to Open Government*.

87   See P. Hennessy and M. Cockerell, *Sources Close to the Prime Minister* (Macmillan 1984).

88   Kellner and Crowther-Hunt, pp. 275–6 (emphasis in original).

89   See e.g. G. Kalko, *Railroads and Regulation 1877–1916* (Princeton University Press 1965); M. Bernstein, *Regulating Business by Independent Commission* (Princeton University Press 1955); James Q. Wilson, *The Politics of Regulation* (New York: Basic Books 1980). Schuch, review of *The Politics of Regulation*, *Yale Law Journal*, **90** (1981), p. 702; S. Breyer, *Regulation and its Reform* (Cambridge, Mass.: Harvard University Press 1982).

90   Wass, p. 105.

91   See M. Harrison (ed.), *Corporatism and the Welfare State* (Gower 1984); W. G. Carson, *The Other Price of Britain's Oil* (Martin Robertson 1982).

92   See Jordan and Richardson, pp. 29–31.

6 Pressure and institutions

The principles of ministerial responsibility conceal both the federal nature of central government and the policy-making functions of the civil service. The same lack of effective 'organic law', of constitutional delineation of the real location of decision-making, applies to the external relationships of central government. In a unitary state, where the legislative competence of Parliament is unlimited and there is little in the way of developed administrative law, constitutional authority to allocate decision-making functions is both concentrated and highly discretionary. The exercise of that authority moreover can sometimes be well nigh invisible.

Despite the constitutional gap, legal form is in fact given to many of the institutions and to some of the processes of disintegrated government. Public corporations, tribunals and advisory bodies are often created by primary legislation and the courts do enforce to some extent statutory allocations of power and requirements of consultation.[1] As we saw in Part One, in terms of constitutional expectations, there lies at the heart of the Dicean paradigm the distinction between a public sphere of accountable civic authority and a private realm of individual autonomous activity. The two are supposed to relate through Parliament, which represents the latter and controls the former on its behalf.

Public and private

The activities of all post-liberal states in relation to the organization of both production and consumption have made the divide between public and private increasingly blurred.[2] In Britain the Dicean paradigm has continued, none the less, to condition constitutional rhetoric and expectations. At the same time the absence of constitutional machinery for planning and monitoring the allocation of decision-making has encouraged an *ad hoc*, pragmatic approach to the design of processes and institutions. As a result their legal form – if any – is a poor guide to their functions and mode of operation. Lawyers who are concerned with constitutional matters must, of necessity, direct their attention to the lack of fit between the real location of decision-making functions and the map of such functions implied by the traditional delineation of constitutional authority. To fail to do so is to break faith with the promise of accountability that constitutes the essence of the rule of law. Even those who, like Bagehot, would acquiesce in the concealment of the efficient parts of the constitution behind a dignified facade have an intellectual duty to identify, as Bagehot sought to do, what exactly it is that the facade conceals.

In this chapter we shall examine the Byzantine structure of networks of quasi-government and quasi-non-government through which much of the authority that the traditional constitutional map locates in Parliament, and those directly responsible to it, is now really exercised.

In Britain the kind of legislature which a different constitutional pattern produced in the USA has not emerged. Congress has a strong, bureaucratic committee and subcommittee structure through which the process of legislation and budgeting is conducted and bargaining between interests takes place. MPs in Britain do represent or have connections with a wide range of outside interests and specifically parliamentary results can sometimes be identified. The committee stage of the Cable and Broadcasting Bill for example and a 1984 debate on civil aviation policy were dominated so far as backbench contributions were concerned by those who declared an interest.[3] For the most part, however, it is the party rather than the specifically parliamentary connection of MPs which is of significance.[4] The channelling of the democratic franchise into mass parties in the nineteenth century and the growth of party discipline eroded the capacity of Parliament to play a creative policy-making role even in relation to the limited range of interests it represented before the extension of the franchise. At the same time Parliament was being excluded from the prelegislative phase of public bills and delegated legislative and administrative powers were largely supplanting private bill procedure. As a result it was the executive that became the primary location for both outward and inward pressure on the boundaries of the state.[5]

The organizational principles of the executive at central government level – confidentiality, mutual trust and pragmatic accommodation – facilitated the developments we are discussing. They also extended themselves into the emerging networks with the result that their existence, let alone their significance, only emerged comparatively recently.[6] We have already referred to Douglas Ashford's remark that 'British administration mastered the principles of co-optation and mutual self-interest long before the "corporate state" became a political science buzzword'.[7] However, while the traditional social mechanisms for creating elite consensus remain of fundamental importance they are increasingly embedded within rather more differentiated and institutionalized forms.[8]

The reason why groups and organizations seek to bring pressure and influence to bear upon government is self-evident. Not only does it have the power to legislate and to acquire and use administrative authority, it can also allocate resources through taxation and spending.[9] At a similar level of generality, there are a number of factors bearing upon central government which encourage responsiveness to such pressures.

A general cultural preference for informal, fluid processes of elite consensus-seeking and co-optation[10] makes it easy for networks that blur the boundary between public and private to flourish. But this cultural preference operates within the context of a liberal-democratic political tradition. The continued existence of private ownership and individual freedoms – while not a matter of constitutional guarantees and thus susceptible to marginal encroachment through processes that lack constitutional form – is a general structural feature of state activity.[11]

The primary constraint, therefore, on centralized decision-making is that to achieve its objectives government must to some extent influence the use of resources that it does not directly control. Obvious examples in the economic field include incomes policy and other interventions at micro-level such as industrial restructuring. Even monetary policy, however, requires co-ordination of the activities of the clearing banks, building societies and other financial institutions.

The absence of direct hierarchical administrative control over the resources needed for making and implementing policy imposes a degree of dependency on government. As state activity increasingly involves not the rational-legal form of administration typical of the liberal *gesellschaft* polity, but the formulation of specific goals and the achievement of particular outcomes, there is a concomitant increase in the complexity of decision-making.[12] Government has traditionally relied on 'producer groups' in particular to supply it with necessary information, technical expertise and judgement that could otherwise be acquired only at inordinate cost, or not at all.[13] 'The form and functioning of British Government are predicated upon the assumption that it will be advised, helped and criticised by the specialist knowledge of interested parties.'[14]

At the level of the legitimation of state activities, electoral success does not guarantee that a government's specific policies will be acceptable either generally or to those whose lack of co-operation or whose resistance can hinder implementation. Bargaining and negotiation with pressure groups and affected interests may thus be ways of winning the active consent of those whose co-operation government needs and/or of avoiding conflicts that may threaten the 'mass diffuse loyalty' engendered by the system of electoral competition between parties.[15]

Accounts of group activity in Britain have distinguished broadly between 'promotional' groups which seek to advance some conception of the public interest and 'sectional' groups which lobby on their own behalf.[16] The classification of groups is of less importance for constitutional purposes than how far the institutions and processes through which the groups operate require open and rational policy debate. It is the appropriateness of an argument in a particular context that matters rather than who makes it and the constitutional problem is the design of contexts which enable sectional and common interests to be distinguished and given their due weight.

In Britain the informal and secretive nature of the policy process and continued reliance on a constitutional framework which ignores the interpenetration of public and private make such contexts all too rare. The negotiations which underlie the decisions of supposedly constitutionally accountable public actors – ministers and through them civil servants – are hidden from view. The effects caused by the absence of any constitutional pattern are not limited to blocking scrutiny and debate of policy outcomes. The structure of processes and institutions and the nature, significance and rationale of changes that may occur within them are also obscured. In particular the terms on which access to public decision-making processes is available to 'private' groups and organizations and how such terms are established, changed and monitored are not matters of open debate, nor have they been systematically examined by constitutional lawyers.

This failure to map the institutions and processes through which interaction between groups and government takes place can only be reconciled with rule of law ideals if a naively pluralistic model of decision-making is assumed in which all interests and potential interests are treated fairly in a 'contest for marginal privilege by a great many pressure groups'.[17] But this is precisely what cannot be assumed. Corporatist models of interest intermediation and policy formation may, for example, provide in many instances a more satisfactory explanation of the pattern of relationships between groups and government than pluralism. While both pluralist and corporatist theories direct attention to the part played by representative groups in policy formation, distinctive features of corporatism are the active role played by *public* power in creating, shaping or giving privileged access to the representative organizations and the role of the latter in policy implementation through disciplining their membership.

From a constitutional perspective both these aspects of corporatism raise questions about accountability for the exercise of public power – its use in creating, shaping and giving privileges to institutions and in bargaining over the concessions which are the price of co-operation. 'Tripartite' relations between government and 'producer groups' – employers' organizations and the trades unions – provide the best known, though perhaps least stable, examples of attempts to use corporatist arrangements for public purposes.[18] It is still unclear how far the general ideological attack on corporatist arrangements that has taken place since 1979 is merely the marginalization of trade union power.[19] The phenomenon of 'self-regulation' by, for example, the advertising industry, the City and the professions involves both of the constitutionally significant features of corporatism. In exchange for the assistance of representative organizations in the process of policy implementation, government has to accept a degree of loss of control over the substance of policy. On the other hand government is frequently instrumental in creating or shaping the self-regulatory bodies, and indeed the attack on 'corporatism' has not embraced self-regulation which is sometimes actively promoted.

In the absence of a constitutional form for consultation, negotiation and bargaining between government, groups and organizations, the dynamics of these constitutional relationships – the 'rules of the game' – tend to receive public debate only at a political level.[20] We cannot therefore assume that the institutions and processes of public decision-making operate pluralistically, nor, without abandoning the constitutional claims of the rule of law, can we consign to the realm of politics questions about the part played by groups in the policy process.

Let us then begin the task of trying to map the institutions and processes of fragmented government by examining the type of agency to which public decisions are allocated when they are not conferred upon government ministers.

The institutions of fragmented government

Choice of agency type

It is possible to list a number of factors which *a priori* constitute potential reasons for using one type of body rather than another.[21] At the level of managerial effectiveness, it has been suggested that non-departmental bodies may offer flexibility, speed and capacity for innovation.[22] On the other hand, the Fulton Report on the civil service favoured hiving-off the more routine tasks, where institutional differentiation might facilitate the establishment and monitoring of performance targets.[23] Policy-oriented reasons that observers have proposed include the idea that *ad hoc* bodies may outflank obstacles presented by existing institutions or facilitate the co-optation of political support through patronage.[24] At a more general level are ideas that government may 'put the action where the talent is', which might be in voluntary or other non-government bodies and that increasing the number of decision-making centres is *per se* a good thing since it spreads power pluralistically.[25] It has also been suggested that government may seek to insulate itself from criticism in politically sensitive areas by using non-departmental or non-government bodies to carry out potentially unpopular policies and that the use of such agencies may reduce the number of civil servants.

However, even taking into account other factors such as the influence of administrative fashion, there is no satisfactory explanation available for the present pattern of non-departmental bodies nor even, in many cases, as to why a particular policy initiative was given one administrative form rather than another.[26] Only in the case of the Morrisonian nationalization formula of the 1940s was the choice of a particular type of institution for a particular set of purposes made the subject of a clear theoretical explanation.[27]

In the absence of any constitutional mechanism for requiring or examining reasons for the allocation of decision-making, this is not really surprising. Nor is it surprising that the list of possible reasons that may influence the allocation contains such theoretically disparate elements. Some of the factors proposed gesture in the direction of broad constitutional concerns, while others point merely to short-term political manoeuvring. This is not a criticism of the sources that have been cited: the jumble of factors accurately reflects the lack of constitutionality. 'Self-regulation' for instance raises theoretical issues of considerable constitutional significance about ways of responding to the technical and legitimation problems of both *gesellschaft* and centralized bureaucratic methods of generating flows of decisions.[28] In Britain there are no mechanisms which could disentangle reasons that could be understood in this context from, say, Treasury objections to the cost of establishing a statutory agency or concern to meet a self-imposed target of reduction in the number of people classified as civil servants.

In similar fashion it is hard to distinguish in the establishment of new structures between concern to facilitate learning processes and a narrowly instrumental intention to implement a pre-established policy or even merely to react with speed to external pressures.[29]

The overall consequence of these ambiguities is that no constitutional mechanism exists to relate decisions about institutional structures to the general context of modern state activity. As a result, not only is the development of the machinery of government subjected to little in the way of scrutiny and debate, but it is, so far as the overall pattern is concerned, unplanned to a significant extent.

Institutional forms

The same lack of constitutional pattern and rationale that is displayed in relation to choice of agency type characterizes also the form and mode of operation of such agencies. As regards institutional form, the endemic terminological confusion – 'quango', 'fringe body', 'non-departmental public body' – is symptomatic of the lack of constitutional status of bodies which do not fit traditional categories. It is by no means clear exactly what is a government department and what is not, but at least the constitutional category exists even if it is fuzzy around the edges.[30] The nineteenth century brought a strong trend, with a clear constitutional rationale in ministerial responsibility, towards the abandonment of *ad hoc* boards and the like in favour of allocating functions to departments.

The reversal of this process in the twentieth century has not been accompanied by any constitutional redefinition to accommodate the increasing importance of non-departmental bodies.

In the United States there was early recognition of the constitutional problems presented by a 'headless fourth branch of government' – the Federal administrative agencies. Acknowledgement of the anomalous status of the agencies led to the creation of administrative law mechanisms that were designed to constitutionalize their activities, most notably 'notice-and-comment' rule-making under the Administrative Procedure Act and the creation of the Administrative Conference of the United States as an overseeing body.[31] In Britain, the Franks Report on Tribunals and Inquiries, while producing important and worthwhile reforms, none the less did not produce any analysis that departed from the traditional categories.[32] Tribunals were assimilated conceptually to the judicial model as machinery for the adjudication of individual rights, separate from the courts but with essentially the same function. Inquiries were treated as a kind of poor relation of tribunals, neither wholly judicial nor yet wholly administrative.

Franks avoided the trap of assuming that the appropriate procedures for judicial and semi-judicial functions were necessarily those of the courtroom but the effect of making the category of 'judicial function' the constitutional focus of the report profoundly influenced the nature of the reforms proposed. Tribunals that fitted the judicial model were put under the aegis of the Council on Tribunals and public inquiry procedures were regularized and formalized.[33] Bodies which did not easily fit the model, however, remained in a constitutional black hole, invisible to the observer but none the less exercising an important role in determining the motions of the public sphere.

Neither did the Report on Non-Departmental Public Bodies by Sir Leo Pliatzky make any progress towards a constitutional understanding of its subject matter.[34] Largely instrumental in its focus, the conceptual apparatus of the report was precisely the old constitutional categories. Despite the discovery of some 489 'executive' non-departmental bodies the assumption which underlies the report is the same as that first clearly enunciated by the Haldane Committee in 1918: that the 'normal' machinery of government is the department headed by a minister.[35] Overseeing of non-departmental bodies was seen as the function of departments themselves, with external scrutiny coming from traditional sources such as the Comptroller and Auditor-General and parliamentary select committees.

The inadequacy of traditional mechanisms for the redress of individual grievances was implicitly acknowledged by the creation of the office of Parliamentary Commissioner for Administration in 1967. While the ombudsman was correctly seen as an important innovation and the ombudsman concept has become, deservedly, increasingly popular, the broader constitutional implications of such machinery have remained largely unexplored. The somewhat shadowy notion of 'maladministration' has not been developed into a set of general principles of good administration and more particularly, the jurisdiction of the Parliamentary Commissioner has not extended much beyond the confines of government departments to embrace quasi-government bodies.[36]

The constitutional invisibility of non-departmental bodies is the more surprising in that they have a long history, even setting aside the nineteenth-century forerunners. The Metropolitan Water Board, Port of London Authority and Development Commission, for example, were all established prior to 1914, while the 1920s and 1930s saw the creation of, notably, the BBC, Central Electricity Generating Board, London Passenger Transport Board, Agricultural Marketing Boards and BOAC. There does however, appear to have been an increased rate of growth in the number of such bodies in the post-Second World War period.[37] The Conservative government elected in 1979 promised a drastic purge of quangos as one aspect of retrenchment of the public sector but the cull of quangos announced in the Report on Non-Departmental Public Bodies and further cuts made in late 1980 had little more than a cosmetic effect. 'The vast bulk of the sacrifices were of moribund or peripheral organizations, not bodies of major importance as executive units.'[38] The creation of new non-departmental bodies has since continued apace (e.g. the Urban Development Corporations) and the abolition of the Greater London Council and the metropolitan counties will result in many more: it was reported in 1984 that the government has 'no ideological objections to quangos'.[39]

Any scheme of classification of public activities produces the result that non-departmental bodies operate across almost the whole range. They provide goods and services and regulate and perform entrepreneurial or commercial activities. They carry out policy programmes directly, license the activities of others, inspect, make rules and adjudicate.

There is no clear fit between the type of activity, however classified, and the legal basis of the agency. Public law methods of establishing non-departmental bodies include of course Acts of Parliament and use of delegated legislative powers but also use of the royal prerogative as in the case of the BBC and the research councils.

In so far as English law recognizes a principle of freedom of association it is in the absence of specific legal constraints on joint activity and the provision of a private law framework for the creation of suitable institutional forms. In addition to the unincorporated association and the company, there are other legal forms available as special regimes: friendly societies, for example, and the charitable trust. The concept of the charity indeed is almost the only legal institution which recognizes that private activity may be 'affected with a public purpose'. The government is as free to make use of freedom of association as anyone else, subject only to the general principle of ministerial responsibility and the need to obtain parliamentary approval through financial procedures for supply expenditure (see Chapter 4 above). In so far as a body is funded entirely from monies voted by Parliament there is a conventional expectation that legislation will be used to establish the body, but a 'Treasury minute' may be used instead (as in the case of the University Grants Committee). Ministers need no specific legislative authority to create a Companies Act company[40] and there is nothing to prevent them from setting up new bodies by 'a mere answer in the House, a memorandum from the minister to himself, a wave of the hand, or whatever else may signify a decision to establish a new body'.[41] The use by government of private law mechanisms to establish non-departmental entities makes for constitutional confusion, since the same mechanisms may be used by private interests to create bodies which, in terms of their purposes, the nature of their activities and their relationship with government, are indistinguishable from those created by government itself. A revised mapping of the location of public decision-making must therefore include such privately-established bodies, for there is no less reason for questions of constitutional accountability to be addressed to them than to other organizational forms, such as government departments, through which public purposes are achieved.

Self-regulation

Perhaps the clearest examples come from the field of self-regulation where the regulatory framework is in a number of cases the result of bargaining on a continuing basis between government and the private interests concerned. Take, for instance, the National Housebuilders Council which registers approved private housebuilding firms, makes site inspections and compensates purchasers of an approved house which develops faults. The NHBC began life in 1936 on the initiative of several leading housebuilders in co-operation with the Ministry of Health 'whose officials wholly fashioned the scheme to meet the government's requirements'.[42] The two housebuilders' trade associations constitute only about one-third of the membership of the Council (their minority status being at the government's behest) and the chairperson and one Council member are appointed by the Secretary of State for the Environment. Civil servants attend meetings of the Council and its committees and the Council has undertaken not to alter its purposes, procedures or required building specifications without ministerial approval. Government now appears to regard the NHBC as such a public policy success that proposals were made in 1979 to hand over to it local authority building control regulation.[43] Other bodies which fall into a similar category to the NHBC are the Advertising Standards Authority, the Press Council and the British Board of Film Censors. In all three cases 'public' regulatory purposes have been achieved by bargained arrangements without any recognition of the status of the regulatory bodies through public law mechanisms. Self-regulation thus represents the pursuit of a public purpose through means which avoid the traditional mechanism of constitutional accountability for public choices.

Sometimes self-regulation is achieved directly through business associations rather than by separately established bodies. The British Agrochemicals Association's code of practice, for example, requires its members not to supply crop protection agents to distributors who are not registered with the British Agrochemical Supply Industry Scheme (which sets out specified standards). The Scheme is an alternative to statutory regulation: 'if it hadn't been set up, government would have intervened and imposed statutory requirements on the industry'.[44] Another example is provided by the codes of advertising practice operated by the various associations of companies marketing drugs. The codes cover advertising both to the public and to doctors and, while they are negotiated with the Department of Health and Social Security, their application and interpretation are in the hands of the associations themselves. Forming a background to these arrangements is the Department's unused authority under the Medicines Act 1968 to impose a statutory system of control.[45] In this instance, self-regulation is clearly a public matter even in terms of traditional constitutional theory since ministers are responsible for the non-exercise of powers they possess. It seems absurd to accept this but then to treat institutions resulting from negotiations in which ministers agree not to *seek* statutory powers as being outside the purview of the constitution.

Self-regulation in the City

The dense and complex network of relationships between central government, the Bank of England and financial institutions also illustrates the role of self-regulation as a means of achieving public policy goals. It has a bearing as well on many of the other themes broached in this chapter so far.

Traditionally the primary institutional focus of relationships between finance capital and government has been the Bank of England which has acted as central banker to the government, supervisor and regulator of many City institutions and the traditional conduit for expressing the views of the City to government.[46]

The Bank underwent a legal change from private to public corporate status in 1946 but this has had little or nothing to do with the subsequent evolution of its function.[47] The Bank's relationship with the City has primarily depended upon mutual trust, adherence to consensual norms and enlightened self-interest: it has thus been suspicious of unbridled competition as well as of formal statutory regulation.

While the Bank has remained the lynchpin of the system and its principle of operation is still informally networked elite consensus, changes in the nature of financial markets have resulted in the process of self-regulation becoming increasingly institutionally differentiated. In the 1950s the Bank and City became concerned about the conduct of company takeovers and a set of rules was established, but without any machinery for monitoring or supervision. Its unsatisfactory operation led the Bank to encourage the creation of the Panel on Takeovers and Mergers and later the Council for the Securities Industry, whose secretariat is provided by the Bank. The clearly expressed alternative to more effective self-regulation was, from 1967 onwards, the threat of statutory controls.[48]

Problems with takeovers represent only one facet of the difficulties caused for the Bank's traditional role by the changing and expanding nature of financial markets and institutions. The secondary banking crisis of 1974 and more recently problems at Lloyds also demonstrated the extent to which traditional consensual expectations were no longer capable of avoiding scandal. These factors together with EEC Directives on listed securities and action by the Office of Fair Trading against the Stock Exchange's anti-competitive practices have resulted in considerable pressure for change. What is proposed in the white paper following the Gower Report on Investor Protection[49] is the extension and legal recognition of self-regulation but without any analogue of the American Securities and Exchange Commission as a statutory oversight body.

Legal recognition of self-regulatory arrangements through conferral of statutory powers on the City's own oversight bodies will make their corporatist nature rather more visible than is usual in the British context.[50] However, the avoidance of scandal is only one aspect of governmental concern with the City. Economic policy in the post-war period has required intervention in financial markets for a variety of purposes. The Bank has successfully pushed for the creation of associations (e.g. of finance houses and hire purchase companies) to facilitate co-ordinated 'self-regulatory' responses to 'requests' from the Bank on the lines of its traditional directive relationship with the clearing banks.

This aspect of self-regulation, the pursuit of governmental economic goals through voluntary corporate responses by financial institutions is no less important under monetarist policies than it was in the earlier post-war period. It does not, of course, come within the ambit of the proposed legally structured mechanisms of self-regulation for investor protection purposes. Likewise, the mechanism of the Building Societies Association's relationship with government, a Joint Advisory Committee which includes representatives of the Department of the Environment, Treasury and Bank of England, has no legal form.[51] What is from government's perspective the most crucial aspect of its relationship with financial institutions and the one which bears most heavily on their real independence of operation will remain legally unstructured.

Self-regulation in the City and elsewhere demonstrates the absence of any clear link between the apparent status of an institution and its real function in relationships with government, of which the central dynamic remains closed and informal bargaining. It is this which makes it so difficult to produce any satisfactory analytical classification of 'quangos'.[52] This conclusion is strengthened when we examine the mode of operation of those non-departmental bodies which have responsibility for establishing and implementing policy in particular areas.

Mode of operation

Let us start by considering the only area of quasi-government which had a rationale in terms of the choice of agency type and something approximating a common form for separate bodies: the nationalized industries. What we shall discover is that the statutory definition of the relationship between the industries and government, and attempts to specify more precisely that relationship through white papers, have failed to achieve the prerequisite of constitutional accountability: public visibility of the real locations and processes of decision-making.

The nationalized industries

The 'old-fashioned nationalization'[53] formula of the 1940s and 1950s was a concept associated above all with Herbert Morrison and the pioneering pre-war example of the London Passenger Transport Board. Morrison's philosophy of an 'arm's length' relationship between corporations and government was embodied in the nationalization statutes which provided for the corporations to have independent legal personality, with limited powers for ministers to give directions to their boards. As to precisely how the boards should act, the statutes gave little guidance. It seemed to be assumed that, freed from the capitalist imperative of profit, the industries would automatically be able to identify and act on behalf of some vague notion of the public interest, with political intervention being limited to directions given in the broader national interest.

What this might mean and how the relationship between the corporations and sponsoring departments should be conducted has been the subject of a number of official attempts at definition.[54] However, apart from the earliest conception – that the boards were responsible for day-to-day matters while the minister was concerned with long-term policy – there is a constant thread in these efforts. That is to produce an analogue of the neo-classical market by specifying a form of decision-making at the level of the individual enterprise which is *economically* rational while ministers intervene to secure 'social' benefits or to protect the 'national interest'. At first this took the simplistic form of expecting boards to behave in a 'commercial' way. Subsequently efforts were made to improve upon this essentially vacuous notion by the publication of financial targets defining more precisely the statutory requirement to 'break even taking one year with another' and later by specifying criteria for pricing and investment decisions.[55]

Attempting to implement the criteria necessitates a working relationship between departments and the corporations going far beyond the issuing of formal directions. A 1967 white paper stressed the annual investment programme and review as the main focus of consultation, while by 1978 it was corporate planning that was seen as providing a systematic framework for reaching agreement on long-term objectives and strategy.[56] However, despite the fact that more recent statutes establishing public corporations have generally provided for a greater formal power of ministerial control than those of the 1940s, there is nothing approaching a public law framework for examining and debating policy decisions or monitoring the effectiveness of their implementation. As the Public Accounts Committee put it in 1983, 'departments have been forced into a situation where they exercise continuous intervention, with a daily dialogue, leading to blurring of responsibilities and possible resentment'.[57]

It was reported in 1982 that the Treasury has set up a Public Enterprise Analytic Unit to monitor the nationalized industries, set strategic objectives and make an exhaustive annual review jointly with the sponsoring ministries.[58] However, given what we have already seen of the Treasury's operations in Chapter 5, it seems unlikely that the new unit will be able effectively to ensure or monitor rational planning by the sponsoring ministries or the industries themselves.

The history of the nationalized industries indicates an even more fundamental problem. Successive governments have intervened through informal means over issues of pricing, investment, borrowing, industrial relations, pay negotiations and plant closures, bypassing the formal legal authority to give directions and making a nonsense of the 'arm's length' approach. As a report from the National Economic Development Office made clear in 1976 the result is that, not only has there been a general failure to establish effective mechanisms for determining policy for the industries and for monitoring performance, but that this has been exacerbated by *ad hoc* government interventions.[59]

In relation to macroeconomic objectives such intervention has now become institutionalized through external finance limits (EFLs), which are determined annually as part of the public expenditure planning system. EFLs have no clear relationship with the required rate of return on assets, financial targets or performance indicators for which sponsoring departments remain responsible.[60] As a result industries themselves have been drawn into the kind of bargaining with the Treasury that departments undertake, and which we examined in Chapter 5.[61]

Increasingly in the past few years the solution to the problems involved in public enterprise has been sought in privatization. As a political programme this has involved more than simply the sale of publicly owned assets[62] but it is such sales that have demonstrated the inherent problems and ambiguities in their sharpest form. The legal mechanisms for making decisions to sell assets have offered little opportunity for critical debate of the intended purposes or of the extent to which such purposes are or might be achieved.[63] Since the government has retained a substantial shareholding in, for example, British Aerospace, Britoil and British Telecom and intends to do the same in the case of British Airways, questions arise about the relationship of government and these hybrid companies.[64] In one sense the problem is not new since state ownership of shares in Companies Act companies has been a frequently preferred alternative to the Morrisonian public corporation as a vehicle for public enterprise (e.g. Rolls Royce, BL and British Nuclear Fuels). There has been little if anything to distinguish the relationship between government and such companies from that between government and the corporations. Taking BL as an example, a *Memorandum of Understanding* drawn up in 1981 provided for the same corporate planning framework for the relationship between the company and the department as is supposed to apply to the public corporations.[65]

The government has given assurances that it will – except in relation to takeovers where the 'golden share' device provides a clear discretionary veto power[66] – treat hybrids in exactly the same way as other private sector companies. Such assurances have, of course, no legal status.

The government has recognized the necessity for regulation of BT in the post-privatization period and presumably any future sales of monopolies will also involve the establishment of a regulatory regime. In the BT case the post of Director-General of Telecommunications has been established to head a new quango, the Office of Telecommunications (OFTEL) whose relations with BT are to be governed by the terms of the licence granted to BT by the Secretary of State.[67] How the triangular relationship between the Secretary of State, OFTEL and BT will develop has yet to be seen. In so far as OFTEL pursues an independent line there is the possibility that it will be outflanked, as was the Office of Fair Trading (OFT), by the bargain struck between the government and the Stock Exchange to end the OFT's restrictive practices case against the Exchange.[68] On the other hand, there has been speculation that OFTEL might be subject to 'agency capture' or be 'leant on' by ministers.[69] Whatever the outcome may eventually be, it will emerge without debate and scrutiny in any public forum.

We shall conclude this section of the chapter with a brief examination of the procedures used by three other non-departmental agencies: the Housing Corporation, the Independent Broadcasting Authority and the Civil Aviation Authority.

The Housing Corporation was created by statute in 1964 to act as a promotional body and conduit for public finance to the voluntary housing movement.[70] A major expansion of its role and importance occurred in 1974 when the government decided to inject large amounts of public money (with a substantial grant element) into housing associations to act as third force in the provision of rented housing. To be eligible for public support from the Corporation, associations must be registered and it is the Corporation which maintains the register and decides whether or not to accede to an application for registration.[71] The body recognized by central government since 1935 as representing housing associations, the National Federation of Housing Associations (NFHA), fought successfully to prevent the 1974 Act containing restrictive registration provisions and instead the Corporation was given rule-making power to establish criteria in consultation with the Housing Association Registration Advisory Committee (HARAC), a statutory body appointed by the Secretary of State. Criteria that were sufficiently detailed to amount to an effective confining and structuring of the discretion to register were devised and published, but in practice were abandoned in favour of an unannounced policy of registering almost all associations in the shortest possible time.[72] The government, anxious to achieve rapid success for the 1974 Act's policy initiative, for which the co-operation of the NFHA was essential, was content that the initial registration process be regarded as a 'coarse sieve' with reliance on post-registration supervision to prevent impropriety in the use of public funds.[73] A factor which facilitated the abandonment of the criteria was that the Act contained no provision for any kind of notice-and-comment or other form of public consultation when the criteria were being established. HARAC consisted, for the most part, of NFHA members: thus the criteria must have seemed to be essentially a private set of arrangements between the Department of the Environment, the NFHA and the Corporation which could be dispensed with by mutual consent.

The Department of the Environment has the ultimate responsibility for the Corporation's development programme, with the shadow of the Treasury in the background, but it is unclear just how much of an independent policy-making role the Corporation is supposed to have.[74] There is no suggestion that the provisional programme, prepared by the Corporation in consultation with the NFHA, should be reasoned nor is there any requirement for the Corporation to answer cogent criticism. At the level of individual housing associations there is no provision for an appeal mechanism when an association's allocation is reduced nor even a duty to give reasons.

In relation to the Independent Broadcasting Authority,[75] perhaps the most fundamental point which needs to be made is that the legal mechanism which the legislation requires the Authority to use in allocating a scarce public resource – broadcasting frequencies – is the private law of contract. Certain limited gestures towards openness in the holding of public meetings before the last round of television franchise awards in 1980 were clearly no more than public relations exercises and the IBA's decision-making processes remain closed to public scrutiny and debate. The 'contractual' nature of the legal framework encourages the private and unaccountable exercise of the IBA's powers and there are strong indications that even the limited canons of administrative law procedural requirements could not be imposed on the IBA through the courts.[76] There are no competitive hearings, no worthwhile reasons are given for non-renewal of franchises, nor for the award of franchises to successful applicants, nor do any appeal mechanisms exist.

Events have resulted not only in the IBA being accused of unfairness (e.g. in its treatment of Southern TV in the 1980 round of television franchise awards) but have also cast doubt on its ability to promote any coherent view of the public interest. In particular the sorry tale of the breakfast television franchise appears to indicate that the IBA neither understands the realities of commercial pressures on those it is supposed to regulate nor the limitations on its own capacity to intervene effectively once such commercial pressures have been allowed to dictate the course of events.[77]

By way of contrast, the Civil Aviation Authority (not confined by its statutory remit to the use of private law forms despite the functional similarities between its role and that of the IBA) has been a rare example in Britain of a multi-function agency which has gone a long way towards creating a public law framework for discharging its responsibilities, in particular the development of civil aviation policy and the exercise of allocative discretion. It has used open hearing procedures for the allocation of routes and licences and takes its decisions against a background of published policy statements. As a major centre of aviation policy expertise it has used procedures for development of longer-term policies and strategies which have involved a participative 'learning' dimension and which have enabled the CAA to resist informal processes of departmental interference. These aspects of the CAA's work have not, however, been taken as model for the design of other agencies. Nor have the broader public law implications been understood by the courts which have categorized its allocative role in terms of the old constitutional category of a 'quasi-judicial' function.[78]

The institutions of fragmented government: a summary

In considering non-departmental bodies we have for the most part been examining institutions through which public policy is formulated and implemented and in which public and private are inextricably linked: 'the institutions of compromise'.[79] The exception is the traditional public corporation form of public enterprise where the key constitutional problem is the lack of definition of the relationship between admittedly – and legally defined – public actors. The policy of privatization, far from rolling back the frontiers of the state in a way which sharpens the distinction between public and private, instead injects the confusion which exists elsewhere into the world of 'traditional quasi-government'.[80] Chairpersons of nationalized industries have been appointed who are explicitly committed to privatization before they have even taken up their posts and who expect to continue as chairpersons of the boards of the new 'private sector' companies, often with enhanced emoluments. At another level, the British Steel Corporation acted as the government's agent in restructuring the steel industry as a whole and administering government assistance to private steel producers. Not only did this involve, as the documents published by Granada Television at the time of the 1981 steel strike made clear, the disappearance of any structured difference in the policy-making function of BSC management and the government, it also involved, through the creation of 'Phoenix' companies jointly owned by BSC and 'independent' steel producers, complex and confidential bargaining with the private sector.

The institutions of fragmented government are characterized by interaction between the discretionary granting of access to the policy process and the closed and unaccountable nature of the framework for the conduct of that process. The same interaction can be observed if we shift the focus of our attention to institutions such as advisory committees and to procedures such as consultation and the holding of inquiries which are all capable of making inputs into the policy process at a time when agendas have not yet hardened and options remain open.

The processes of public choice

Advisory bodies

The *Report on Non-Departmental Public Bodies* identified 1561 advisory bodies, two-thirds of which were accounted for by twenty-two networks of between eight and 200 or so separate bodies.[81] Such 'permanent' advisory committees are supplemented by *ad hoc* entities which are sometimes given public legal status as Royal Commissions or are appointed under statutory powers.[82] Others are 'departmental committees', 'working parties' or 'steering groups' with no formal status. Between 1945 and 1969 there were on average sixty-four of these *ad hoc* committees sitting each year.[83] Some committees provide technical or scientific advice, others are used to test policy initiatives before representatives of affected interests and some constitute forums for bargaining. Such committees are, it has been argued, an important channel of access for groups,[84] but the terms of access are very much in the hands of government. Appointments are invariably in the discretion of ministers. Sometimes the power of patronage is used to ensure group representation but in other cases it is 'sound' people who are wanted, those who will co-operate automatically with the tacit, consensual and informal workings of elite consensus. If group representations can be ensured through 'sound' people so much the better.[85] It is significant in this connection to note, for example, that the Secretary of State for Social Services vetoed the advice given by civil servants to appoint a leading campaigner for the rights of the mentally ill to the Mental Health Commission. Similarly, the Secretary of State for Energy departed from usual practice in not re-appointing the chairperson of the London Electricity Council when that body began litigation to challenge increases in the price of electricity imposed as a consequence of negative external finance limits and members of health authorities have allegedly been sub-ject to politically inspired vetoes on re-appointment.[86]

There is no very sharp distinction between permanent advisory bodies and *ad hoc* committees nor between internal departmental committees and those which have external participation. In general, however, a wholly internal committee has the advantage for government that it is easier to limit and direct the scope of debate without taking public responsibility for so doing. There is no obligation to hold meetings of any advisory committee in public nor to make public the evidence which departmental or other advisory committees receive.[87] Consequently, there may be no opportunity for rebuttal of evidence, the scope and depth of public debate on a report may be restricted, and in fact, the publication of committee reports is discretionary and often delayed.[88]

Some of these points are illustrated by the example of the Hunt Committee on cable television. The Home Secretary set out the terms of reference of an inquiry into the *broadcasting* aspects of cable television expansion in March 1982 and a three page 'consultation document' was issued the following day. The report was submitted less than six months later.[89] Evidence was received from a number of organizations and individuals but such evidence had to be produced within eight weeks of the publication of the consultation document which consisted of little more than a series of questions on which views and comments were invited. There were no public hearings at which competing views could be tested, no chance for a second round of comments in response to those made in the first, no formulation of provisional conclusions on which a second round of comments could be made, no opportunity to argue that the separation of broadcasting policy from economic and technological issues was misconceived.

In general then, the composition of 'advisory committees' and similar bodies, their agendas, procedures and the treatment of their reports all fall very far short of the constitutional desiderata of machinery for scrutiny and debate of policy.

Inquiry processes – land-use planning

The only field in which the overwhelmingly *ad hoc* and discretionary nature of processes of advice and inquiry gives way to a legally structured framework is that of land-use planning. The origins and development of that legal framework depended crucially on the categorization of compulsory purchase and planning restrictions as derogations from the common law rights of owners of land.[90] It was the property connection which provided institutional opportunities for judicial challenges to decision-making leading to demands for the extension of formalized procedures and rights enforceable ultimately through the courts. Lawyers did not become so heavily involved in any other area of policy-making. The 'new property' of welfare benefits, and allocative decisions in fields such as education or health lacked the common law property connection which existed in relation to land-use planning and consequently have never been subjected to the same degree of public law structuring.[91]

Even within land-use planning the centre of gravity for scrutiny and debate of policy in legally structured forums has remained the individual development control decision. A large body of law has emerged imposing restrictions on relevant considerations, duties to give reasons and to demonstrate substantial evidence to justify decisions. For the most part, this body of law inures to the benefit of would-be developers. 'Public participation' in planning was never conceptualized in terms of public law mechanisms for scrutiny and debate of policy, with the result that the instruments used remain discretionary and are ineffective in opening-up the policy-making process before significant options have already been closed.

We should add that to a large extent the major choices in structure planning have been made in off-the-record negotiations between central and local government: a process facilitated by the organization of the examination in public through largely discretionary decisions by central government.[92]

Individual development control decisions are increasingly made through bargaining and even commercial co-operation between developers and the local authority.[93] The intersection of this framework of negotiation with the legally structured process of preparing local plans and other statutory planning requirements may provide a judicially-monitored impetus towards greater openness. The case law so far suggests only that a degree of circumspection may be required from planning authorities but there is no doubt that greater institutional opportunities exist in this area than in almost any other for requiring *ex parte* contacts between private interests and public authorities to be put on the public record.[94]

The public local inquiry has developed into a forum in which – albeit usually on a discretionary basis – a wide range of interests may appear and through participation gain procedural rights. This development was not intended by government but rather occurred in response to strongly felt public expectations of 'openness, fairness and impartiality'.[95] Outside the framework of appeals against refusals of planning permission, however, the courts remain largely wedded to the notion that at central government level 'policy' need be subject only to political scrutiny and debate. Inquiries are to 'inform the minister' who is responsible to Parliament for the policies adopted.[96]

The initiation of 'big public inquiries' into areas of policy extending well beyond land-use implications remains a matter of a political judgement to use the inquiry forum as a legitimating device. Its use imposes constraints on government, partly through the public expectations thereby engendered. However, the fact that the legal framework is that of a *land-use* inquiry allows considerable discretion to government in the articulation of the inquiry with the policy-making process generally and means that the public expectations of openness, fairness and impartiality are not guaranteed by public law mechanisms but rather are assimilated into the political process.[97]

For all its weaknesses, the legal structuring of land-use planning does at least provide a degree of visibility of public decision-making and limited institutional resources for requiring scrutiny and debate of policy through the giving of reasons, substantial evidence on a public record and opportunities to challenge the cogency of evidence or reasoning.

By way of contrast, we might examine various aspects of the relationship between government and industry. Let us look first at mergers policy and then consider some of the problems of 'the contract state'.

Mergers policy

It has recently been argued that anti-trust or monopoly-control regulation in Britain as well as in the US and the EEC is to a large extent regulation by bargaining.[98] No clear criteria exist for deciding when a proposed merger should be referred to the Monopolies and Mergers Commission (M&MC). The official government position is that 'decisions on merger references are taken on a case by case basis rather than by applying a rigid set of rules'.[99] Even general guidelines have not been established for the acceptability of mergers and no full-scale review of policy has been undertaken since 1978. This situation has led to complaints from companies that decisions have been arbitrary and inconsistent, complaints with which the Director-General of Fair Trading reportedly has some sympathy.[100] In these circumstances it is perhaps unsurprising that ferocious lobbying has taken place both for and against references to the M&MC in particular cases. Thus, for example, it was reported that Sotheby's had hired a firm of professional lobbyists who contacted fifty or so MPs to urge them to press the then Trade Secretary to override a recommendation from the Office of Fair Trading (OFT) that a bid for the firm should be allowed to proceed without a reference.[101] The subsequent referral of the bid for Sotheby's to the M&MC was only one instance of many where the advice of the OFT was not followed.

In relation to the press the general failure to establish the conditions for scrutiny and debate of decisions assumes more serious dimensions, since issues of freedom of expression are involved. The Fair Trading Act permits the Secretary of State to withhold consent to, or impose conditions on, any newspaper sale or transfer after an M&MC investigation. Reference to the Commission is mandatory unless a newspaper 'was not economic as a going concern'. The sale of *The Times* and *Sunday Times* to Rupert Murdoch in 1981 was not referred on this ground: here again *ex parte* lobbying was involved including a meeting between Murdoch and the Prime Minister.[102]

The Secretary of State set out the material on which he based his decision in a memorandum (deposited in the House of Commons library some weeks after the parliamentary debate on the issue). It is arguable at least that in the case of the *Sunday Times* some of the material relied on was wrong and indeed an application for *mandamus* against the Secretary of State was initiated by *Sunday Times* journalists, though subsequently dropped after discussions with the new proprietor.[103] Had the application proceeded, the courts might well have been prepared to review the Secretary of State's procedural judgement,[104] but it is clearly inadequate from the point of view of ensuring public scrutiny and debate of decisions that the only check on the Secretary of State's discretion, exercised after strong *ex parte* lobbying, should be unaccountable private initiative in seeking judicial review.

The contract state

English law has no general concept of a 'public law contract' as a regime to govern commercial relationships between government or other public bodies and private firms.[105] In the United States concern that the contract mechanism was being used, in effect, to delegate public decision-making to private bodies led to debate over accountability in 'the contract state' and to discussions of 'federalism by contract'.[106] In Britain, with the exception of the IBA's relationship to its franchise companies, contract has not been the form in which public functions have been devolved upon non-departmental bodies. However, this is not to say that the character-istic issues of the contract state do not also occur here in abundance. Indeed, if privatization in the form of contracting-out functions previously performed by public bodies continues to be developed, loss of control over and accountability for policy may become prominent aspects of concern over public contracts in Britain.

It has, however, been financial questions that so far have been the key issue in government contracting in Britain. Although some government contracts are for goods and services which are widely available through competitive markets, very many more are not. Frequently the public sector is the sole or dominant purchaser (e.g. of defence equipment, much health care equipment and supplies, nuclear installations) and the contract may require research and development, new investment and a close degree of integration of the progress of the contract into the policy framework to which it relates. In many cases a single or very limited number of suppliers exist who may have a general economic importance in addition to their role in supplying the public sector (e.g. the pharmaceutical industry, nuclear engineering suppliers, defence contractors). In such circumstances 'contract' as a legal mechanism has nothing to do with the neo-classical competitive market: it is simply an empty vessel into which the results of administrative bargaining can be poured.

Following the scandal of excessive profits made by Ferranti and Bristol Siddely, a Review Board on Government Contracts was established through a memorandum of agreement between the government and the Confederation of British Industry in a classic piece of bipartite corporatism.[107]

The Board consists of five members, two nominated by the CBI and two others and the chairperson by the Treasury: all the nominations must be mutually acceptable to the Treasury and the CBI.[108] The Board has a number of functions. First, it carries out periodic general reviews of the formula for calculating profits and the target rates of profit for government contracts. It also produces an annual report to the Treasury giving the overall percentage profit made by government contractors. Dispute resolution is also part of the Board's remit: government contracts contain a clause providing for reference by either party to the Board in respect of profits made or losses incurred on individual contracts. The memorandum of agreement between the CBI and the Treasury sets out principles on which the Board is to base its appraisal and the procedural framework which is to govern the process.[109] It is also possible, of course, for departments and contractors to settle disputes over profits or losses through direct negotiation without recourse to the Board. In a sense, the Review Board represents only the tip of the iceberg since individual departments also have complex negotiated regulatory machinery for establishing profit targets and formulae for their calculation.[110] The existence of the Review Board on Government Contracts and similar arrangements are a necessary recognition of the fact that 'contract' is not a magic wand which dissolves away all the administrative problems attendant upon the pursuit of public goals. The Board and all the other bargained arrangements between business and government that constitute the administration of commercial relationships between private firms and the public sector exist in a shadowy constitutional limbo. Having no public law form and 'private' in the sense of being largely invisible in their operation, they represent yet another aspect of 'quasi-government' which urgently needs constitutionalization.

Conclusion

This chapter has necessarily been programmatic in its mapping of the institutions and process through which the constitutional authority derived from Parliament is in fact exercised. That this is so is a consequence of one of our central themes: the absence of an adequate constitutional framework and the *ad hoc*, pragmatic nature of the British method of institution building. Our intention has been to set an agenda, to indicate the need for new constitutional mechanisms of accountability and to identify the problems to which they need to be addressed. We have considered the structure and the procedures of the heterogeneous mass of organizations outside central government departments that fulfil public policy tasks. We have looked briefly at processes of inquiry that constitute vehicles for development of policy and sometimes even its public discussion. Considered as machinery for distinguishing between and weighing public and private interests in the making of policy these intermediate organizations and processes are clearly defective. Furthermore, they are vulnerable to the problem that also besets Parliament and central government: the confusion of the public interest with short-term sectional and political concerns.

Even where particular bodies constitute valuable policy-making resources capable of responding to 'hard look' concerns they are too often isolated and undercut in their actual operation. They are by-passed through informal networks, their agendas are set and their activity is initiated by unaccountable discretionary decisions taken elsewhere. They lack an audience with a clearly defined duty to give their reports a hearing and inject them into the machinery of state.

Considered as channels through which groups and interests can gain access to the policy process, the same weaknesses appear in the institutions and processes of fragmented government. The terms of access are rarely the subject of any public debate. They may be subject to unilateral and unaccountable changes and, in so far as they are negotiated, it is through processes in which those who have most to offer or threaten – on a variety of levels – get preferential treatment. 'Issue networks' or 'policy communities'[111] are structured through a complex process of mutual accommodation and adjustment, of which differential access and marginalization are important features. Consultation can be essentially a process of exclusion and favoured groups are those who can participate in establishing agendas and setting the terms of debate before formal consultation processes begin.[112]

In Chapter 5 we saw that the politico-administrative mechanisms of Whitehall are no more effective than the institutions of fragmented government in ensuring the adoption and implementation of policy for the public interest. In constitutional terms this means that Parliament does not render accountable everyone who, through express or implicit delegation from those directly responsible to it, exercises public authority. In the United States a perceived failure of traditional theories of legitimation of the delegation of power from Congress to the Federal agencies met with a judicial response. The Federal courts expanded standing and participation rights in relation to judicial review and agency decision-making and formulated new procedural requirements.[113] In the next chapter we turn to the response of courts in Britain to the changing map of the real constitution.

References

1   On which see Chapter 7 below.
2   G. Poggi, *The Development of the Modern State* (Hutchinson 1978); R. Scase (ed.), *The State in Western Europe* (Croom Helm 1979).
3   The *Observer* 1 July 1984. See also the Report of the Select Committee on Members' Interests. HC 97 (1984/85) and G. Alderman, *Pressure Groups and Government in Great Britain* (Longman 1984), ch. 3.
4   See Grant Jordan, 'Parliament under pressure', *Political Quarterly*, **56** (1985), pp. 174–82.
5   See S. H. Beer, *Modern British Politics*, 2nd edn (Faber 1982), pp. 65–8, and G. Alderman, *The Railway Interest* (Leicester University Press 1973).
6   Consider for example the neglect of pressure group activity in Britain until the late 1950s and the sudden emergence of 'quangos' as a subject of political interest in the 1960s and 1970s.
7   *Policy and Politics in Britain* (Blackwell 1981), p. 57.
8   See e.g. M. Moran, 'Finance capital and pressure-group politics in Britain', *British Journal of Political Science*, **11** (1982), pp. 381–404; W. Grant, 'Large Firms and Public Policy in Britain', *Journal of Public Policy*, **4**, 1–7.
9   See T. Daintith, 'The executive power today', in J. Jowell and D. Oliver (eds.), *The Changing Constitution* (Oxford University Press 1985).
10 K. Dyson, *The State Tradition in Western Europe* (Martin Robertson 1980), p. 280.
11 See C. Offe, *Contradictions of the Welfare State* (Hutchinson 1984); J. Habermas, *Legitimation Crisis* (Heinemann 1976).
12 See Alice Ehr-Soon Tay and Eugene Kamenka, 'Beyond bourgeois individualism, the contemporary crisis in law and legal ideology', in E. Kamenka and R. Neale (eds.), *Feudalism, Capitalism and Beyond* (Edward Arnold 1975).
13 Beer, pp. 321–5.

14 S. E. Finer quoted in Beer, p. 322.
15 Habermas, *Legitimation Crisis*, p. 36. See e.g. M. Holmes, *Political Pressure and Economic Policy* (Butterworths 1982).
16 There is a considerable discussion in the literature on the question of classification. See e.g. S. E. Finer *Anonymous Empire*, 2nd edn (Pall Mall 1966); W. J. M. Mackenzie, 'Pressure Groups in British Government', *VI British Journal of Sociology* (1955); J. D. Stewart, *British Pressure Groups: their Role in Relation to the House of Commons* (Oxford University Press 1958); A. Potter, *Organised Groups in British National Politics* (Faber 1961); G. Alderman, *Pressure Groups and Government in Great Britain* (Longman 1984).
17 B. Crick, *The American Science of Politics* (RKP 1959), p. 118.
18 For the largely informal, secretive and pragmatic history of tripartite 'corporate bias' in Britain see K. Middlemas, *Politics in Industrial Society* (Andre Deutsch 1979). And see *idem, Industry, Unions and Government* (Macmillan 1983).
19 N. Lewis and P. Wiles, 'The post-corporatist state?', *Journal of Law and Society*, **11** (1984), 65–90, p. 87. cf. A. Cawson, *Corporatism and Welfare* (Heinemann Educational Books 1982), at p. 41: 'To dismiss the significance of corporatism because of the instability of one of its forms – tripartism – is to overlook the much more firmly embedded structures of corporate representation in a far wider area of social policy-making.' See also Malcolm Harrison (ed.), *Corporatism and the Welfare State* (Gower 1984).
20 Corporatism in Britain therefore was never likely to take the form of a public law framework in which representative organizations were accorded formal state recognition of their legitimacy. cf. P. Schmitter, 'Still the Century of Corporatism?', in P. Schmitter and G. Lehmbruch (eds.), *Trends Towards Corporatist Intermediation* (Sage Publications 1979); and 'Reflections on where the theory of neo-corporatism has gone and where the praxis of neo-corporatism may be going', in G. Lehmbruch and P. Schmitter (eds.), *Patterns of Corporatist Policy-Making* (Sage 1982).
21 C. C. Hood, 'Keeping the centre small: explanations of agency type', *Political Studies*, **26** (1978), 30–46; G. Ganz, 'The allocation of decision-making functions', *Public Law* (1972) 215, 299.
22 Hood, and see B. L. R. Smith and D. C. Hague, *The Dilemma of Accountability in Modern Government* (Macmillan 1971), pp. 74–5.
23 Cmnd. 3638 (1968).
24 Hood, 'Keeping the Centre Small'; Smith and Hague.
25 Smith and Hague. On the potential role of voluntary bodies as more effective methods of policy-delivery than statutory agencies see *The Future of Voluntary Organisations: Report of the Wolfenden Committee* (Croom Helm 1978).
26 Hood, 'Keeping the Centre Small'.

27   See H. Morrison, *The Socialization of Transport* (Constable 1933). W. A. Robson, *Nationalized Industry and Public Ownership*, 2nd edn (Allen and Unwin 1962).

28   See G. Teubner, 'Substantive and reflexive elements in modern law', *Law and Society Review*, **17** (1983), p. 239. See further below on reflexive or 'soft' law techniques, Chapter 10.

29   J. Bradshaw, 'The DHSS–Rowntree Memorial Trust Family Fund: an innovation in quasi-government', in A. Barker (ed.), *Quangos in Britain* (Macmillan 1982).

30   C. Hood, A. Dunsire, K. S. Thompson, 'So you think you know what government departments are', *Public Administration Bulletin* (1978).

31   On 'notice-and-comment' rule-making see below Chapter 8. For ACUS see B. Schwartz and H. W. R. Wade, *Legal Control of Government* (OUP 1972), pp. 180–4.

32   Cmnd. 218 (1957).

33   Tribunals and Inquiries Act 1958.

34   Cmnd. 7797 (1980).

35   Cd. 9230 (1918).

36   See generally on the Parliamentary Commissioner for Administration; The Whyatt Report, *The Citizen and the Administration: the Redress of Grievances* (Justice 1961); *Our Fettered Ombudsman* (Justice 1977); R. A. Gregory and P. G. Hutchesson, *The Parliamentary Ombudsman* (Allen and Unwin 1975); and P. Birkinshaw, *Grievances, Remedies and the State* (Sweet and Maxwell 1985). See also Fourth Report of the Select Committee on the PCA on *Non-Departmental Public Bodies* HC 619 Session 1983–4. On principles of good administration see *Administration Under Law* (Justice 1971).

37   C. C. Hood, 'Governmental bodies and government growth', in A. Barker (ed.), *Quangos in Britain* (Macmillan 1982).

38   C. C. Hood, 'Axeperson, Spare that Quango . . .', in C. C. Hood and M. Wright (eds.), *Big Government in Hard Times* (Martin Robertson 1981), p. 120.

39   Speech of Lord Gowrie, the *Guardian*, 20 November 1984.

40   Cmnd. 7797.

41   Barker, *Quangos in Britain*, p. 7.

42   A. Barker, 'The National House Builders Registration Council', in D. C. Hague, W. J. M. Mackenzie and A. Barker, *Public Policy and Private Interests, The Institutions of Compromise* (Macmillan 1975).

43   *The Times*, 17 December 1979 quoted in Hood, 'Axeperson, Spare that Quango . . .'.

44   W. Grant, 'Neo-Corporatism and the Study of Business Interest Associations: An Interim Report', *University of Warwick Department of Politics Working Paper No. 35*, p. 20.

45 J. A. Sargent, *The Organisation of Business Interests in the UK Pharmaceutical Industry* (Berlin: International Institute of Management 1983).

46 See Moran, 'Finance capital and pressure-group politics in Britain'.

47 On which see esp. M. Moran, 'Monetary policy and the machinery of government', *Public Administration*, **59** (1981), pp. 47–66.

48 See Hague, Mackenzie and Barker, pp. 328–32; A. Page 'Self-regulation and codes of practice', *Journal of Business Law* (1980), p. 24.

49 See L. C. B. Gower, *Review of Investor Protection, Report Part 1*, Cmnd. 9125 (1984).

50 Previously the legal underpinnings of self-regulation have been in the case of Lloyds a *private* Act (see Hodgson, 'Self-regulation at Lloyds', *Political Quarterly*, **51** (1981), p. 488), and for bodies such as the Stock Exchange, exemption from statutory licensing requirements.

51 For the origins, purposes and present functioning of the Committee see M. Boleat, *The Building Societies Association* 2nd edn (the Building Societies Association 1981), pp. 20–3. See also M. Boddy, *The Building Societies* (Macmillan 1980).

52 See Hague, Mackenzie and Barker, esp. pp. 10–32 and 409–21; Barker, *Quangos in Britain*; N. Lewis, 'Who Controls Quangos and the Nationalized Industries?', in Jowell and Oliver (eds.), *The Changing Constitution*.

53 The phrase is taken from Hague, Mackenzie and Barker.

54 See J. Redwood and J. Hatch, *Controlling Public Industries* (Blackwell 1982), pp. 5–10.

55 *The Financial and Economic Obligations of the Nationalized Industries* Cmnd. 1337 (1961).

56 *Nationalized Industries: A Review of Economic and Financial Objectives* Cmnd. 3437 (1967); *The Nationalized Industries*, Cmnd. 7131 (1978).

57 Public Accounts Committee, 7th Report 1983/4. *Departments of Industry, Transport and Energy, The Monitoring and Central Activities of Sponsor Departments of Nationalized Industries*, para. 45. See also Reports by the Comptroller and Auditor-General on Departments of Energy, Transport and Trade and Industry: *Monitoring and Control of Investment by the Nationalised Industries in Fixed Assets* HC 284 1984/5.

58 *Financial Times*, 7 April 1982.

59 *A Study of UK Nationalized Industries* (HMSO 1976). See also the Serpell Report: *Committee on the Review of Railway Finances* (HMSO 1983), esp. paras. 10, 14.

60 See 8th Report of Treasury and Civil Service Committee 1980/81 HC 348.

61 The *Economist*, 5 March 1982.

62　'Contracting-out' of services and charging users for services previously financed through taxation are other significant aspects.

63　See N. Lewis and I. Harden, 'Privatisation, de-regulation and constitutionality: some Anglo–American comparisons', *Northern Ireland Legal Quarterly*, **34** (1983), pp. 207–29. And see Reports of the PAC; HC 189 10th Report 1981–2 on the sale of shares in British Aerospace, BP, Cable and Wireless and Amersham International, and 17th Report 1983–4 HC 443. See also M. Webb 'Privatisation of the Electricity and Gas Industries', in D. Steel and D. Heald (eds.), *Privatising Public Enterprises: Options and Dilemmas* (RIPA 1984).

64　D. Steel, 'Government and the new hybrids', in Steel and Heald, *Privatising Public Enterprises*, and *idem* 'Government and the new hybrids: a trail of unanswered questions', *Fiscal Studies*, **5** (1984), pp. 87–97. D. Heald, 'Will the privatisation of public enterprises solve the problems of control?', *Public Administration*, **63** (1983), pp. 7–22. For an account of earlier examples of 'hybridity' see G. Ganz, *Government and Industry* (Professional Books 1977), esp. ch. 7.

65　20th Report of the PAC, Session 1981–2 HC 407.

66　Golden shares exist e.g. in Britoil, Cable and Wireless, Amersham International and BT.

67　Telecommunications Act 1984; *The British Telecom Licence* Department of Trade and Industry (HMSO 1984).

68　See statement by the Secretary of State, *Hansard* HC Debates, 27 July 1983 cols. 1194–5.

69　Steel and Heald, *Privatising Public Enterprises*.

70　Housing Act 1964. See generally N. Lewis and I. Harden, 'The Housing Corporation and "voluntary housing"', in Barker (ed.), *Quangos in Britain*.

71　Housing Act 1974, s. 13.

72　D. Noble, 'From rules to discretion: the Housing Corporation', in M. Adler and S. Asquith (eds.), *Discretion and Welfare* (Heinemann 1981).

73　See 5th Report of the Public Accounts Committee HC 327 1978–79 reply to Q. 188.

74　*Housing Corporation: Approved Development Programme for England, Memorandum of Authorisation* (DoE 1981).

75　See N. Lewis, 'IBA Programme Contract Awards', *Public Law* (1975), pp. 317–40.

76　*Gaming Board of Great Britain ex parte Benaim and Khaida* [1970] 2 QB 417 at 430; *Cinnamond v British Airports Authority* [1980] 2 All ER 368 at 374.

77　See the *Economist*, 26 May 1983.

78 See G. Baldwin, 'A British regulatory agency and the *Sky-train* decision', *Public Law* (1978), 57–81, *Laker Airways Ltd. v Dept. of Trade* [1977] QB 643.
79 Hague, Mackenzie and Barker.
80 ibid.
81 Cmnd. 7797 para. 7.
82 See generally R. E. Wraith and G. B. Lamb, *Public Inquiries as an Instrument of Government* (Allen and Unwin 1971).
83 T. J. Cartwright, *Royal Commissions and Departmental Committees in Britain* (Hodder and Stoughton 1975).
84 J. J. Richardson and A. G. Jordan, *Governing under Pressure: The Policy Process in a Post-Parliamentary Democracy* (Martin Robertson 1979), pp. 72–3.
85 On the 'list of the great and the good', see Anne Davies, *What's Wrong with Quangos?* (OCPU 1979), pp. 47–56.
86 See the *Guardian*, 5 July 1983; 30 July 1984. See also C. C. Hood, 'Axeperson, Spare that Quango ...', at pp. 112–13 on the abolition of advisory bodies whose advice proved politically embarrassing.
87 Contrast the position in the United States where the Federal Advisory Committees Act requires openness. See further below Chapter 8. The Public Bodies (Admission to Meetings) Act 1960 applies to meetings of various executive bodies. Again compare the more extensive requirements of the US Government in the Sunshine Act discussed in Chapter 8.
88 As, for example, in the case of the Informal Working Group on Effective Prescribing ('The Greenfield Report' on generic substitution of brand-name drugs in the NHS). Publication of the Report was delayed for over a year and there is evidence that the government had not intended to publish it at all. See C. Medawar, *The Wrong Kind of Medicine?* (Consumers Association and Hodder and Stoughton 1984).
89 *Report of the Inquiry into Cable Expansion and Broadcasting Policy*, Cmnd. 8679 (1983).
90 See P. McAuslan, 'Planning law's contribution to the problems of an urban society', *Modern Law Review*, **37** (1974), p. 134; 'The ideologies of planning law', *Urban Law and Policy*, **2** (1979), 1; *The Ideologies of Planning Law* (Pergamon 1981).
91 On the absence of legal structuring in local government service delivery generally see N. Lewis and I. Harden, 'Law and the local state', *Urban Law and Policy*, **5** (1982), p. 65, N. Lewis and P. Birkinshaw, 'Taking Complaints Seriously', in M. Partington and J. Jowell (eds.), *Welfare Law and Policy* (Frances Pinter 1979), 'Local Authorities and the Resolution

of Grievances, Some Second Thoughts', *Local Government Studies*, **5** (1979), p. 7.

92 See e.g. L. T. Bridges, 'The structure plan examination in public as an instrument of inter-governmental decision-making', *Urban Law and Policy*, **2** (1979), p. 241; L. T. Bridges and C. Vielba, *Structure Plan Examinations in Public; a Descriptive Analysis* (Birmingham University Institute of Judicial Administration 1976), Roy Darke, 'Public participation and state power: the case of South Yorkshire', *Policy and Politics*, **7** (1979), p. 337.

93 J. Jowell, 'Bargaining in development control', *Journal of Planning and Environment Law*, 414 (1977), 'Limits of law in urban planning', *Current Legal Problems*, **63** (1977).

94 See *Steeples v Derbyshire County Council* [1984] 3 All ER 468, *R v Amber Valley District Council ex parte Jackson* [1984] 3 All ER 501.

95 See Wraith and Lamb. The phrase 'openness, fairness and impartiality' is taken from the Franks Report on Tribunals and Inquiries.

96 *Bushell v Secretary of State for the Environment* [1981] AC 75; *Kent County Council v Secretary of State*, 75 *Local Government Reports* 452.

97 On the Windscale inquiry see B. Wynne, *Rationality and Ritual* (British Society for the History of Science 1982), McAuslan, 'The ideologies of planning law'. See generally on big public inquiries, *The Big Public Inquiry* (Council for Science and Society/Justice/Outer Circle Policy Unit 1979).

98 A. Boyer, 'Form as substance: a comparison of antitrust regulation by consent decrees in the USA, reports of the M & MC in the UK, and grants of clearance by the European Commission', *International and Comparative Law Quarterly*, **32** (1983), p. 904–30.

99 *A Review of Monopolies and Mergers Policy*, Cmnd. 7198 (1978).

100 *Financial Times*, 18 March 1983. See also N. Green, 'Crisis in the Monopolies and Mergers Commission', *Business Law Review*, **4** (1983), p. 303.

101 The *Guardian*, 5 July 1983.

102 Harold Evans, *Good Times, Bad Times* (Coronet 1984).

103 ibid.

104 cf. *R v Secretary of State for Trade ex parte Anderson Strathclyde plc* [1983] 2 All ER 233.

105 On the *contrat administratif* in French law see L. Neville Brown and J. F. Garner, *French Administrative Law*, 3rd edn (Butterworths 1983), pp. 125–31.

106 See B. L. R. Smith, 'Accountability and independence in the contract state', in B. L. R. Smith and D. C. Hague, *The Dilemma of Accountability in Modern Government* (Macmillan 1971); D. K. Price, *Government and Science* (New York University Press 1954).

107 M. Edmonds, 'Government contracting in industry: some observations on the Ferranti and Bristol Siddely contracts', in Smith and Hague; C. Turpin, *Government Contracts* (Penguin 1972).

108 Turpin.

109 ibid., pp. 196–7.

110 J. Sargent, *The Pharmaceutical Price Regulation Scheme* (Berlin: International Institute of Management 1983); Medawar, *The Wrong Kind of Medicine?*

111 H. Heclo, 'Issue networks and the executive establishment', in A. King (ed.), *The New American Political System* (Washington DC: American Enterprise Institute 1978); Richardson and Jordan, *Governing Under Pressure*.

112 Richardson and Jordan, p. 45, and see e.g. S. Haywood and D. J. Hunter, 'Consultative processes in health policy in the United Kingdom: a view from the centre', *Public Administration*, **60** (1982), p. 143.

113 See generally R. Stewart, 'The reformation of American administrative law', *Harvard Law Review*, **88** (1975), pp. 1667–1813.

7 The courts and the constitution

Introduction

In this chapter we consider the role that the courts play in the British constitution, pursuing as usual the strategy of immanent critique. The strategy is ideal-typical: we shall draw on the views of judges and constitutional commentators to produce a version of the place of the judiciary in the British constitution that is recognizable as mainstream. However, we shall claim neither to encompass every possible nuance nor that the constitutional claims we identify are expressly put forward by any person or group in exactly the form that we present them. Constitutional theory is implicit as well as explicit and our task is to identify a coherent theory and to analyse the implications of its central concepts. Then the empirical assumptions on which it rests can be examined, paying particular attention to changes that have occurred over time in both ideology and actuality. Finally the conceptual implications set against changed empirical circumstances lead us to argue that fidelity to constitutional claims requires practical change.

An influential modern jurist has argued that the activity of judges should itself be understood as a form of immanent critique.[1] While it should already be clear that Ronald Dworkin's conception of constitutionality as a larger set of claims is not the same as our own, there is at least a similarity of method in seeking to identify implicit theories of legitimation. For Dworkin however the boundaries of immanent critique are set by a concept of law which limits his analysis to the activities of the 'least dangerous branch' of government – the courts – in identifying existing institutional rights of parties to litigation. Our net is more widely spread. We have argued in Chapter 3 that *gesellschaft* legal institutions constitute an historically specific form of law rather than its essence. The ideals and values immanent in the concept of the rule of law transcend the nineteenth-century conception of the autonomy of law from politics and administration and of a strict divide between the public and private spheres.

The idea of legal autonomy is present in Dworkin's work as an institutional division of labour between courts and other organs of government. Courts are charged with the task of weighing arguments of principle directed to discovering the rights of parties to litigation.[2] Legislatures, while making judgements of principle, also use arguments of policy to 'justify a political decision by showing that the decision advances or protects some collective goal of the community as a whole'.[3] The authority to make such policy decisions flows from the democratic representativeness of the legislature: a characteristic which courts lack and which thus disentitles them from using arguments of policy to justify their decisions.

Dworkin's theory of adjudication is directed to what he calls 'standard civil disputes' and to constitutional cases within the framework of the American constitutional system.[4] In relation to the latter the central issue for Dworkin is the idea of 'constitutionalism': 'the theory that the majority must be restrained to protect individual rights'.[5] We are not concerned to discuss whether in 'standard civil cases' (or in public law decisions) judicial reasoning is appropriately to be characterized as policy- or principle-based, although, in modern circumstances, 'private law' forms can operate to conceal crucial issues of public policy making. Nor is our focus on the existence of substantive individual moral rights which limit the political authority of majority decisions, though we do not deny the importance of such rights nor of the debates over the appropriate role of the judiciary in their protection in the United States, Britain and elsewhere. Rather, alongside the case which has been powerfully stated by other constitutional writers for protection of individuals against the power of the state, we have sought to place arguments for reconstitutionalization of the processes of public policy-making. Representation, including democratic representation, is not only a matter of politics: it also has a constitutional dimension. The rule of law – and hence the values immanent in the specific conception of the Rule of Law embodied in the idea of legal autonomy – demands not only constraints on public power but also the positive structuring of processes and institutions through which the use to be made of that power is decided. The dominance of Parliament by the executive, the fragmentation of government and the interpenetration of public and private – the collapse of the empirical basis of the nineteenth-century liberal model of constitutional legitimacy – mean that the 'collective goal(s) of the community as a whole' can no longer be regarded as the exclusive province of a democratically responsible legislature. Fidelity to the rule of law ideal that the use made of public power should be legitimated through mechanisms of accountability requires that we treat the means for the establishment of such collective goals as an urgent concern of constitutional law.

It is important to emphasize that, although a focus on constitutionality as *process* is by no means new, the direction of our argument differs from that of other procedurally-oriented writers. We are not seeking to argue that procedural emphasis avoids the philosophical problems raised by attempts to justify substantive moral values as objectively valid.[6] We have sought to by-pass such issues, as we indicated in Chapter 1. Again, we are not attempting to duplicate, though we would not dissent from, arguments that ground the traditional liberal freedoms in the logic of the democratic process.[7] Our claims are at the same time both more limited and more wide-ranging. *If* we take seriously traditional constitutional rhetoric about the rule of law, about accountable and responsible government, then we must seek to infuse those values into the complex processes through which public policy is actually made. Our task in this chapter is to ask how far the British courts have responded adequately to the shifting and uncertain map of the policy process that we have outlined in previous chapters and to what extent they could have done and could do better.

The historical background

As we have seen in Part One of the book, the key notion which underpins the place of the courts in most accounts of the constitution is the rule of law, central to which are ideas of the common law and of the independence of the judiciary. The central unresolved problematic in traditional accounts of the constitution is the nature of the relationship between the courts and the authority of Parliament as the representative of the (politically significant) nation. The words in parentheses are important since democratic accounts of representative legitimacy are of comparatively recent origin and certainly post-date the seventeenth-century political settlement which continues to underpin the orthodox conception of the respective role of the courts and Parliament. In the next sections we examine that conception and the assumptions on which it was based before considering the impact of nineteenth-century political economy and the specific conception of the rule of law propagated by the doyen of the nineteenth-century constitutional theory, A. V. Dicey.

The seventeenth-century settlement

In the battles between the Crown and the common lawyers in the first part of the seventeenth century the issue at stake was the scope of the royal prerogative and the control of its exercise: an issue which was framed by Chief Justice Coke in terms of the King being beneath and not above the law. While recognizing the existence of 'absolute' or 'extraordinary' prerogatives exercisable by the King on what a modern lawyer would call an unreviewable discretionary basis, the courts decided in the early part of the century that the so-called 'ordinary' prerogative was institutionally and procedurally confined. Thus the imposition by the Crown of taxation incidental to the absolute prerogative powers to regulate foreign trade and to defend the realm was held lawful. However powers to dispense justice and to make laws were exercisable only through the courts and Parliament respectively.[8]

We have already seen that the potential for conflict inherent in the claim that common law was in fact superior to statute never emerged. After 1688 the common lawyers accepted the supremacy of Parliament in that every statute enacted by the Crown-in-Parliament has been applied as law, and judicial dicta to the effect that Parliament is the supreme law-making authority are so legion as to make exhaustive citation unnecessary. Statutes must, of course, be interpreted, but that is another question and one to which we shall return later.

However, for the common lawyers the supremacy of Parliament was not a 'rule of recognition'[9] which might confer legitimacy on legislation of any sort whatsoever. Fundamental to the alliance of the common lawyers and Parliament was the belief, described in Chapter 2, that Parliament, by virtue of its composition, was a self-limiting institution. Statutes were *un*common, designed to deal with some specific 'mischief' that required a change in the common law as expounded by the judges.

The seventeenth-century constitutional settlement thus contained two legitimating principles that were compatible given the institutional framework in which they were embedded: the maintenance of the common law, 'which was nothing else but the rule of established customs . . .' and the legislative supremacy of a representative Parliament, which was essentially a denial of the Crown's claims to cast off traditional limits on its authority.

The absence of public law

The defeat of the Stuarts meant the demise of the Old Tory conception of the Crown as an independent authority and diviner of the public interest and thus of a unified conception of public power capable of development into a theory of the state.[10] The overthrow of the conciliar courts (in particular the Star Chamber) reduced the emergence in Britain of a distinct administrative law on the later pattern of the Conseil d'Etat in France to a remote possibility.[11] The essentially medieval concept of the Crown remained the basis of constitutional authority and the consequences for both law and politics were profound. The emergence of Parliament as the key political forum, of representation as the basis of political legitimacy and of the idea that executive power was an emanation of, or an agency of, Parliament were not accompanied by any corresponding legal reformulations. The responsibility of ministers to Parliament retained as its theoretical basis their status as advisors of the Crown until, quite gradually, legislation began to confer new powers directly on individual ministers. As we have seen in Chapter 5, the emergence of the cabinet and of the office of Prime Minister received no legal formalization whatever: the powers of government continued to be personified in the over-life-size figures of ministers rather than being attributed to institutions and structures.

In the absence of any necessity to re-examine the fundamental basis of public power, there was no pressure on the legal profession to develop new constitutional theory. Rather, the traditional pattern of the profession was maintained, organized around the Inns of Court whose medieval roots continued to condition legal thinking. Legal practice developed in the direction of pragmatic adaptation of procedural formalism in the service of private interests.[12] Thus, to quote Dyson's splendid encapsulation of the argument of this section:

On the one hand the judiciary has a fierce independence; on the other hand law is not regarded as the great interpreter of the pattern of politics.[13]

The legal paradigm becomes gesellschaft

While public law remained undeveloped and unsystematic because it had no dynamic part to play in the dual system of legitimation inherent in the logic of the seventeenth-century constitutional settlement, private law developed rapidly in a way that facilitated and accommodated market economic relations and later the growth of an industrial economy.

The roots of economic liberalism among lawyers can be traced back at least as far as Coke. The transition from a system of law, which in its economic aspects previously had marked *gemeinschaft* characteristics, to one in which individual freedom of contract was a primary organizing theme was gradual, with significant developments occurring in the eighteenth and nineteenth centuries. In political theory the idea of property as an exclusive right, an absolute or near absolute individual freedom to use and alienate began completely to supersede older notions of limited and common rights only in the seventeenth century.[14] But in the eighteenth century 'one legal decision after another signalled that lawyers had become converted to the notions of absolute property ownership'.[15] In the field of contract it was not until the nineteenth century that the courts accepted the idea that the fairness or otherwise of a bargain should not be relevant to its enforcement and as late as 1792 it was maintained by the Vinerian Professor of Law at Oxford that the doctrine of *caveat emptor* was 'now exploded'.[16] It is clear therefore that market-oriented concepts such as freedom of contract, typical of the *gesellschaft* type of legal ordering, can scarcely be thought of as essential to the nature of English law and they most certainly post-date the establishment of the seventeenth-century constitutional pattern.

While it would be exceedingly difficult to find any direct link between constitutional doctrines and developing economic relationships there is none the less a degree of fit between the *gesellschaft* form of law and the constitutional pattern we have described which has considerable significance: the triumph of *gesellschaft* reinforced rather than challenged the assumptions on which the seventeenth-century constitutional settlement had been founded.

The Weberian analysis of formally rational law as conducive to the development of capitalist economic relations has been reworked by Habermas to distinguish between a number of different aspects of rationality.[17] At the level of 'internal rationality' *gesellschaft* law seeks to operate through classifications of fact situations according to pre-existing rules and the development of autonomous legal concepts rather than by evaluation of specific outcomes. This has normative implications in that decisions are not made on the basis of prejudices against or in favour of specific individuals. This links up with the broader aspect of *gesellschaft*'s 'norm rationality' which centres around the value of individual freedom and autonomy and the protection of a private sphere within which judgements are made by individuals. The existence of private autonomy is necessary for the market economic relations which constitute the 'system rationality' of *gesellschaft* – its external social function. If we compare these features of *gesellschaft* with the constitution founded on parliamentary supremacy and judicial protection of customary rights, a number of points at which the two complement and reinforce each other emerge. First, there is the emphasis on individual freedom and autonomy which harmonizes with the constitutional focus on individual rights. Second, development of formalism in the law's internal rationality[18] discouraged concern with result-oriented administrative activity involving discretion which could not be fitted into the model of law as comprising fixed rules and autonomous concepts. Formalism also meant the conscious eschewal of the consideration of values in judicial decision-making, thus removing the need to find a substitute for a conservative interpretation of 'custom' as the normative basis of common law.

Dicey and the rule of law

We have already indicated that Dicey, for reasons that are not obvious to the student of politics, has retained a central position in the minds of constitutional lawyers even though his views have been strongly challenged for more than half a century.[19] Bagehot is in many ways more perceptive and acute and J. S. Mill had identified one of the crucial issues of the relationship between common law and a democratized version of representation much earlier.[20] However, Mill's concepts continue to be reworked and reanalysed as part of contemporary debate,[21] whereas Dicey's version of the rule of law, while still taken by commentators as a starting point, is subjected to criticism rather than critique. The deficiencies of Dicey's formulation are pointed out but the result is either to deny the concept any validity at all or to make it a synonym for a general political morality in which the place of law remains unspecified.[22] Meanwhile the courts continue to appear to conceive their own role largely in the terms that Dicey formulated.

In fact Dicey was concerned to present the rule of law as a distinct aspect of legitimation connected with, but separate from, the supremacy of Parliament,[23] with which it is often conflated in contemporary political rhetoric. When Dicey wrote, the assumptions of 1689 had already been undermined by the growth of state functions carried out through administrative mechanisms and by the transformation of parliamentary representative legitimacy into democratic claims. Dicey ignored the former development in his analysis of the rule of law and thought the concept of constitutional convention adequate to accommodate the latter within the traditional law of the constitution.[24] The claims he made for the rule of law, if taken seriously, require analysis of the place of law both in administrative activity and as part of the democratic principle of legitimation. Dicey's well known formulation of the 'kindred though distinct' elements of the rule of law contains assumptions which it is important to make explicit. Certain key elements are obvious: a stress on the role of the courts, concern for 'ordinary', 'private' law and a focus on absence of punishment outside the framework of courts applying common law as the crucial protected interest of individuals. It would be a mistake, however, to conclude that Dicean constitutional concerns were too narrow, that the only reason for protection of a sphere of private autonomy was for the sake of the individuals concerned. From an historical perspective, the perspective of the seventeenth century, the protection of private autonomy had been the key battleground for defeating the growing political claims of the Crown. To govern requires money: in so far as money could be raised without Parliament (by taxes or by coercion of individuals) absolutist rule was possible. Thus the rule of law in Dicey's sense was a necessary precondition of the exercise of political control over the Crown through the possibility of the denial of supply by Parliament.[25]

Dicey did not fail to recognize that changes had occurred in the political and institutional context within which rules enforceable in the courts have their effects. He did, however, ignore the significance of a sphere of discretionary administrative power created by statute. He failed to see that statute not only could create but had created a sphere of *public* autonomy, of powers significantly unstructured by fixed rules. Quite simply, Dicey believed that the necessity to embody powers in enactments interpreted by judges in the ordinary courts was sufficient to ensure that arbitrary executive power could not be derived from statute. As for the residue of power, exercisable by the executive under the royal prerogative, conventions existed to regulate their mode of exercise. The majority of these conventions Dicey regarded as indirectly legally enforceable in that a failure to observe them will ultimately result in a government being obliged either to act illegally or to resign because it cannot obtain supply from Parliament.[26]

In essence then Dicey rested his account of the constitution on the twin pillars of legitimation that emerged in the seventeenth century: the preservation of common law by the courts and the supremacy of a representative Parliament. The only major addition is the concept of convention which ultimately constitutes the mechanism of political accountability to the electorate.[27] The analysis is sophisticated in that the two elements are seen as indirectly mutually supportive, but no attention is given to the growth in the nature and scope of state functions nor to the concomitant diminution in the importance of Parliament itself as a policy-making body.

It is easy to recognize the theoretical attraction for Dicey in the equation of his three claims for the rule of law: that it means the security of individual rights (i.e. traditional common law rights); that it is in essence the 'right of the courts to punish any illegal act by whomsoever committed'; and that these together entail 'the absence of arbitrary power on the part of the Crown, of the executive, and of every other authority in England'.[28] The advantage is the same as that in making convention the source of non-legal rules confining discretion – the basis of legitimacy is custom or tradition – and thus commitments to a rational political morality can be avoided, while at the same time the scope of legitimation embraces the entire compass of state activity. The challenge presented by the growth of state functions, which makes implausible Dicey's neglect of the problem of discretion, is to create institutions and mechanisms capable of legitimating the exercise and non-exercise of public power. Custom and tradition alone cannot suffice: in conditions of change they need reinterpretation or they will rapidly come to mean no more than the way in which power is in fact exercised. If this is so then the question arises: where are the forums for legitimate interpretation and reinterpretation of constitutional requirements?

The place of courts in the constitution

Ultra vires *and natural justice*

In the United States the answer would of course be that constitutional amendment is a matter for Congress and the states whereas interpretation is for the courts. For most commentators, as for the Supreme Court itself, the task of interpretation is itself seen as a more or less creative one.[29] In Britain too the courts have responded to some of the questions which Dicey neglected – to the problem of discretion generally and more recently (and inadequately) to the provision of goods and services by the state to individuals through non-market mechanisms. However, to a very large extent the courts have failed to break away from a paradigm which is essentially Dicean in the analysis of problems and attempted solutions. In particular, they have failed to develop a general theory of their proper role in structuring policy-making processes. As we should expect, this has led to inconsistency and incoherence. Much of what the courts do and have done is inconsistent with the Dicean version of their role, but an alternative account, more faithful to the concern for legitimacy, would also require considerable modification to the principles and approach adopted by the courts.

By the late nineteenth century the pattern of the judicial response to the growth of administrative powers exercisable under statutory authority was relatively clear. The doctrine of *ultra vires*, that administrative bodies must not exceed the strict powers conferred by Parliament, was borrowed from company law and developed to limit official power. The courts' control of administration thus appeared as simply an aspect of statutory interpretation, a necessary and limited function which, in the heyday of formalism at least, could be argued to make Parliament itself responsible for the substance of decisions.

In relation to the procedures adopted by executive decision-takers the courts were more ambivalent. The so-called rules of natural justice – the duty to give a fair hearing and an unbiased decision – were imposed in contexts assimilable to the model of criminal or civil adjudication. But the basis for this, especially when natural justice was applied also to 'private' institutions deriving their powers from contract, could not easily be presented as statutory interpretation. The alternative view, that natural justice is a matter of common law, of the design by the courts of procedures for the fair exercise of power, was occasionally asserted but later denied in favour of the view that central government at any rate should be largely the master of its own procedures.[30] Subsequently, even in relation to local government, the courts declined to apply natural justice except where a 'judicial' decision-making framework (in general a third party deciding a formalized dispute) already existed.[31] This in effect left the question of whether natural justice should apply to be decided by the success or otherwise of affected interests in lobbying for the insertion of formal procedures at the time the relevant legislation was being drafted. This abdication by the courts from a general concern for administrative procedure extended also to the handling of complaints. No general requirement for adequate grievance-handling mechanisms has ever been developed.[32]

It is not difficult to understand why, given the Dicean paradigm as a starting point, judicial control of administration should have developed more readily through the concept of *ultra vires* than through natural justice. It is important to emphasize that the distinction here is not straightforwardly between 'substance' and 'procedure', though it is sometimes presented in this way. *Ultra vires* too can be procedural (since statutes often contain express procedural requirements) but even so-called 'substantive' *ultra vires* is supposed to be concerned not with the *merits* of decisions but with their *legality*. The question is not whether a particular matter has been correctly decided but whether the administrative authority in question had power to decide as it did.[33] This analysis fits well with the courts' acceptance of the supremacy of Parliament: subordination to the legislature entails that courts must not usurp power which Parliament has conferred on another body. A reinforcement of judicial deference to the legislature was the growth of the idea of individual ministerial responsibility to Parliament as a means for the redress of grievances and thus as a guarantor of the legitimacy of individual decisions in fields from which the courts themselves were excluded. As we have seen in previous chapters, by the end of the nineteenth century the quango form of public administration had been very largely superseded by the department headed by a minister responsible to Parliament and the device of the parliamentary question was becoming increasingly popular. The courts themselves relied heavily, especially in wartime, on the doctrine of ministerial responsibility as the source of legitimation for wide discretionary powers whose exercise they themselves were not prepared to question.[34]

In the case of natural justice, however, there is no legitimate basis for judicial review comparable to that for *ultra vires*. To appeal to the implied intent of the statute is a transparent fiction, but to make common law the basis of judicial intervention is to invite questions about the nature of common law itself. To present it in Dicean fashion as 'nothing else than the rule of established customs modified only by Acts of Parliament' will not do where new administrative schemes are being created, for *ex hypothesi* no 'customs' exist and it is the nature of the scheme created by the Act of Parliament which is itself in question. But to treat the common law as a source of principles which require application to changing circumstances is in this context to recognize the need for a theory which defines and gives coherence to the (necessarily limited) role of the courts in trying to ensure that power is exercised legitimately. Such a theory must of course go beyond the mere invocation of 'tradition' to encompass, at least, immanent critique.

The inadequacies of ultra vires

The fundamental weaknesses of the *ultra vires* doctrine in relation to discretionary powers of the executive have received a sporadic, *ad hoc* and inadequate response, especially from the courts.[35] *Ultra vires* suffers from two inherent limitations if it is understood simply as a matter of statutory interpretation. First, it can have relatively little impact on broad statutory grants of discretionary power, and, second, it applies only to powers derived from statute. If on the other hand *ultra vires* is something other than statutory interpretation then the argument made above in relation to natural justice applies here also. A developed theory of the role of the courts in relation to administrative processes is required, including a definition of their function in overseeing policy formation – something from which the courts have always recoiled.

As we shall see the courts have developed principles concerning executive abuse of discretion which cannot, without absurdity, be attributed to the intention of Parliament. Thus the question of the source of legitimacy of judicial decisions does indeed arise here just as in the case of natural justice and we will pursue these matters shortly.

However, even if we look at what the courts have done in practice rather than merely at the theoretical limitations of *ultra vires* as an aspect of statutory interpretation, we find that there are vitally important gaps in the extent to which public activity is subject to judicially monitored norms. To put it another way, there is a sphere of 'public autonomy' which the courts have regarded as none of their business. This sphere of public autonomy derives from three sources: the royal prerogative, statutorily conferred discretion and the ordinary rights and liberties which public legal persons enjoy as much as private ones.

The royal prerogative

Dicey defined the prerogative as 'the residue of discretionary authority, which at any given time is legally left in the hands of the Crown'.[36] The traditional view has been that while it is for the courts to determine the existence and extent of a prerogative power they will not question the appropriateness or adequacy of the grounds on which the power was exercised.[37]

There is no point here in attempting to give a full account of the extent of prerogative powers as they exist today.[38] It should be noted though that in addition to such general matters as the dissolution of Parliament, creation of peers, conduct of foreign affairs (including the declaration of war) and a very vague and broad power to act in times of emergency, the prerogative also covers a large number of other matters which are of considerable significance for particular individuals and interests, such as, for example, the issue and withdrawal of passports. Another power which has perhaps been unduly neglected is the creation of corporations by royal charter: as the universities have recently discovered such corporations are vulnerable to pressure from the government of the day exercised through powers reserved in their charters.[39]

Various of the powers exercisable under the prerogative would be considered non-justiciable even in jurisdictions such as the United States where the scope of judicial review is generally broader, but this is most certainly not true of the issue, for example, of passports. There can be no doubt that the exclusion of prerogative powers from judicial review has left unstructured by law a number of aspects of administration which are no different in principle from others governed by statute. However, there are now signs that the courts may be prepared to subject justiciable prerogative powers to review on the same grounds as statutory powers. In the case concerning the removal of trade union membership rights from workers at GCHQ Cheltenham, a majority of the House of Lords took the view that the power to regulate the civil service could be reviewed, albeit that on the facts of the case the failure of the government to observe requirements of fair procedure was justifiable on grounds of national security.[40] If 'justiciable' prerogative powers are indeed assimilated to statutory ones then this represents a welcome step. As we shall see later, however, the performance of the courts in relation to the control of statutorily conferred discretion itself falls a long way short of meeting constitutional requirements.

Private law rights and liberties

The essence of the *ultra vires* principle is that the powers of a body *created* by statute are limited to those conferred on it by statute or which are reasonably incidental to powers so conferred. But in relation to bodies which are not created by statute the doctrine has more limited effect. Powers specifically granted by statute are subject to review certainly, but in other respects the liberty of action permitted by the law to private persons applies: that anything may be done which is not made unlawful by statute or common law. Thus in examining the Dicean account of the rule of law we might for example compare the landmark eighteenth-century case of *Entick v Carrington* with *Malone v Metropolitan Police Commissioner.*[41] In the former case it was held that entry and search of property pursuant to a general warrant was unlawful because such warrants were authorized neither by statute nor common law. The plaintiff therefore recovered damages for trespass. In *Malone* on the other hand the plaintiff complained that his telephone had been tapped by the police but it was held that this could not found an action for damages since no private right had been infringed. Tapping a telephone at the exchange does not constitute an actionable trespass while no general right to privacy has been developed in English law. *Malone* should also be contrasted with cases in which the courts have developed the concept of breach of confidence to restrain publication of information, and have required identification of the sources of information or documents obtained in breach of rights of property or confidentiality.[42] The attempt to found a claim on the basis of confidentiality was rejected in *Malone* though subsequently an injunction has been granted in a case of tapping by private persons.[43] This makes it clear that the refusal to provide a remedy in *Malone*, despite the fact that the European Convention on Human Rights requires that telephone tapping be subject to legal safeguards, was a deliberate choice not to restrict the sphere of public autonomy.

Public expenditure

The limited effectiveness of the *ultra vires* doctrine is also exemplified by the case of central government expenditure. (As we shall see later, *local* government spending is subject to tight control by the courts.) The Exchequer and Audit Department Acts 1866–1957, which require the Comptroller and Auditor-General to oversee expenditure by government departments and to report to the Public Accounts Committee of the House of Commons, do not create duties enforceable by citizens in the courts.[44]

We have discussed elsewhere the weaknesses of parliamentary control of public expenditure, but it is important to note here that it is not possible to question in the courts either the legality of central government expenditure, or the failure to spend, on the basis of the Appropriation Act procedure. It is possible to incur expenditure simply on the basis of Appropriation Act authorization but, by convention, continuing expenditures are usually covered also by specific legislation which may be a source of rights and duties enforceable in the courts.[45] However, such legislation often confers wide discretionary powers on public officials and it is to the question generally of the courts' response to legislatively conferred discretion that we must now turn our attention.

Statutory discretion

Despite the theoretical basis of *ultra vires* in statutory interpretation, the courts have in fact developed a number of principles for the control of discretion, for limiting the sphere of public autonomy created by statute. Arguably some of these are derivable by analysis of the concept of discretion itself (e.g. that discretion must not be fettered by rules of policy) but for the most part they are clearly judge-made law (e.g. the fiduciary duty of local authorities to their ratepayers). The principles of natural justice are usually treated separately in the literature but, although this has an historical justification, modern natural justice is very much an aspect of the control of discretion. The main problem with the principles the courts use is that they are often primitive and under-developed, and have not been consciously related to any clear understanding of their nature and purpose. Partly as a result they are too often context-dependent and thus are not true principles at all. In relation to land-use planning, for example, the courts have treated the duty to give reasons for decisions as a requirement to be rigorously enforced, whereas in the field of supplementary benefits they have conspicuously failed to take as vigorous a stand.[46]

Furthermore, because of the lack of a clear understanding of the nature and purpose of judicial review, the courts have vacillated between a helpless quietism and an active interventionism which has too often appeared to depend on the judges' views of the merits of particular policies rather than upon a view of their role in the constitutional order of things. The point is not that judges are biased or that they ought to have taken a different view of the merits of particular disputes, but that the decisions were unprincipled and were not based on any standards that transcended the particular case at hand.

These problems are not of course unique to Britain and in the United States debates surrounding the nature and basis of adjudication, particularly constitutional adjudication by the Supreme Court, have a long history. Concerns of the kind expressed here, about the role of principles as opposed to views on the substantive merits of disputes have been central to the literature which developed as a result of the Warren Court's perceived activism.[47] In Britain debate has been rather more low-key and critics of the courts have focused on the identification of the judges' hidden agenda of substantive values.[48] If we look at the writings of judges themselves, we do find a recognition of the need to rethink the legitimacy of judicial decision-making in a post-formalist age, although their definition of the problem gives no special attention to public law matters.[49] This is not the place for a full critique of these (often highly positivistic) judicial contributions. For our purpose it is sufficient to note that, whatever the particular mode of expression, all turn ultimately on a distinction between matters on which there is a community consensus – on the basis of which it is legitimate for judges to make decisions – and matters of social or political controversy that the courts should leave to Parliament. Clearly this kind of approach is wholly inadequate to define the scope and basis of judicial review. Indeed all it really does is to restate in a slightly modified form the seventeenth-century constitutional formula with 'consensus' substituted for 'established customs'. But this simply will not do, for if 'consensus' means an actual empirical coincidence of ideas then it is very doubtful if on disputes which reach the courts any universal consensus ever exists. Even if it does, or if 'consensus' means a majority view, why should judges be thought better at registering the existence of consensus than the political processes of democracy? If on the other hand 'consensus' refers to the implications of principles which underlie constitutional arrangements based on government with the consent of the governed, we are no further forward, since the question at issue is precisely what those principles do in fact imply for judicial review. We thus return once again to the need for a rational theory to justify judicial review, not as an externally imposed requirement but as an immanent necessity of the judges' attempts to control the exercise of discretion. To these attempts we shall now address ourselves in rather more detail, taking as our first example the control of local authority expenditure.

Public expenditure – local government

The application of the *ultra vires* principle to local government expenditure has been particularly strict as a result of a special limitation invented by the judges. Local authorities have been restricted in the exercise of discretionary powers by a 'fiduciary duty' owed to ratepayers to pay particular attention to their interests when deciding how much to spend on particular policies. The impact of the fiduciary duty on local government has gone far beyond the cases which have reached the courts because of the requirement that local authority accounts be audited and the possibility of surcharge of individual councillors.[50] At a time when central government is attempting to restrict local expenditure, especially by the use of grant penalties, it was perhaps inevitable that the fiduciary duty would be invoked in particular fields. In the event it was a London Borough rather than an auditor or group of ratepayers who used this gound of challenge to question the Greater London Council's policy of reducing London Transport charges by 25 per cent in fulfilment of an election pledge.

The case of *Bromley LBC v Greater London Council* is complex since the decision of the House of Lords rested not only on the issue of the fiduciary duty but also on the interpretation of the relevant statute. The Lords decided that subsidies might be paid, and indeed budgeted for in advance, but only within the context of a policy which aimed so far as practicable at ensuring that fare revenue covered costs. It is worth emphasizing the openness of the statutory interpretation question as it confronted the House of Lords. It was by no means inevitable that the court should have reached the result that it did and the strongest argument that was offered for the interpretation actually adopted was that it was consistent with an earlier case, *Prescott v Birmingham Corporation*, in which it had been held that the common law fiduciary duty required local authorities to run transport undertakings on business lines and that there were no clear words in the statute to make the principle of that case inapplicable.[51] There is no self-evident reason why the court should have preferred to interpret the statute so as to preserve the effect of *Prescott's* case rather than applying the classic test adopted for reviewing most other areas of policy: *viz.* whether the GLC had acted in a way that no reasonable local authority could have acted, i.e. the so-called *Wednesbury* test.

There are a number of presumptions of statutory interpretations to which the courts appeal in order to preserve traditional common law rights. These

no longer have anything to do with the intent of the legislature: they are a means of controlling that intent. Together they form a sort of common law 'Bill of Rights'. English . . . judges have no power to declare Acts unconstitutional merely because they depart from the good old ways of thought; they can, however, use the presumptions to mould legislative innovation into some accord with the old notions. The presumptions are in short 'an ideal constitution' for England. . . .[52]

It should be fairly clear by now that we regard it as necessary for judges to make decisions on the basis of a theory of 'an ideal constitution'. The problem is, what should be its contents? The decision in the *Bromley* case appears to elevate the fiduciary duty of local authorities to their ratepayers to the status of part of the 'ideal constitution'. However, the fiduciary duty might have been taken to mean simply efficiency: cost-effectiveness rather than breaking even. Why then should the court have adopted the latter interpretation? If we take the assertions of the court about fiduciary duty at face value then it was quite simply acting as a court of appeal from the political process, intervening to prevent the putting into effect of a policy which had been presented to the local electorate (which had in turn given a majority to the party offering it) in order to protect the pockets of a favoured group, the ratepayers.

This interpretation may indeed be correct but there are, in some of the judgements, indications of rather different lines of reasoning. If the GLC had reached a result that was unlawful in its substance because it infringed the rights of ratepayers then it is irrelevant *how* and *why* that result was reached and yet such questions, about the legitimacy of *processes*, were expressly raised by certain judges. If it was the legitimacy of the processes of policy-making that was really of fundamental concern, then invocation of the fiduciary duty to ratepayers was a singularly inept means of expressing it.[53] On the other hand to recast the decision in terms of *process*, and modes of review appropriate to ensure legitimate policy-making, is to adopt a much broader role for judicial review.

Let us examine the procedural issues mentioned in *Bromley*. First, by way of criticism of the argument that the GLC had a 'mandate' for its policy, it was pointed out that the greater part of the rates is paid by commercial ratepayers who have no votes as such. What is the logic of this? That the democratic process can in certain circumstances illegitimately override or fail to take into account the interests of affected parties. It is possible to question whether that is a good description of what happened in the case of the GLC's fares policy but that is not the point. The principle that the courts should police the policy-making process in order to ensure that all affected interests are taken into account is a potential basis for judicial review with the most far-reaching implications. It also brings with it a host of problems, not the least of which is the fact that to make such review of procedural failures effective can require the court to evaluate the substance of decisions. This second-guessing of political processes can only be prevented from degenerating into a wholesale subordination of politics to the courtroom if ways can be found to limit the role of the courts to the protection of certain specific rights and to acting as a final quality-control mechanism for open and participative policy-making processes.

Perhaps surprisingly some inchoate and confused recognition of the possibility of judicial review for this purpose does emerge from some of the *Bromley* judgements. It was said in particular that, by regarding itself as bound to introduce the 25 per cent fares reduction by virtue of a manifesto commitment, the GLC had failed to exercise its discretion. Another way of expressing the same idea was that there had been a failure to take into account relevant matters, in particular the loss of central government grant consequent upon the policy adopted.[54] In the Court of Appeal this line of criticism had been developed in a rather different direction. The figure of 25 per cent had not been explained and was entirely arbitrary – later attempts to defend it in terms of the promotion of an integrated, cost-effective transport system were simply *post hoc* rationalization.[55]

These criticisms can be related to certain well known principles of judicial review of discretionary powers[56] and we need to pursue their implications much further. It is notorious that in English administrative law the various categories of review 'overlap to a very great extent' and 'all run into one another'.[57] To some extent this is inevitable but in an important measure it is also owing to a failure to understand the differences between, and the complex interrelationship of, procedural and substantive review. This failure has had a particularly deleterious effect upon the development of judicial review in Britain as compared, for example, with the United States. We shall attempt to illustrate and explain this contention as we proceed.

Judicial review of policy-making

Let us start with the proposition that the GLC's selection of the figure of 25 per cent for fares reduction was arbitrary and that defences of it were *post hoc* rationalization. In American law, review for lack of 'substantial evidence' is well established but in Britain a similar principle is only slowly emerging, and its development has been uneven.[58] In the case of *Secretary of State for Education v Tameside Metropolitan Borough Council*,[59] for example, the court came very close to allowing the test of the reasonableness of a factual conclusion to amount to an appeal on the merits against a policy decision.

To avoid this happening it is necessary to distinguish carefully between a number of different matters:

1 There are questions of fact, or of inferences to be drawn from facts, on which the court wishes, in effect, to allow an appeal;
2 There are similar questions where, for whatever reason (typically because the court is an inappropriate forum, because it lacks expertise or adequate procedures), review should be limited to checking that a factual conclusion is rational to the extent of being supported by at least some evidence;
3 Finally, there are 'policy' issues.

English courts have for the most part treated the idea of policy in the most crude fashion, failing to make even the most basic distinctions between value judgements, objectives designed to serve those values, policies to achieve objectives, and measures to implement the policies.[60] If such distinctions are made it is possible to see both that a test of rationality can be applied to the links between different elements in (3) and that questions of fact (of type (1) or (2)) will be involved in the explanation of those links.

Consider now the question of the GLC treating itself as bound by the election commitment and, correlatively, entitled by its mandate to introduce the 25 per cent fares cut. The implication of the rejection of this defence as a failure to take into account relevant matters and a fettering of discretion is that the court considered that the fact of an authority's being democratically elected did not *ipso facto* make the policies it espoused legitimate. The nature of the processes through which the policies were chosen was also of relevance: some degree of rationality is required. The implications of this proposition are enormous. If the requirement that policy-making processes be rational is to be more than simply a pious hope and if the role of courts is to involve more than arbitrarily chosen forays into specific areas inviting the conclusion that they are motivated by political prejudice, then administrative law needs to be considerably developed in a procedural direction. In the first place, the doctrine that there is no general duty in English law to give reasons for decisions needs to be recognized for what it is: a wholesale licensing of arbitrariness and irrationality.[61] To reverse the position would be no greater step than many involved in other 'landmark' decisions in administrative law.[62] Half a step towards this was taken in *Padfield v Minister of Agriculture, Fisheries and Food*[63] in which it was suggested that if a *prima facie* case of abuse of discretion can be made out, then in the absence of a statement of reasons by a minister for a decision, a court would be entitled to assume that no good reasons existed. But in fact this creates a Catch 22 situation since 'the burden of demonstrating a wrongful exercise of discretion must rest on him who asserts it'.[64] In the absence of a statement of reasons or other access to official thinking such a *prima facie* case can rarely be established.[65]

More broadly, in many areas of policy-making the burden of demonstrating the procedural fairness and rationality of decision-making needs to be imposed on the decision-maker. In particular it should be for the policy-maker to show that a 'hard look' has been taken at the policy adopted. The absence of a general 'hard look' requirement in English law was never more clearly demonstrated than in *Bushell v Secretary of State for the Environment*.[66] Objectors at an inquiry into the route of a proposed section of motorway were allowed to give evidence concerning traffic forecasting methodology but were not permitted to cross-examine the government department's experts. Subsequent to the inquiry the official forecasting methodology was revised but the inquiry was not reopened.

The House of Lords held that there had been no breach of natural justice because the methodology was not a matter fit to be debated in the forum of the public local inquiry. The Secretary of State was prepared to consider representations as 'part of the continuous consideration of any of the department's proposals': in other words the department promised that it was meeting hard look standards, but in private. The court was prepared to accept that there was no necessity for the department to *demonstrate* how it received criticism and reassessed its policy.

What can be achieved by courts in practice is illustrated by the 'hybrid rule-making' decisions of the American Federal courts which established a general duty on Federal agencies to demonstrate to the courts that a rational process of decision-making took place with adequate opportunities for participation. We examine hybrid rule-making and the 'hard look' doctrine in Chapter 9. The essential point is that the design of procedures is primarily up to the agency, with the court acting as a quality-control mechanism primarily in relation to the adequacy of the procedures adopted rather than the substantive rationality of the decision. Courts should, of course, be prepared to recognize that restraint in the performance of their reviewing role may well be appropriate. Indeed this is part of the rationale of the hybrid cases in relation to substantive review.[67] Restraint may well be appropriate where other mechanisms of procedural review exist, but this must depend on those mechanisms being real rather than fictional as is for the most part the case with ministerial responsibility. The House of Commons may be the most appropriate place for debating the wisdom of going to war over the Falklands, raising tax rates or other burning issues of the day in which ministers are personally involved. But the Minister of Transport in all probability knows no more personally about the methodology of traffic forecasting in motorway planning than the average citizen and to say that this is a matter of policy for which he or she is responsible to Parliament is simply to treat ministerial responsibility as a shield to protect private and unaccountable government, to preserve and enlarge the sphere of public autonomy where the rule of law does not apply.

Consultation requirements

To a limited extent the courts have recognized the importance of procedures in the formation of policy by enforcing express statutory consultation requirements as mandatory, so that breach of them makes the subsequent act or decision void.[68] However the significance of this is limited by a number of factors. First, the courts have in general refused to impose a duty to consult in the absence of an express statutory provision. A limited number of exceptions to this have emerged through the creative application of principles of natural justice. Where a public body has volunteered substantive or procedural limits on its own discretionary powers, it may be held unfair for it to depart from these without good reason.[69] However valuable these limits on the discretion of public bodies are, they are unsystematic and do little to open up the policy-making process since they have depended on the giving of specific assurances as the foundation of the 'legitimate expectations' which they seek to protect. The case concerning the banning of trades unions at GCHQ Cheltenham offers the potential for further development of procedural duties founded on 'legitimate expectations'. The House of Lords would, if the national security issue had been absent, have been prepared to grant the plaintiff trades unions a remedy on the grounds that the Prime Minister had acted unfairly in failing to consult unions or staff before deciding to ban union membership at GCHQ. A legitimate expectation, it was said, 'may arise either from an express promise given on behalf of a public authority *or from the existence of a regular practice which the claimant can reasonably expect to continue'*.[70] The importance of the GCHQ case should not, however, be overstated. What was said in the *Padfield* case concerning reasons was hailed in 1968 as the harbinger of a new dawn of judicial review which has signally failed to appear. It is unlikely in the extreme that the ability of government to manipulate the terms of access to the policy process in the ways described in Chapter 6 will be significantly affected by the GCHQ case.

Similarly it is unlikely that the reasoning of the judge in *Steeples v Derbyshire County Council*[71] will be developed into a coherent set of principles to deal with the problem of *ex parte* relationships between public authorities and private interests. In the *Steeples* case a local authority had entered into a contractual relationship with a developer to whom it subsequently granted planning permission for a controversial project to which there was considerable public opposition. This was held to be contrary to natural justice in that it might appear that there existed a real likelihood that the authority had taken into account an irrelevant consideration – its contractual obligation – in granting the permission. Most interestingly the judge suggested that the authority could have removed the impression of unfairness if it had held a public meeting at which the development proposals and the reasons for them had been explained and at which objectors could have had an opportunity to present their views.[72] The logic of *Steeples* is that a public authority may be obliged to develop procedures to subject its own policies to critical appraisal and testing where it is reasonable to suppose that *ex parte* or bargained relationships may have unduly affected decisions. In the context of the dense network of informal relationships which characterizes British public administration this could have significant impact in opening up procedures. However, *Steeples* is an isolated decision and there are many other cases in which the courts have refused to use natural justice or fairness to prevent the formal and public procedures of land-use planning being subverted by the processes of private government.[73]

An important aspect of consultation is of course the provision of information to the body being consulted. The courts have done little to make this a significant requirement of openness but instead have emphasized that the duty to provide information in consultation is limited by traditional divisions of institutional responsibility. For example, even where there is a statutory duty to consult, central government need not provide information to local authorities on matters for which the latter have no specific statutory responsibility.[74] In general the courts have been hostile to attempts to obtain more freedom of information, especially in relation to central government. They have been eager, as we have seen, to allow private law rights, such as those of confidentiality and property, to be used by the government as a means for preserving the sphere of public autonomy from critical comment by outsiders.[75] When the British Steel Corporation successfully applied to the court for an order naming a 'mole' who had leaked information to a television company Lord Wilberforce repeated the old constitutional nostrums: 'the legitimate interest of the public in knowing about its (BSC's) affairs is given effect to through information which there is a statutory duty to publish and through reports to the Secretary of State who is responsible to Parliament'.[76]

A further crucial aspect of taking consultation seriously is that cogent comment on a proposal should be answered. British courts have not, however, interpreted statutory duties to consult in this way nor has the requirement of substantial evidence been developed. Again in the case of land-use planning where regulations specifically provide for a statement of reasons when a minister disagrees with the conclusion reached by an inspector after a public local inquiry, the courts do treat the requirement seriously but they do not impose it elsewhere as a common law matter. An example of the consequences is *R v Secretary of State for Trade ex parte Anderson Strathclyde plc.*[77] The report of the Monopolies and Mergers Commission recommending, by a majority, that a proposed merger be not allowed contained detailed reasons for both the majority and minority views on the public interest. The Secretary of State's decision to allow the merger to proceed was simply announced in a press release which dealt with none of the substantial points raised in the report and merely recorded the bare facts of the minister's disagreement with the majority's view. The Divisional Court refused to quash the decision

> it was a matter for the minister, in his unfettered discretion, to choose between those two views [i.e. the majority and minority of the M&MC], taking into account any other relevant matters . . . . He preferred the view of the minority. Whether he was right or wrong about that is a matter of political judgement, and not a matter of law.
>
>   . . . it is no part of the function of this court to go into the merits of whether or not this proposed merger should be allowed. Our sole function is to consider whether the minister, in refusing to stop the merger, acted lawfully. That involves answering two questions and two questions only. (1) Did the minister have the power under the Fair Trading Act 1973 to take the course he did? . . . (2) In exercising the power did he take into consideration any matter which he should not have taken into consideration?[78]

The refusal by the court to be drawn into an evaluation of the merits of the decision cannot be faulted but the assertion that the reviewing function is thereby limited to questions of *ultra vires* and substantive abuse of discretion is a *non sequitur* displaying a lamentable lack of general principles concerning legal structuring of procedures for subjecting policy to critical testing.

Conclusion

What we have attempted to demonstrate in this chapter is that the criteria of legality which are applied by the courts do not amount to the rule of law in the sense of the exclusion of arbitrary public power. Not only have the courts largely failed to respond in any

principled fashion to the increase in number and scale of government functions, they have not even begun to take account of the
new map of public decision-making through quasi-government and
quasi-non-government bodies. Indeed, when the matter has arisen
even tangentially the courts have gone out of their way to disclaim
jurisdiction.[79] To a considerable extent the courts remain trapped
within the Dicean paradigm, invoking familiar and comforting
doctrines which no longer have the effect that once could be
plausibly claimed for them. Unsure of their own legitimacy when
the boundaries of customary common law and interpretation of the
intention of Parliament are transcended, the courts have failed to
prevent the growth of the sphere of public autonomy. When they
have intervened, a lack of sophistication in dealing with public law
matters has too often meant a failure to understand the subtle
differences and links between substance and procedure. This in turn
has sometimes led to accusations of political prejudice which have
reinforced doubts about judicial legitimacy at large. However, the
courts frequently do express concern about the requirement for the
legitimacy of public action. In doing so they commit themselves
logically to the development and widespread application of principles which are now perceived only sporadically and as through a
glass darkly. In logic, however, they are required to accept responsibility for encouraging the development of open and participative
policy-making processes as the appropriate means of advancing rule
of law values in modern conditions – conditions where government
is multi-layered and fragmented and problems are complex and
interlinked. Too often the judiciary appear to think that ritual
invocation of the *Wednesbury* test of reasonableness constitutes an
adequate response to the need to define a role for the courts in
maintaining rule of law values.

That the courts must develop and apply such principles should be
increasingly obvious to them now that they have abandoned one of
the key elements in Dicey's account of the rule of law: *viz.* 'equality
before the law or the equal subjection of all classes to the ordinary
law of the land administered by the ordinary courts'. The decision in
O'Reilly v Mackman[80] was the culmination of a remarkable process
(in which the contributions of judicial, delegated and primary
legislation were highly confused) creating a British version of one of
the elements that Dicey so detested in *droit administratif*. The
courts will now, in their discretion, refuse to exercise their jurisdiction in 'ordinary' proceedings where this would enable the plaintiff

to evade, 'the safeguards imposed in the public interest against groundless, unmeritorious or tardy attacks on the validity of decisions made by public authorities in the field of public law'.[81] The safeguards offered to public authorities by the form of proceedings which must be used include the need to obtain leave to bring proceedings and various procedural obstacles which place most complainants at considerable disadvantage. The bringing of *locus standi* requirements (i.e. that a complainant must show a sufficient interest in the subject matter of the proceedings) effectively under the discretionary control of the courts further emphasizes the fact that Dicey is dead but that the legitimate basis of a new conception of the courts' role is yet to be articulated.[82]

As in the United States a greater judicial assertion of authority over policy-making is likely to lead to aggravation of the doubts the courts feel in relation to their legitimacy in a polity which claims to be democratic. But, as we have indicated, democracy itself is a procedural concept and an account of judicial review that builds on the idea of law as the structuring of procedures for policy-making can make the courts a necessary and integral part of a democratic polity.

References

1   R. Dworkin, *Taking Rights Seriously* (Duckworth 1977), esp. chs. 4 and 5.
2   That these are 'institutional' rather than 'background' rights constitutes the other dimension of legal autonomy in Dworkin's work. See ibid., pp. 101–5.
3   ibid., p. 82.
4   ibid., p. 100 and ch. 5.
5   ibid., p. 142.
6   See esp. J. H. Ely, *Democracy and Distrust* (Harvard University Press 1980); D. J. Galligan, 'Judicial review and democratic principles: two theories', *Australian Law Journal*, **57** (1983), pp. 69–79.
7   Ely, ch. 4.
8   *Case of Impositions (Bate's case)* (1606) 2 State Trials 371. *Case of Ship Money, R v Hampden* (1637) 3 State Trials 825. *Prohibitions del Roy* (1607) 12 Co. Rep. 63; *Case of Proclamations* (1611) 12 Co. Rep. 74.
9   H. L. A. Hart, *The Concept of Law* (OUP 1961).
10 K. Dyson, *The State Tradition in Western Europe* (Martin Robertson 1980), pp. 36–44. See also S. H. Beer, *Modern British Politics*, 2nd edn (Faber and Faber 1982).

11 The comparison between Conciliar jurisdiction and the Conseil is specifically drawn by Dicey p. 371.

12 J. D. B. Mitchell, 'The causes and effects of the absence of a system of public law in the United Kingdom', *Public Law*, **95** (1965), at pp. 97–8.

13 Dyson, p. 41.

14 C. B. MacPherson, *Democratic Theory* (Oxford 1973), pp. 124–5.

15 E. P. Thompson, *Whigs and Hunters* (Penguin 1975), p. 241.

16 P. S. Atiyah, *The Rise and Fall of Freedom of Contract* (Oxford 1979), pp. 147, 173 and 180.

17 See G. Teubner, 'Substantive and reflexive elements in modern law', *Law and Society Review*, **17** (1983), p. 239.

18 See Atiyah, pp. 388–9.

19 Sir Ivor Jennings, *The Law and the Constitution*, 5th edn (University of London Press 1959).

20 J. S. Mill, *On Liberty* (Penguin 1982). Originally published 1859.

21 See e.g. H. L. A. Hart, *Law, Liberty and Morality* (OUP 1963). Dworkin, *Taking Rights Seriously*, ch. 11.

22 Jennings, pp. 60–2 is an example of the former; E. C. S. Wade and G. Phillips, *Constitutional and Administrative Law*, 9th edn by A. W. Bradley (Longman 1977), pp. 92–3 of the latter.

23 A. V. Dicey, *An Introduction to the Law of the Constitution*, 9th edn by E. C. S. Wade (Macmillan 1939), pp. 183–4.

24 ibid., pp. 430–1.

25 The rule of statutory interpretation that express words are necessary to empower a public authority to raise money from the subject (see S. A. De Smith, *Judicial Review of Administrative Action*, 4th edn by J. M. Evans (Stevens 1980), p. 100 and cases there cited) is still strictly adhered to, although the historical rationale is ignored; see e.g. *Congreve v Home Office* [1976] QB 629.

26 Dicey, pp. 439–54.

27 ibid., p. 430.

28 ibid., pp. 184, 471 and 189.

29 See e.g. A. Bickel, *The Least Dangerous Branch* (New York: Bobbs Merrill 1962) and *The Supreme Court and the Idea of Progress* (New York: Harper and Row 1970); Ely, *Democracy and Distrust*; Dworkin, *Taking Rights Seriously*.

30 *Cooper v Wandsworth Board of Works*, (1863) 14 CB (NS) 180. (Crucial to this case was the assimilation of the administrative process in issue to the model of 'punishment' for an 'offence'); *Local Government Board v Arlidge* [1915] AC 120.

31 See De Smith, *Judicial Review*, p. 164–72.

32 See P. Birkinshaw, *Grievances, Remedies and the State* (Sweet and Maxwell 1985).

33 Doctrinally it is necessary to distinguish *review* from appeal on the merits. Provision for appeal to courts on the merits from an administrative

decision is restricted to certain licensing matters. Appeal on a point of law is now quite common but the differences from review are not important for the argument presented here. See generally, H. W. R. Wade, *Administrative Law*, 5th edn (OUP 1982), pp. 34–6.

34   See e.g. the *Arlidge* case (footnote 30 above); *Carltona Ltd v Commissioners of Works and Others* [1943] 2 All ER 546.

35   Not only from the courts; it is significant that the *cause célèbre* of Crichel Down, which was pre-eminently a matter of the exercise of discretionary powers by a government department resulted in the setting up of the Franks Committee to examine *tribunals* and *inquiries*.

36   Dicey, p. 424.

37   *A–G v De Keyser's Royal Hotel* [1920] AC 508; *Laker Airways v Department of Trade* [1977] QB 643, and see De Smith, pp. 286–90.

38   For a brief summary see Wade and Phillips, pp. 234–9.

39   The Department of Education and Science, acting through the Privy Council, canvassed the idea of refusing to consider any proposals to amend university statutes which did not also include a clause enabling the university to dismiss academic staff on grounds of redundancy or financial exigency. Other bodies created by Royal Charter include, for example, the BBC.

40   *Council of Civil Service Unions v Minister for the Civil Service* [1984] 3 All ER 935. See also *R v Criminal Injuries Compensation Board ex parte Lain* [1967] 2 WLR 864.

41   (1765) 19 State Trials 1020; [1979] ch. 344.

42   *A–G v Jonathan Cape Ltd* [1976] QB 752; *BSC v Granada Television Ltd* [1981] AC 1096; *Secretary of State v Guardian Newspapers Ltd* [1984] 3 All ER 601.

43   *Francome v Mirror Group Newspapers Ltd* [1984] 2 All ER 408.

44   See the evidence of Professor J. D. B. Mitchell to the Public Accounts Committee HC 137 Session 1981–2 appendix 20, at p. 188. The National Audit Act 1983 does not affect the position.

45   Expenditure on the universities is probably the best known example of 'appropriation only'; see 3rd Report of the PAC for 1948/9 HC 233.

46   See e.g. *French Kier Ltd v Secretary of State* [1977] 1 All ER 296 and on supplementary benefit see Tony Prosser, *Test Cases for the Poor* (CPAG 1983), pp. 48–53.

47   Some of the best known work is: H. Wechsler, 'Toward neutral principles of constitutional law', *Harvard Law Review*, **73** (1959), p. 1; A Bickel, *The Least Dangerous Branch* and *The Supreme Court and the Idea of Progress*; Ely, *Democracy and Distrust*; Dworkin, *Taking Rights Seriously*.

48   See e.g. J. A. G. Griffith, *The Politics of the Judiciary*, 3rd edn (Fontana 1985). P. McAuslan 'Administrative law, collective consumption and judicial policy', *Modern Law Review*, **46** (1983), p. 1.

49   See e.g. Lord Devlin, 'Judges and law-makers', *Modern Law Review*,

39 (1976), 1. See also A. Patterson, *The Law Lords* (Macmillan 1983) for a discussion of these and other judicial views.

50 See e.g. *Roberts v Hopwood* [1925] AC 578 and the case on which discussion here focuses, *Bromley London Borough Council v Greater London Council* [1982] 1 All ER 129.

51 *Prescott v Birmingham Corporation* [1955], ch. 210.

52 J. Willis, 'Statute Interpretation in a Nutshell', *Canadian Bar Review*, **XVI** (1938), 1 at p. 17. See e.g. *Mixnam's Properties Ltd v Chertsey UDC* [1965] AC 735, *Grunwick v ACAS* [1978] AC 277.

53 This would not be surprising: the *Bromley* case is unusual in that not only was it criticized in a predictable way on the fiduciary duty issue but it was also quickly subjected to the indignity of 'explanation' in a lower court in order, effectively, to reverse its interpretation of the relevant statute by pretending that it had not said what it plainly did say – that any policy which deliberately made subsidy a policy objective was *ultra vires*. See *R v London Transport Executive* [1983] 2 All ER 262.

54 See the judgements of Lords Diplock and Brandon at pp. 165, 182.

55 See the judgements of Lord Denning at p. 135 and of Lord Justice Oliver at pp. 141–2.

56 Discretion must not be fettered by self-imposed policy rules; See esp. *British Oxygen Corporation v Board of Trade* [1971] AC 610. It must be used to promote the purposes of the statute; *Padfield v Minister of Agriculture* [1968] AC 997. On relevant and irrelevant considerations see *Associated Provincial Picture Houses v Wednesbury Corporation* [1948] 1 KB 223 (the *Wednesbury* case). Arbitrariness can be categorized as any of the above or as unreasonableness (on which see the *Wednesbury* case and cf. the 'arbitrary and capricious' standard of review under the US Administrative Procedure Act).

57 Per Lord Greene MR in *Wednesbury*.

58 On American law see K. C. Davis, *Administrative Law of the Seventies*. (New York: Rochester 1976). In English law it is an error of law for an inferior tribunal to base a decision on 'no evidence' (see De Smith, pp. 133–4). When this is extended to cover evidence which cannot *reasonably* support an administrative decision something akin to the substantial evidence test begins to emerge.

59 [1976] 3 All ER 665.

60 Most corporate planning theory works with something like this set of distinctions (which is of course ideal-typical and highly schematic).

61 For a clear statement of the doctrine see *McInnes v Onslow-Fane* [1978] 3 All ER 211; *Payne v Lord Harris of Greenwich* [1981] 1 WLR 754.

62 e.g. The effective nullification of statutory exclusion of judicial review in *Anisminic v Foreign Compensation Commission* [1969] 2 AC 147.

63 [1968] AC 997.

64 Per Lord Justice Oliver in the *Bromley* case at p. 143.

65   For an example of the Catch 22 in operation see *Cannock Chase District Council v Kelly* [1978] 1 WLR 1.

66   [1980] 1 All ER 608.

67   See e.g. *Weyerhauser v Costle* 590 F. 2d 1101.

68   Other kinds of procedural requirements are often treated as 'directory' so that breach of them need not *per se* result in voidness. See De Smith, pp. 142–51.

69   See *R v Liverpool Corporation ex parte Taxi Fleet Operators Association* [1972] 2 QB 299, *Attorney General of Hong Kong v Ng Yuen Shiu* [1983] 2 All ER 346, *HTV v Price Commission* [1976] ICR 170.

70   *Council of Civil Service Unions v Minister for the Civil Service* [1984] 3 All ER 935 at 944 per Lord Fraser (emphasis added).

71   [1984] 3 All ER 468.

72   At pp. 494–5.

73   See e.g. *Covent Garden Community Association Ltd v GLC* (1981) *Journal of Planning and Environment Law* 183; *R v Hammersmith and Fulham Borough Council ex parte People Before Profit Ltd* (1982) 80, *Local Government Reports* 322.

74   *Rollo v MTCP* [1948] 1 All ER 13; *Port Louis Corporation v AG of Mauritius* [1965] AC 1111.

75   See cases cited at note 42 above.

76   *BSC v Granada* [1981] AC 1096 at p. 1168.

77   [1983] 2 All ER 233.

78   Per Dunn L. J. at p. 243.

79   See e.g. *Cinnamond v British Airports Authority* [1980] 2 All ER 368 at 374 (dictum concerning the Independent Broadcasting Authority).

80   [1982] 3 All ER 1124.

81   Per Lord Diplock at p. 1131. cf. Dicey, pp. 201–3.

82   See *IRC v National Federation of Self-Employed and Small Businesses Ltd* [1981] 2 All ER 93 and *R v H M Treasury ex parte Smedley* [1985] 1 All ER 589.

Part Three

Reconstitutionalizing the Business of Governing

In this part we seek to address what we have called 'the reconstitutionalization of the business of governing'. In other words we deal, albeit in a preliminary fashion, with the nature and measure of constitutional reform necessary to realign our governing institutions with the cultural claims and expectations of the rule of law.

First, we deal with the kind of institutional changes needed to confine public decision-making processes within acceptable bounds. We examine the conditions under which rules, laws, policies and plans currently emerge and suggest approaches to the institutional establishment of a context in which rational, informed decision-making could take place. We draw upon both American and British sources and experience in advocating changes in political and legal structures.

Second, we discuss the question of the standards of debate required for open and rational decision-making. We speak briefly but forcefully to the issue of freedom of information and then at greater length to the criteria for public affirmation of the quality of policy debate. In particular, we espouse the 'hard-look' doctrine of American administrative law as the most satisfactory way of judging the quality of the decision-making process. We envisage an expanded role for law as the supreme constitutional guarantee.

Finally, we speculate upon the character of a rule of law re-born to underpin constitutionality in the complex conditions of late twentieth-century Britain. Using the expansive concept of law adopted in Part One we outline the role of a reinvigorated rule of law in realizing the aspirations of both democratic government and full citizenship. We regard a British Administrative Procedure Act as a necessary precondition of satisfactory constitutional readjustment.

8 An institutional approach to power and discretion

It should be clear that we regard traditional governing institutions as inadequate to guarantee canons of openness and accountability without some radical reconstitutionalization. We do not have a green-field site for constitution-building and in any event the stability of British political traditions is so widely and rightly admired that our suggestions for delivering on the promises under-lying the concept of the rule of law are intended to build upon existing foundations. In particular the need to retain (and indeed strengthen) the authority of Parliament is a paramount considera-tion. It is evident that the very considerable discretionary power exercised by the executive branch in alliance with its clienteles is not the subject of institutional patterns of control directed to producing genuine policy debate and informed decision-making. This chapter is dedicated to examining some of the procedural implications for putting our governing habits in touch with a reborn rule of law.

Accountability to the nation as an undifferentiated whole lies at the base of our polity and access to official information guaran-teed by law would do much to enhance the dignity of this aspiration. Accountability through Parliament has remained and will remain a central belief. On the other hand, it will almost certainly prove necessary for the raw information to be put to deliberative tests mediated by authorized agencies and, ultimately, by the courts. Openness is the key to any concept of accountability in the sense of the decision-maker being called to account through reasoned ex-planations and, increasingly, in the sense of making policy decisions through a process of informed rational debate. Giving meaning to accountability requires the identification of appropriate 'constitu-encies' to be entrusted with the task of exposing decision-making processes to close scrutiny. This argument needs development and we shall address ourselves to it in a later section. The quality and nature of the information to be scrutinized we leave over until Chapter 9.

There are a number of ways in which Parliament might be reformed to improve the quality of its executive and agency 'oversight', to use an American expression, but given the very different natures of Parliament and the US Congress it is doubtful whether even the American degree of effective oversight can be achieved here in the immediate future.[1] The present inadequacies concern as much oversight of quasi-government and quasi-non-government bodies as the departments of state. Indeed, one of our complaints has been that, for all the achievements to the credit of court-imposed notions of fairness, we have signally failed to develop an extensive doctrine of bureaucratic 'due process' even in relation to complaints about executive conduct which do not impinge directly on the policy area. Decision-making procedures of an open and ordered nature are not a systemic part of British public life: we have not as a general practice injected due process into the administrative machine, partly because of the dominance of the Dicean version of the rule of law.[2]

Over and above this basic need is the issue of procedures for informing discretion and decision-making where, as we have seen, our courts have relatively little to say. Land-use planning aside, our legal order largely fails to address the need for public authority to be 'nourished by effective criticism'.[3] We have for too long clung to a notion of law which at best seeks to confine government within the limits of rules and have failed to explore law's potential for releasing the critical energies of interested constituencies. Furthermore, constituencies or client-groups vouchsafed access to government proposals commonly operate in the constitutional shadows, and their participation is not visibly on the basis of information which has to be defended against some test of rational purpose. Least of all does our legal order systematically seek to inject notions of due process and critical debate into the province of 'private governments', or what we have earlier referred to as the 'new feudalism'. Given the networks and alliances between the public and private realms which we have described in Chapter 6 this is a matter of some significance, not least in terms of governmental decisions *not* to take action.

Non-decisions

The concept of the 'non-decision' has now become well-established in the political and social science literature.[4] Bachrach and Baratz pay greater attention to non-decisions as 'the mobilization of bias' than perhaps would we but they address questions which vitally concern us when they speak of the 'suffocation' of demands for change and of failure to act because of strong pressures exerted by those powerfully inimical to change.[5] In Britain enthusiasm for studying the phenomenon has not extended to constitutional lawyers although, as we shall see, there have been remarkably interesting developments in the United States where the courts have occasionally been prepared to review agency inaction. For the reasons explained earlier, we can for all effective purposes usefully speak of the delegated omnicompetence of the executive. In this context non-exercise of power is a matter of considerable importance both in terms of conduct under specifically delegated authority and more generally in terms of decisions not to intervene programmatically to regulate the affairs of groups and institutions.[6] Thus, to take concrete examples which we shall mention again, there are matters of pressing importance involved when the Department of Trade and Industry (DTI) decides not to refer a monopolies situation or a merger proposal to the Monopolies and Mergers Commission (M&MC) after advice from the Office of Fair Trading.[7] It is a matter of even greater moment when the DTI decides whether or how to regulate the City of London.

These issues are simply unaddressed by appeals to the formalistic nineteenth-century version of the rule of law, while the traditionalist concept of law almost certainly acts as an impediment to taking these issues on board. Even if formalist notions were capable of 'controlling' the state in a simple-minded sense, they would still leave untouched major centres of private bureaucratic power and the quasi-polities with whom modern governments have sinuous relationships.[8] British pressure groups, professional associations and clienteles do not generally work through political parties and elections to advance their aims but through the executive. Whitehall in particular operates under peculiarly sheltered conditions, not least in terms of the special relationship of ministers to civil servants, that facilitate closed bargaining.

This is to say much more than that we should interest ourselves in the non-exercise of political and legal power, but it is certainly to say that as well. Political scientists have commented on the policy-making constraints of British politics, on how difficult it is for new policies to emerge which challenge political traditions, and have described the incrementalist nature of much of our public conduct. Non-decisions and procrastination are a significant part of British traditions but whereas most other democracies have engaged in institutional experiments to deal with new conditions, the British have largely avoided any similar response.[9] It is true that such experiments where they have occurred have enjoyed mixed success but at least the attempts have been made in the recognition that genuine problems of legitimation arise out of the sets of circumstances we are describing.

We shall speak in this chapter to the kinds of experiments which we regard as necessary and outline the range of possibilities which are needed to supplement our formalist traditions. In so doing we shall rely heavily on developments in American Federal administrative law, not with a view to suggesting wholesale importation, but in order to indicate how an expanded concept of law and of the rule of law can contribute to institutional design for constitutional legitimation. Law is coterminous in our view with legitimate institutional power but we shall not attempt to lay down a blueprint for institutional developments, pointing instead to a programmatic set of inquiries which seeks to relate the promise of the rule of law to the reality of executive power today.

There is nothing in our constitutional literature which addresses non-decisions except the truistic doctrine that discretion means that a decision-maker may or may not act and that in so doing he or she must at all times be guided by 'proper considerations'. American administrative law, on the other hand, has identified the problem and although the Federal courts have allowed antiquated doctrines to bar review in many administrative law areas, there is at least a strain of cases in which non-action or non-implementation of agency programmes may be judicially reviewed by the courts.[10] The definition of 'agency action' reviewable under the Administrative Procedure Act includes 'failure to act',[11] and in recent times concern has begun to be expressed for those for whose benefit an agency is supposed to act, but does not.[12]

It will be most appropriate to examine this issue in detail when we explain the standard of review which courts adopt when operating the 'hard look' doctrine, a matter which we have reserved for

Chapter 9. However, a number of prefatory remarks can be made. The first is that the degree of independence and visibility exhibited by the Federal agencies is such that traditionalists in Britain would argue that our system of parliamentary government makes comparisons difficult or even irrelevant. To this we would respond in a number of ways. One is that the articulation between presidential and congressional power and that of the agencies has become much more apparent and controversial in recent years than formerly. Another is that even in a Congress characterized by the sturdy independence of senators (in particular) and developed oversight mechanisms, it has become apparent that the range and complexity of administrative discretion cannot be handled by the political process unaided if meaning is to be given to democratic principles.[13] Furthermore, given the massive concentration of executive power in Britain compared to the United States, the challenge to find institutions which bring decision-making into the sunlight is especially acute. Suggestions for scrutinizing inaction and non-decisions in Britain only seem incredible because we do not have developed traditions of using the legal system for producing reasoned decision-making. It is unused, for example, to calling up to scrutiny the records upon which executive power relies for the purpose of seeing whether alternative avenues have been adequately explored. Legal devices, broadly conceived as in Chapter 3, can contribute to rational policy debate and to cognitive development if we are prepared to make the effort. The issue is crucial for the restoring of democratic expectations in the political process and the devices which we explore are illustrative of the kind of debate which ought to be engendered concerning the relationship between law and government.

In Britain, as in the United States, regulations are often necessary to give substance to legislative policies and to provide detailed guidance as to what conduct is expected of private parties. In Britain, departments or quangos may or may not make regulations, rules or delegated legislation, may or may not take effective action to prosecute programmes. In both countries, though to differing degrees, these tasks may be delegated to various executive or regulatory agencies and the breadth both of rule-making and of enforcement power thus delegated presents substantial potential for abuse through non-implementation. Lehner instances the Federal Clean Air Act which gave the Environmental Protection Agency powers in relation to the emission of pollutants. In some cases the statutory limits were precise and in other cases the Agency enjoyed broad discretion. In either circumstance the Agency might fail to establish methods of measuring emissions, fail to list acceptable reasons for not reducing emissions or fail to establish schedules for reporting such emissions. Likewise in either case the Agency might fail to hold fact-finding hearings pursuant to which rules might be promulgated. In response

the courts have required agencies to produce contemporaneous records sufficient to show the public and the courts its data, methodology and reasoning. Agencies are thus on notice to keep an up-to-date record of anything that may be of concern to the public. Overall, this increase in documentation and congressional direction gives precision even to non-implementation and thus discounts a concern that these actions are too indefinite for judicial review.[14]

Now critics have berated the Federal courts for their timidity given the institutional opportunities available, yet the institutional potential for such developments in Britain does not exist to anything like the degree presented by Federal law. There is the rub. Neither records, open meetings, access to files nor indeed any attempt at opening up the networks of decision-making through legal restrictions on *ex parte* dealings are central features of our constitutional law. These institutional responses to discretion are matters to which we now wish to pay some attention.

Let us turn briefly to the regulation of finance capital. The City in general and the Bank of England as an institution have over time resisted pressures for incorporation into the machinery of government,[15] but in the last two decades the Bank has become increasingly integrated into the processes of Whitehall decision-making to the point where its relations with the Treasury have come to resemble those of a government department.[16] Now had there been some public acceptance of a policy-linkage then perhaps one might have expected the establishment of a semi-autonomous institution with clear constitutional parameters, so that debate and disagreement might have become part of the stock in trade of a national examination of our economic and financial affairs. In the absence of such formal constitutional features, a degree of incorporation causing the Bank to resemble a part of central government was a more likely outcome. On the other hand, pressures towards incorporation only exist because of the Bank's downwards influence over the various factions of finance capital in circumstances where constitutional visibility is yet again only dimly perceptible.[17]

Some of the City's dislike of regulation, though clearly not all, can be attributed to an excessively parochial attitude towards law and the legal order. If legal control is equated with *gesellschaft* notions, then it is easy to sympathize with the Bank and the City and indeed some deregulation of Wall Street financial institutions has occurred in recent years. But if a broader concept of law is adopted, then whatever resistance might be encountered from the quasi-polities of British life, the picture begins to look very different. If what is being demanded is essentially a constitutional *concordat* with open lines of accountability drawn between the various constitutional actors, then it is less easy to reject a measure of answerability, especially if a substantial measure of self-regulation is conceded.[18] Debate concerning the shape and nature of lines of responsive accountability is in its infancy. It will be demeaned if defensive reactions to demands for open behaviour are encouraged by equating civic enfranchisement with the tight rule-bound structure of a formalist legal tradition.

The networked and clientelist patterns which so characterize the ways of British government are at the heart of constitutional un-accountability. The absence of clear constitutional frameworks has made even tracing the behaviour patterns of decision-makers seem an almost insurmountable problem. The City is not perhaps unique in this respect, but it may well be *primus inter pares*. To describe the power exercised by the Bank and City has always been extraordinarily difficult because so much influence has rested on an elusive capacity to influence the terms of political argument rather than on a crude ability to shape the outcome of overt decisions.[19] It is the elusiveness rather than the capacity which is of major interest to us as constitutional lawyers. Without open meetings, or constraints on *ex parte* dealings, lobbying and the like, we are well down the road to disguising the potential capture of legitimate, formal, elected government. The Bank of England is not a particular target for attack, but it is very noticeable that its influence is rarely signposted by constitutional scholars and it has been the subject of very little legal control. The nationalization statute is as skimpy as most such legislation and it is only since the Banking Act of 1979 that the Bank's extraordinary centrality in the financial affairs of the nation has been implicitly recognized in any distinctly legal sense. The Bank, in the argot, has traditionally assumed 'prudential supervision' over the City. From time to time it has intervened in the affairs of the financial community, albeit usually after some little local difficulty in the square mile, as in relation to the establishment of the Panel on Takeovers and Mergers, and at a later date the Council for the Securities Industry (CSI). The CSI is a perfect example of how self-regulation is inseparable from pressure group organization since it includes representatives of most City associations while relying for its secretariat on the Bank.[20]

The Banking Act 1979 places the Bank of England at the heart of regulation of deposit-taking, but, in spite of a number of very useful provisions for the protection of those who are refused licences or whose licences are revoked, a great deal of discretion remains with the Bank. There is much talk these days of the growth of financial supermarkets or of parabanking activities emerging which are difficult to predict with any precision given the current state of the money markets and of technology.

Innovation of this kind underlines the need for a parallel response from the supervisor, keeping under review both the legislative basis for supervision and the appropriate form of supervision, to ensure that new techniques of banking are both properly conducted and supervised.[21]

Granted there is much going on in the City which we would not wish to second-guess, a public interest in exposing networked decision-making in circumstances where more than a 'soft' standard of judicial review is required is certainly not evident in the Banking Act. The likelihood must remain that any review of the Bank's supervisory role will be essentially a private matter if indeed it takes place at all: 'the whole object of the legislation is to perpetuate, at least through an opaque glass, the undoubted but confidential wisdom of the past'.[22]

The 1979 Act requires the Bank of England to produce to the Chancellor of the Exchequer an annual report which sets out the principles on which the Bank is acting under the legislation. Although much useful guidance has been offered on criteria for granting deposit-taking licences, very little information has thus far been provided concerning developments in financial markets and the continuing supervision of the Bank in these and allied matters.[23] Now accepting the necessity for a high degree of confidentiality in the international banking system, it is still unsatisfactory that any review conducted by the Bank might be less open than, say, the Wilson or Gower Committees.

The City is largely ignored by constitutional lawyers in conditions where its role becomes ever more important in the fortunes of the nation. Even where the City is thought to be a meet subject for constitutional attention, its position in the middle of a financial and governmental spider's web is not sufficiently remarked. Much activity escapes constitutional attention simply because it is not necessarily manifested as a crude attempt to shape the outcome of overt decisions, but operates rather as an 'elusive capacity' to influence the terms of political argument. The processes of bargaining which cause decisions not to be made or the agenda to be narrowed escape traditional lawyering simply on account of its theoretical barrenness.

Add to this the failure to examine quasi-polities or private governments, and suddenly delegated self-regulation has poured through the constitutional net. The world of finance capital is an extraordinarily dense and esoteric place and the proper balance between regulation, self-regulation and governmental aloofness from the affairs of the financial community is not something which we are currently in a position to assess. What is clear, however, is that this balance has not become the focus for constitutional debate in the way that its real nature demands.

Policy-making in Britain: institutional defects

Whatever the political accommodations to interested publics in the policy-making process in Britain, the legal system has only infrequently been seen as having a contribution to make. Land-use planning is the shining exception to the general proposition, though a number of other *ad hoc* legal mechanisms are dotted around our system of administrative law. What has not been attempted in any systematic manner is the refashioning of legal institutions as part of what an American commentator has termed a 'surrogate political process'.[24] The logic of Part Two of our essay is that, even on the basis of government through Parliament in a non-federal constitution, the political process as argumentation, as discourse, as learning process needs at the very least to be buttressed by machinery which informs the mind of Parliament.

The courts have, for the most part, restricted their interventions to the area of individual rights and have shown themselves to be uneasy about injecting principles of democratic procedure into the administrative regime. There has been no attempt to insist that decision-making be articulated with reasonable clarity and accompanied by reasons for choices adopted, that the significance of facts thought crucial be identified or that policies effectuate or are consistent with detectable general standards.[25] There seems to us to be no way of satisfying such demands except through reviewing courts applying a reformed British administrative and constitutional law. These matters are, after all, high constitutional issues. They are the contemporary enlargement of notions of non-arbitrariness and the banishment of caprice, and the means of delivering prediction and accountability in political affairs. The creation of a record by which to judge the behaviour of policy-makers is the kernel of contemporary institutional forms of legality and if guarantees of a speaking polity can be ultimately grounded outside the courts then we should be very surprised.

Our earlier arguments should by now bear testimony to the fact that there exist two major obstacles to democratic debate in the policy arena. The first is that constituencies or publics are too frequently merely clienteles, so that, however sensible it may be to canvas a range of opinions, there exists a tendency in our political culture to classify insiders and outsiders. At the very least this is both complacent and inefficient. As a US Senate committee has stated, 'it has long been established that the making of policy decisions from a narrow perspective with limited sources of information can lead to inadequate and unwise decisions'.[26] More importantly from the point of view of democratic politics, it is a culture and practice with scanty claims to legitimation. If these points are well taken, then the issue of relegitimizing through legal processes, which at least retain the classical virtue of relative autonomy, is placed firmly on the constitutional agenda.[27]

Second, the quality of the information afforded even to insider publics is determined by those who set the agenda for debate. In spite of major failures by the British judiciary the potential for giving substance to consultation requirements is greatly enhanced when the political obligation is supervised by the judicial branch. This is undoubtedly true in the United States and forms much of the argument in Chapter 9 in relation to 'hard look' and the production of a record. Peter Self has pointed out that in Britain, as in other developed countries, the routinized nature of the relations between interest groups and decision-makers leads to the pragmatic assumption that a fair balance of power exists.[28] To counter this assumption he suggests devices for the greater involvement of broader constituencies and, although pointing up the weakness of some of the devices adopted by Federal administrative law, recognizes the need for greater experimentation. Self suggests machinery for direct public consultation, social surveys of needs and attitudes and cost–benefit analysis. This is not the place to examine these matters in fine detail. It must be recognized that cost–benefit analysis is not a substitute for political and ethical discussion of real interests,[29] but it is important to give consideration to using social cost–benefit analyses as a way of breaking down the structure of non-decisions that work to the disadvantage of disenfranchised groups.[30]

Argument concerning both the unrepresentative nature of representative democracy and the place of interest groups in improving or facilitating representation in government has raged fiercely for some time,[31] but the issue is surely *how*, not *whether* we seek to broaden the base of decision-making since openness must mean open to all, with at least the opportunity for the 'all' to make a contribution. The relationship between scholarship in law and social and political administration ought to concern precisely the matter of experimentation in institutional terms for delivering on canons of accountability, i.e. ensuring that open information, properly reasoned and principled, is addressed by relevant constituencies. Self's summary of the present position pinpoints the issue nicely:

It is apparent ... that the actual knowledge of politicians about the requirements of the public is often deficient, and democratic theory no longer seems to hold that the politicians' interpretative right is an exclusive one. Thus, the range of public demands which must be considered in administration has undeniably widened, and the administrator has come to play a more central role over their elucidation.[32]

Much of the cynicism with which such arguments are greeted is explicable by the experience of many whose critical comments have been absorbed and submerged by the participative process in the past. We should not be surprised at this since, if it is their earnest desire, the decision-maker will always be one jump ahead of the general public. But the choice is simple: either to accept both effective exclusion and potentially poorly informed decision-making, or to bend the will to the problem of being outflanked by bureaucracies while seeking to persuade that early disclosure of proposals is the natural ally of better decision-making. American legal experience and experiment in relation to restrictions on *ex parte* negotiations and contacts and to 'sunshine' legislation has been directed to ensuring the 'timely intervention' of publics before bureaucratic attitudes have hardened and to ensuring that neither the presentation of proposals nor the background to them is perfunctory. Again, freely accessible information is vital and the British experience is, of course, dismal.

The burden of our essay so far has been that the rule of law imports open and accountable conduct and that our governing institutions, whatever their considerable merits, are inadequate to the task of matching the constitutional expectations thereby engendered. Although most of the law-jobs to be performed under the constitutional umbrella are presently carried out only in what Llewellyn called a 'barebones' fashion, some of them are less attended to than others. We shall have cause to address them all in turn, but the drift of the last few arguments has been that 'preventive channelling' and 'goal orientation' have operated in Britain with scant regard to our constitutional or rule of law expectations. The legal system has made little contribution to informed and reasoned policy debate nor has it operated as the quality control mechanism of our public life so as to cause the executive at large to conduct its affairs according to 'principles of good administration'.[33] The greatest single failure of British public law is not to oversee the terms of the surrogate political process – not to ensure, merits entirely aside, that a rational foundation for decision-making exists in light of the opportunity for concerned publics to contest the issues at stake.

If not entirely random, the allocation of decision-making functions (law-job 3) at least lacks overall shape and design so that institutions and processes are unpredictably accountable to affected parties according to no clear jurisprudential pattern. Sometimes we have tribunals, sometimes not, sometimes the writ of ombudsmen runs, sometimes not. The picture is as blurred and uneven in local government as in central government, in relation to quangos as to the nationalized industries.[34]

As to the institutional side of law-job 1 it is remarkable that there is no requirement for the administration at large to publish any form of grievance procedure tailored to its own internal needs, as is the case in the field of employment generally.[35] Such a requirement, important *per se*, would also have other dimensions, both for the purposes of internal quality control and, as a form of participation too. Once more American experience is instructive.

The Senate committee which in 1977 examined public participation in regulatory agency proceedings focused some part of its
attention on complaint handling as a method of formulating general
agency policy. Although agency performance was found to be
uneven and in many cases deeply disappointing, it could be said that
most prepared some kind of statistical report on their complaints-
handling systems. Such material was capable of yielding information about regulated industries and agency performance and
hence of becoming a major component of agency accountability. In
some instances it was apparent that consumer complaints had
formed the basis and impetus for rule-making activity and had led
to a clarification of priorities through developing patterns of
complaints.[36]

Rule-making: the American contribution to public law jurisprudence

Most of the major democracies have made unique contributions to
constitutional law – the French through the whole corpus of *droit
administratif* which has been influential throughout Western
Europe; the Swedes, through the ombudsman; the British, through
the system of administrative tribunals. The great American contribution is undoubtedly rule-making.[37] Rule-making seeks to involve
a wide constituency as a matter of right in some of the Federal
agencies' most distinctive and significant policy-making. Because
Congress had delegated broad law-making powers to independent
agencies, it was thought necessary to restate democratic principles
involving their behaviour through reformed legal processes.

For all the defects of the rule-making provisions of US Federal
law they constitute the single most marketable commodity currently
available for producing procedural means of accountability and
participation. Developments in the last two decades make this
strain in American administrative law even more pertinent to the
British experience than a cursory glance at the Administrative
Procedure Act would lead the casual observer to expect.

Section 553 of the US Administrative Procedure Act provides for
'notice and comment' rule-making. Proposed rules or subjects for
rules should be publicly advertised so as to give interested parties
the opportunity to participate in the rule-making process through
presentation of written data, views or arguments, with or without
opportunity for oral presentation. After consideration of the relevant matter presented, the agency must incorporate in the rules

finally adopted a concise general statement of their basis and purpose. In certain circumstances formal trial-type hearings are required which necessitate a detailed record supported by substantial evidence.[38] Formal notice-and-comment requirements would be generally welcomed by us in a British setting, though we recognize the possibility of tokenism as an official response. On the other hand, the trial-type proceedings are rarely suitable mechanisms for resolving policy-laden disputes. Replicating the courtroom is the least desirable response to the problems we have been attempting to describe. At the risk of sounding trite, something in between these extremes would be the most acceptable solution to the problem of causing the administrator or the minister to enter into genuine dialogue with the electorate in its manifold forms. That something in between has been the crucible of Federal administrative law in recent years and is best summarized as 'hybrid' rule-making: hybr d because it injects elements of trial-type procedure, judged appropriate for the purpose of creating participative dialogue, into notice-and-comment rule-making.

Even the British regulatory agencies, let alone government departments, very rarely engage in rule-making on the American pattern. Indeed, the Civil Aviation Authority aside,[39] practically none of our quangos develops its policies and goals through a process of publicly structured debate, whatever level of consultation, formal or informal, may occur. They certainly do not engage in rational defences of adopted positions with an obligation to assess and respond to alternative positions, however important the decisions which they take may be.

It is at the level of relating the legal order to the problems of a modern administrative state that most diagnostic work needs to be done. It is facile to suppose that the legal systems of the modern world can be concerned only with facilitating the market and protecting property rights since the economic activities of private entities are regulated to varying degrees, and even the existence of markets depends increasingly on *active* state intervention not mere facilitation. Given that the law-jobs are scattered around the whole catacomb of governmental and quasi-governmental activity, there exists no choice between use of law and non-use of law. Rather we are looking at how the range of expanded state activities is conducted and through what mechanisms. The decision-making processes of British government lack legitimate authority in so far as they fail to address the institutional needs of expanded state

forms. Open conduct and rule-governed behaviour have constituted the claim for our being a nation governed under the rule of
law, but whatever the substance of the older claims, they clearly
could only be expected to relate to a minimalist state whose functions were primarily to create the condition for markets to flourish.

To argue for the maximum feasible reduction of arbitrariness in
policy-making we shall need to go beyond formal regularity and
reach out towards processes which produce rational outcomes
based upon standards which have been put to the test of open
criticism. In other words, regulating for public purposes is to strive
towards clarifying notions of the public interest. That process of
clarification will involve testing alternative strategies for the implementation of mandates and reconstructing those mandates in the
light of what has been learned. This, of course, involves more than
the business of making rules. Policy-making requires the definition
of goals, establishment of performance criteria, formulation of
guidelines and the like. To exclude these matters from our conception of the legal is to deprive the agencies charged with the task of
searching for public purposes of the legal system's expertise in the
practical and intellectual art of setting standards.[40]

Corporate planning

A system for the goal identification of an enterprise is fulfilling one
of the primary law-jobs so that for present purposes we shall need to
treat corporate planning as a somewhat flexible concept. In local
government the issue was brought into vogue by the Bains Report
as an accompaniment to the reforms introduced in 1972. It represents an attempt to secure unity of purpose in the affairs of large
organizations through adjusting activities to changing needs and
problems.[41] This involves making assumptions explicit, methodi-
cally reviewing policy and attempting to measure outputs. It is a
concern with what has become known as 'meta-policy-making'.[42]
For the most part, however, and with some noble exceptions, much
of what has passed under the name of corporate planning has been
little more than corporate management, with more energy spent on
implementation than on formulation of policy. This has been
accompanied by a phenomenon which we have touched upon at
several points in this essay, *viz.* a marked tendency towards seeking
managerial/technical solutions to problems.

In the early 1980s, however, in some areas of local government

there were signs of disenchantment with the way in which pro-
fessional/bureaucratic values had tended to stifle political choice.
The changed political and economic environment in which local
government was required to operate tended, in some instances, to
force policy planning into centre-stage.[43] This occasionally led to a
realization by some authorities that piecemeal approaches were
unacceptable and that a system of total policy-making and management was required if any real degree of local autonomy from central
government was to be preserved. In the very recent past the pace of
change in central–local relations has quickened and we would
hesitate to make forecasts about the anatomy of those relations in
the near future, but at times explicit policy-making systems with
rigorous processes of policy review have emerged from the local
government end. In some authorities policy plans appeared in the
early 1980s which aimed to establish and agree service priorities
outside the annual budget cycle, while ensuring that the latter was
closely integrated into the overall policy-planning process. Increasing financial pressure had the effect in some authorities of causing
them to preface their budgetary processes with policy review and
priority setting. This was accompanied by a concern to question
how political values and priorities can be fed into corporate processes which have traditionally been seen to be officer-managed
activities. The developments were sometimes accompanied by
attempts to secure external or consumer input, not least in an effort
to politicize their services against attack from the centre.[44]

At central government level the picture which emerges is one of
failure to engage in promotional value planning in most areas of
policy-sensitive activity and an overwhelmingly defective institutional framework for addressing these issues. Elsewhere the same
strains have been identified in the nationalized industries. The
National Economic Development Office report of 1976[45] had found
that the major problem of the industries was the lack of a systematic
framework for reaching agreement on long-term objectives and
strategies. The 1978 white paper which formed the governmental
response to the proposals,[46] while rejecting the institutional prescriptions, nevertheless accepted that more effective corporate planning was desirable to ensure greater policy-making efficacy and that
such planning should be participative. In fact, as is cogently argued
in a forthcoming book,[47] corporate planning has since that time not
become the central vehicle of relations between interest groups and
government. It has not, for example, provided a stable environment

for British Rail, while in British Steel corporate planning has been a largely closed process. Little information has been made available to enable informed criticism to take place and precious little consultation with those affected has taken place either. Civil aviation has a record better than many other areas, but the review of British aviation policy undertaken by the Civil Aviation Authority in 1984 had too narrow a focus. It was said at the time of publication of the much-criticized report that in a rational world it would have made considerable sense to review the entire direction of the industry 'in one mega-investigation' of an undertaking which currently brings in a surplus of over £400 million a year to the British economy.[48]

One more illustration and we shall close the account. On the appointment of a new chairperson of the Central Electricity Generating Board by the Secretary of State for Energy in 1983, it was reported that a secret agenda had been set between the two which was to form the basis of the Board's emergent corporate plan. The terms of the appointment were said to have demanded the honouring of 'seven secret pledges' one of which was to exploit the full potential of nuclear power at the expense of the coal industry.[49] If true, this episode displays an alarming degree of constitutional insouciance. Whether or not it is true, given the way our great public industries conduct their affairs, there is no guarantee that the Board's corporate plan will experience the advantage of open debate and the testing of alternative hypotheses. We ought, however, to add that the Board's procedures and plans have been much more exposed than those of many public industries in recent years, not least during the course of the Sizewell Inquiry.[50]

There is no formal record produced by British agencies or boards which a reviewing court could examine for the purposes of testing critical assumptions to see whether they were rationally supported. There is no general participative requirement which could guarantee that oppositional stances and positions were scrutinized. We shall look at the critical exceptions to this picture in a moment, but it is safe to say that even quasi-non-government, lying as it does in a constitutional vacuum, is not brought to account by the processes of the law. We find it surprising that there is no outcry about the freestanding nature of these mini-governments and can only assume both that ministers feel they can have their way and their sway with these bodies and that the dominant clienteles are equally contented. There is no detectable desire on the part of the clienteles to entrench a system of legal protection similar to that which their American counterparts were influential in establishing at an earlier period. Perhaps capture can be effected without recourse to formal structures for targetting decision-makers. Whether that is an over-cynical view or not, there is no doubt that the present system makes few gestures to constitutional legitimacy while it seems to offer few promises of an instrumentally efficient new dawn.

If we have accurately assessed the constitutional position of quasi-government in its broadest sense, what are we to make of ministerial power and ministerial and clientelist concertation? We have already sketched the main lines of legal responsibility and accountability where they exist, but the broader expectations of openness and accountability upon which the symbolic force of the rule of law is based are clearly not honoured. Quite apart from the absence of freedom of information legislation there are relatively few specific institutional constituencies to which executive power must report and justify itself. What we shall wish to argue is that once, constitutionally speaking, the agencies of quasi-government have put their houses in order, theirs is a territory of major potential for establishing a rule of law revival. In other words, if we are concerned, as we must be, with mechanisms of accountability for participative decision-making then we must look beyond parliamentary institutions, however much they might be capable of making reformed contributions to these matters. The constitutional lines to be drawn between the executive and any such mechanisms will require very serious attention and we should be surprised if these intermediaries (quangos by whatever name) could usefully function without paying serious attention to the reformation of administrative law.

Accountability and constitutional redress

We have argued at various points that accountability is an assumed feature of the British way of public life and we should now defend the assertion a little more stoutly before trying to invest the concept with constitutional meaning. The rule of law and its later associations with democratic forms of government have depended in full measure upon the visibility of organized public life. In the legal system itself the *gesellschaft* idea depends heavily upon the existence of generalizable rules known in such a way that life can be fashioned with them in mind. The notion of a supreme Parliament elected and recallable has strong associations with open debate, 'responsibility' being the price which the elected pay for their power. Whatever the exceptions which the political sophisticate might choose to defend, it is impossible to deny that open conduct is the lynchpin of our system of legitimation. However, the relationship between openness and being called to account has to be examined closely.

When talking specifically about political canons of accountability it might be argued that if open government is the characteristic pattern, periodic electoral choice will suffice as the touchstone of *ex post* accountability: accountability for past action and inaction. We have in Chapters 4 and 5 explained both the accountability orthodoxies and their shortcomings in a contemporary setting. None the less, the logic of our immanent critique is to point up the shortcomings and set them alongside the ideology and the aspirations. In one sense therefore, we are prepared to accept the stronger claims for representative government provided always that electoral choice is informed by 'intermediate' or 'programme' conduct being defended periodically in Parliament, where after all the executive is supposed to respond. However in order for Parliament to have an account properly rendered to it, it must be provided with the means of receiving and interpreting the accounts. Parliament has long recognized this through various procedures of the House, from question time through supply or opposition days to the select committee structure. There is surely then no denying that our immanent constitutional expectations include some enduring notion of accountability. The questions are: what sort of accountability and through what procedures?

Accountability in the constitutional law textbooks seems to us to dwell too much on nineteenth-century ways of thinking. It is associated rather too closely with the office of the Comptroller and Auditor-General and with the idea of keeping public officials in their place by means of meticulous financial discipline. Limiting the powers of government and keeping down the level of taxation were its rationale and in this respect it partakes of a somewhat negative flavour. We are not demeaning financial rigour and yet, as all but the most wilfully stubborn would admit, the nature of modern governments is such as to cause financial canons of accountability *simpliciter* to require considerable supplementation.[51] Programmes, plans, relationships of a contractual and less formal nature, and bargaining in its many forms operate in conditions of huge complexity and against a backcloth of uncertainty as to the implications of policy choices. In this respect the idea of a range of constituencies acting as the public watchdog for and through Parliament requires careful development.

Openness is undoubtedly essential for, although accountability is indispensable to regimes of every kind, it does not entail openness in the way that the latter entails accountability. Thus, it has been well said that officials in dictatorial and absolutist states are often even more strictly accountable than in open systems more dedicated to a version of the separation of powers. This is hierarchical accountability – upward, not downwards and outwards – to the most jealous and potent line manager, the dictator. But our love affair with the rule of law is of a very different kind:

> public accountability . . . is actually or potentially a rich and open source of knowledge about how government services function in actual practice, and hence of ideas about how they ought to function. It casts a spotlight upon institutions which are shy of the public's gaze, but whose qualities and imperfections have a steady cumulative effect upon our daily lives.[52]

Normanton goes on to argue that a report or explanation by the responsible officials is inadequate to render a proper account given the likelihood of self-justification and vindication by the persons concerned. It is the very essence of accountability that the initiative must be held by those who question the decisions being taken. They therefore need an independent source of information to ensure that no vital problem remains unmentioned or uninvestigated.[53]

In terms of *ex ante* accountability, accountability *before* irrevocable policy decisions (or non-decisions) occur, Parliament can only make informed choices if alternative programmes rationally defended are presented to it. There seems little likelihood that the executive can be trusted to perform this task itself. Responsibility to the nation as a whole then can only be expected by ensuring that the opportunity for participating in the debate which leads to policy choice is afforded to constituencies which have a chance of creating rational discourse.

The institutions of accountability

The object of the accountability exercise is to ensure openness at all stages of the policy process and to provide explanations for action taken and conduct reserved. It is the constituencies for receiving the explanations which are the heart of accountability and it is these which require particular attention. A satisfactory taxonomy of accountability procedures would require programmatic development, but a mix of openness and justification to constituencies such as advisory bodies and other agencies specifically emplaced both to report to Parliament and to be consulted by it, is clearly required.

If accountability requires that public business should be observable then we would expect to start with opening up the meetings of public authorities. This is not a general legal requirement in Britain, although the Public Bodies (Admissions to Meetings) Act 1960 is a major exception, particularly in relation to local government, though other bodies are also mentioned in the schedule to the Act. This legislation requires that most public business conducted by the bodies subject to it shall occur in open proceedings and is something of a rarity in our legal system. Although a number of bodies have been added to the schedule from time to time, the Act's history is not entirely progressive since, for example, the Water Act 1983 excludes water authorities, previously covered, from the openness requirements. As to most other public bodies they will conduct their business in public out of a sense of civic duty if at all: the law lends little assistance.

The freedom of information campaign has begun to canvass changes in this position, but it would be fair to say that little public debate has occurred in relation to 'sunshine' legislation. In the United States the 1977 Government in the Sunshine Act[54] applies to all agencies of the executive branch of the Federal government headed by at least two members, and also their subcommittees and advisory committees. The Act circumscribes what can be dealt with collectively without an opportunity for the public to be present and provides that every portion of every meeting of an agency shall be open to public observation unless the subject matter is statutorily exempted. There are also procedures for closing meetings and for the announcement of open and closed meetings; requirements that records be kept of closed meetings; procedures for public access to those records and ground rules for judicial review of alleged violations of the Act. The Act has been described as ranking 'among the most significant in the history of the Federal administrative establishment'.[55] It represents a clear threat to *ex parte* negotiations or closed bargaining and seems to us to be the ground floor of the new constitutional tenement.

We should expect that the setting up of watchdog agencies would

of itself provide no guarantee of open debate and genuine accountability and indeed some of the American agencies which we admire
in certain respects have been accused of being captured by their
clients. Indeed, the creation of the Interstate Commerce Commission
in 1887, which set light to the whole regulatory agency idea, has been
described as an example of a special interest group co-opting the
government to cartelize an industry.[56] American administrative law
has been concerned in the last twenty years with trying to use
inventive legal processes to overcome these natural tendencies.
Legal scholars in Britain seem either unaware or insouciant of these
phenomena as they operate in our own back yard. We have pointed
to the broad range of non-parliamentary bodies which in some
measure or another are concerned with doing the public's business
and we find it odd that they are largely left free-standing. They are
accountable only in the loosest political fashion without any real
pressure from Parliament or the judiciary to adopt internal processes which would minimize the possibility of arbitrary results.

As the Fulton Committee on the Civil Service pointed out some
time ago, we need something of a general reappraisal of our
inherited forms of government and social and economic organization if we are to give accountability real meaning within the
operations of our governing institutions as a whole.[57] Since Fulton
reported we have come to understand more clearly how difficult are
the problems of social and economic policy and have learned to add
a body of policy analysis to the better established market analysis
literature.[58]

A review of the machinery of government was outside Fulton's
remit, but it may be recalled that a recommendation to examine the
constitutional implications of a further degree of hiving off was
made. The Committee was not persuaded that we had necessarily
drawn properly the line between matters for which ministers were
and were not directly responsible.[59] Despite this limited focus
Fulton clearly recognized that, if such an examination were to take
place, then its knock-on effects for the rest of the machinery of
government might be considerable.[60] It is at the level of intermediate bodies that we think perhaps most can be achieved in adding a
legally responsive dimension to the general problem of accountability.

We have observed that there are many and varied requirements
for consultation, sometimes mediated through green and white
papers, sometimes formal and sometimes not, though it is fair to say
that in purely legal terms most attention has been paid to delegated

legislation, an important, though limited, aspect of executive behaviour. There are therefore several major problems in relation to consultation or *ex ante* accountability. First, we have an unsatisfactory range of processes for consultation: we need to devise mechanisms for settings other than legislation. Second, there is little in the way of guarantees of the quality of consultation in the sense of encouraging a policy debate based upon the need both to justify assertion and the rejection of considered recommendations. Finally, we have not sufficiently addressed the question of the constituencies appropriate to ensuring the effective working of these mechanisms. The remainder of this chapter and part of the next will be directed to examining these issues.

There exists a very large number of British advisory committees and it is possible to build upon these structures in order to contract the distance between rule of law ideology and reality. It is clear from Chapter 6 that the range of such bodies and their variegated roles makes generalization about their potential contribution to policy debate and to both *ex post* and *ex ante* versions of accountability less than fruitful. Some are obviously extremely influential and powerful and some conduct their affairs more openly and more discursively than others, but we can make a generalization that will stick in terms of distinctly legal contributions to their deliberations. It is normally the case that the conduct of their business is sheltered to a greater or lesser degree; it is normally the case that they do not have the right to call for background papers from the executive body concerned and that their enabling legislation, if any, does not require a hard look debate so as to ensure that executive assertions are justified against some measurable test of a factual nature. There is little point in listing all the advisory bodies which fit these broad categorizations, and the educational policy area will provide sufficient illustration.

When the Board of Education was set up in 1899 a consultative committee was set up alongside it since it was felt that government required expert advice to assist in the assessment of educational needs. Since that time a large number of departmental and other committees have been set up to examine various aspects of policy and to advise those in central government with special responsibility for education. It is not easy to provide answers to questions such as how far they have shaped policy, or how far they have simply been the instruments by which an already determined policy is legitimized.[61]

The view has been expressed by senior civil servants that it makes little difference whether or not advisory bodies are set up since departments will 'consult all the people we do think are interested all the time'.[62] There is also considerable evidence that much of this type of committee structure will be directed to producing consensus, which may or may not be a good thing, but does tend to be the enemy of innovation. The balance sheet of advantage and achievement in relation to these bodies, especially in the educational field, is extremely difficult to draw, but we have not begun to attempt to look for methods of producing policy-making records which could be made the subject of a rigorous standard of external review, judicial or otherwise.[63]

The *ex parte* problem

One of our strongest commitments thus far is to attempt to place *ex parte* communications on the record. There are genuine needs of confidentiality which must be met but a system which lays claim to democratic characteristics and to the treating of like as like cannot but baulk at the idea of covert government and subterranean bargaining. The law of land-use planning recognizes the issue in circumstances where quasi-judicial means of inquiry are emplaced[64] but the matter seems never *systematically* to have entertained the public lawyer.

Rule-making with fully institutionalized public participation is a response to the problem of unchecked discretionary power whether we are talking about client relationships directly with government departments or through quasi-government bodies. In the latter situation, however, the institutional issue has to be addressed in terms of distinctly 'triangular' relationships. Intermediate bodies placed between government and the broader electorate may have potential for acting as representative constituencies capable of generating debate and the testing of critical assumptions. We shall begin to sketch out the shape of these ideas shortly, but it is important to stress that intermediation does not of itself prevent the displacement of covert and bargained behaviour into other channels.

Let us return to the 'capture' theme. The literature is too voluminous to catalogue,[65] but two distinct problems need to be addressed. The first is that *ex parte* or informal negotiations may occur with the agencies, but informally and outside the statutory framework. The second is that, even within that framework, the resources of the regulated tend to outweigh so disproportionately those of their opponents that they can dictate the terms of debate within the agency. Citizen participation has been felt by official committees to be some counterbalance to the latter problem and experiments have occurred which we shall examine later. There have been a number of responses to the former problem including the possibility of introducing legislation to regulate lobbying or *ex parte* contacts, while the issue has been confronted most directly by the 'sunshine' legislation and the Federal Advisory Committees Act which preceded it.[66] Whatever the danger of capture by regulated groups in a regulated political environment, it is almost certainly heightened where, as in Britain, *ex parte* contacts, lobbying and clientelist patterns of behaviour constitute the means of testing opinion and garnering information.

The ex parte *problem confronted*

Notice-and-comment rule-making has been outflanked on numerous occasions by the simple expedient of informal negotiations and bargains struck in lieu of official agency proceedings.[67] The Administrative Procedure Act places restrictions on *ex parte* contacts between interested parties and the decision-maker in formal, trial-type, agency proceedings, but no such constraints are imposed by the legislation in respect of informal rule-making. None the less there have been occasions when the courts have been prepared to prohibit such conduct.[68] The position currently adopted by the courts is that a democratic system of government in which policy-making is undertaken substantially by unelected administrators should be accompanied by openness, accessibility of officials and their amenability to the general needs of the public. Nevertheless, they also recognize that effective regulation demands a continuing relationship with the regulated industries in order to make possible the successful implementation of particular programmes and policies. Even so there has been much more concern, in striking an effective balance between these two groups of factors, to address the problem of agencies simply mediating between powerful interest groups and ignoring weaker ones. The Administrative Conference of the United States concluded that a general ban on private contacts was undesirable, as was a requirement that every such communication be summarized and exposed on the public record.

Nevertheless, recognizing the validity of concern about *ex parte* contacts, it called on agencies to place in a public file all written comments addressed to the merits of a proposed rule received after issue of a notice of proposed rule-making. It also proposed experimental procedures, including the use of summaries and public meetings to disclose oral communications containing significant information or argument respecting the merits of a proposed rule.[69]

The independent regulatory agencies appear to have the most restrictive policies regarding contacts during rule-making. The Civil Aeronautics Board requires that all substantive *ex parte* oral contacts be summarized and placed in a public file, while both the Federal Communications Commission and the Federal Trade Commission have tightened up their rules. The Consumer Product Safety Commission has produced the most rigorous requirements for openness of agency meetings and disclosure of communications. Notice must be given of virtually all meetings between agency employees and outside persons, the public may attend any meeting and summaries are kept of all meetings and telephone conversations between agency employees and interested parties.[70] Elsewhere in the agencies, important experiments have taken place which are not dissimilar to the judicial limitations imposed in Britain upon the minister's or inspector's contacts with parties after the close of a land-use planning inquiry.

We are not in a position to draw conclusions concerning the efficacy of these developments nor indeed of the many changes which have been forced upon the administration by the Government in the Sunshine Act. What does excite us is the belief that these experiments have potential value in the British context, especially given the extent to which networked decision-making characterizes our executive behaviour. Of similar potential value is the experience of the Federal Advisory Committees Act 1972.

In the US as in Britain, advisory committees are devices employed to solicit advice and information from private parties and other governmental and public institutions in formulating policies, to gain the benefit of fresh ideas, to secure the co-operation and assent of affected groups in administering programmes and to provide a measure of public participation. Until 1972 many important advisory committees exhibited all the features of a closed policy-making system which shut out significant public interests. Since then the position has been transformed. The Federal Advisory Committees Act requires annual reports listing advisory committees, their membership and notice in the Federal register of proposed meetings. It also requires that meetings should normally be open and that records, minutes, drafts, agenda, transcripts and other documents prepared by or for the advisory committee are to be made available to the public, subject to the exemptions of the Sunshine Act. Committee membership is required to be fairly balanced in terms of the points of view represented and the functions to be performed.[71] As with 'sunshine', the freedom of information legislation and general agency conduct, the Federal courts are charged with interpreting the Act and ensuring compliance with its primary concerns. Litigation has not been fierce, but the steady body of legal doctrine emerging indicates that judicial competence to advance the interests of open and accountable government should not be underestimated.

These developments ought to be of major interest to constitutionalists in Britain. Traditional principles and considerations should be moving us towards opening up and placing on the record issues of major policy planning. Quite apart from a commitment to democratic principle, covert brokerage of politicians and civil servants is inevitably in conflict with attempts at comprehensive forms of planning which require a harmonization of interests along systematic lines and on a fairly durable basis.[72] The great corporate power of outside interests in Britain has not been systematically addressed and brought within our system of constitutional law.[73] Correspondingly, leading politicians can justly complain that these interests are not publicly accountable for what they say, are not obliged to give evidence to support the positions they adopt, and are not compelled to speak openly to the relationship between their own and wider interests.[74]

Towards new institutions

As far as quasi-government and quasi-non-government are concerned, including for these purposes the nationalized industries, broad suggestions for bringing their behaviour more in line with the spirit informing the rule of law could usefully be made. The position of the great departments of state and their relationships with their client groups is more intricate and perhaps more constitutionally controversial. None the less, if once the empirical evidence to which we have drawn attention concerning the actualities of the British governing processes is allowed to be used as part of an immanent critique then it is equally clear that legal processes of a refined sort will need to be adapted to cater for the clear dissonance between reality and ideals. Let us turn first of all to quasi-government broadly conceived.

We should repeat that we are not attempting to provide a blueprint. Nevertheless, if we examine the administrative machine as a whole in light of the law-jobs theory and attach as a legitimating accompaniment the rule of law ideals we shall be forced to examine the generic concept of rule-making very closely. The major decisions, policies, and rules of quasi-government and the nationalized industries, for example, should be reasoned and based upon informed discussion. We doubt very much whether any open guarantee of that occurring can be expected without at the very least notice-and-comment requirements, though very often a more considered set of consultative practices would seem to be necessary. It ought to be axiomatic by now that complaints or grievance mechanisms should be a universal requirement, though without prejudice to the form that they should be expected to take in any particular policy or functional areas.

The recent determination by government to exercise a more stringent form of control over quasi-government gives point to our arguments, though sadly most of the efforts seem to be directed to tightening central control without the effective level of policy debate for which we are arguing. Thus, a Cabinet Office Report in late 1984 announced that the financial management initiative, discussed in Chapter 5, would be extended to quangos. The intention would seem to be to furnish them with clear objectives which they will be expected to achieve in as cost-effective a manner as possible.[75] At the time of writing there are moves to introduce the same kinds of considerations into the conduct of the nationalized industries, thereby perhaps finally laying to rest the ghost of the Morrisonian arm's length relationship. In fact, since the Competition Act 1980 the industries have been overseen by the Monopolies and Mergers Commission. By the autumn of 1981 government had decided that the Commission would carry out annually announced programmes of efficiency audits in place of the *ad hoc* references that had been the initial practice. Up to six references per year could be expected with each nationalized industry being subject to at least one reference every four years. The influence of the M&MC has already been considerable in this area and its reports indicate that it is possible for an independent audit agency to reveal shortcomings in performance even without predetermined standards agreed through some version of the political process. However, as one commentator has argued

The time has come ... for accountability to be regarded as a co-operative and improving process, whereby, in the course of explaining their policies, practices and performance to a basically friendly but impartial, expert critic, managements perceive more clearly their strengths and weaknesses and the hazards and opportunities of their situation.[76]

This, however, would go nowhere near as far as the important proposals made in the 1976 NEDO report on the nationalized industries and would not meet the need for a publicly informed dialogue surrounding either annual reports or more importantly perhaps, corporate plans.

The APA requirements relating to American regulatory agencies seem to us to represent a natural starting point for accountability mechanisms for quasi-government at large. There seems no obvious reason why both grievance requirements and rule-making standards should not be imposed unless government is inarticulately promising numerous clienteles that the prize for their closeted co-operation in governmental designs is the absence of public scrutiny. Explicitly or implicitly such promises are no doubt frequently made, but they accord ill with rule of law sentiments and with democratic traditions and expectations. As to corporate plans, similar discourse structures, centring on the requirement for the agency or body concerned to take a hard look at major objections, could and should be established.[77]

It is easy to attack the record of administrative law in the United States by reference to a spectrum of accusations ranging from undue influence through capture to corruption. Even so, the presumption must be that the honourability of British government and the general respect accorded to legal processes would ensure that new forms of legal accountability directed to ensuring open debate would neither reproduce the worst effects of American social and industrial mores nor be totally without beneficial effect. If concern is expressed that new institutions will be disproportionately exploited by interest groups then other experiments directed at redressing the balance are available for inspection. Proposals for independent consumer agencies, for offices of public counsel, schemes of financial assistance for group participation and the monitoring of complaints handling as forms of participation have been widely studied. These are only some of the mechanisms which might repay careful study by lawyers who are concerned to bring nineteenth-century concerns with arbitrariness, excessive discretion and colourability to bear on the problems of the contemporary age.[78]

The fact that our analysis of the British constitution has taken the form of an immanent critique and that we see the need to build on the stable foundations of a rich parliamentary and democratic heritage suggests that the proposals for reform here canvassed are for the most part not alien to British traditions, but simply contemporary accompaniments to them. For instance, we have looked systematically at the vast array of government and advisory committee reports published annually by the Stationery Office and have concluded that, although much of the information is skimpy and self-justifying, it is clearly capable of being put to work to help in creating a more democratic and accountable corpus of constitutional law. Two major gaps can, however, be identified. The first is the general lack of constituencies charged with the task of scrutiny on behalf of the universal public or sets of publics. The second is the absence of machinery or body of doctrine to ensure that debate between constituencies and decision-makers is not to be treated perfunctorily or as a mere formality. The standard to be set for gauging the quality of the debate and the tone of responsiveness and accountability is not the permissiveness of the *Wednesbury* test, the classic formula of the English courts that a policy decision can only be quashed if it is 'so unreasonable that no reasonable body could have made it', but rather some version of the hard look doctrine.[79]

Agencies, committees, and government departments could be required to review rules, policies and practices at periodic intervals and to eliminate or modify any conflicting, inconsistent, redundant or inactive provisions. The agencies, committees and departments would then as now be answerable in ultimate constitutional terms to Parliament, but the changes which we regard as vital, if immanent expectations are to be honoured, would significantly increase the real capacity of Parliament to act as a constitutional focus. It is by no means impossible to devise ways in which similar principles might be brought to bear upon the executive power wielded by ministers and their departments.

Developments in the Department of Health and Social Security show how we might begin to think about assembling constitutionality out of a combination of revised legal technology, homage to our rule of law heritage and exposure of the lack of contemporary political discourse. There have, over the years, been many varieties of departmental inquiry, formal, semi-formal, and secret, but few that have come near to our vision of systematic rule of law governance. Yet there is much upon which we can build. In 1984 the Secretary of State for Social Services announced the setting up of four major reviews of social security which together were intended to constitute a substantial re-examination of the social security system.[80] Some of the reviews identified key issues for consultation, though they were not intended to be exclusive, and all called for written evidence with a view to refining procedures for either receiving oral evidence or a further round of written submissions. All included 'independent' members and later in 1984 the procedures looked likely to be extended in some measure to the Department of the Environment.[81] Although the terms of reference are heavily circumscribed it would be churlish for a constitutional lawyer not to welcome this measure of innovation. Such a degree of openness is bound to be an improvement upon purely departmental reviews, suffering as they must both from a tendency to exclusiveness and from the opportunity to 'massage' such information as they already possess. None the less, some considerable criticism of the reviews has appeared and not, in light of our preceding argument, without justification. We will not here catalogue the deficiencies of the process but concentrate on one crucial issue. No mechanism was enlisted to secure that due and serious consideration had been paid to uncomfortable and original points of view. We are back in the land of hard look and find ourselves without contemporary resources to ensure that an independent body acts as umpire enforcing the rules of a democratic polity – one which observes, listens, reasons and then decides.

Even more significant perhaps, if the phenomenon of executive discretion is to be tackled, is the Social Security Advisory Committee (SSAC). British government is awash with advisory committees as we well know and the SSAC may not be unique, but, given its centrality in policy-making terms and its particular constitutional configuration, we believe it holds out considerable potential.

The SSAC is the main UK public body responsible for giving the government independent advice on social security matters. Section 9 (4) of the Social Security Act 1980 gives it the statutory right to be provided with information reasonably necessary for the proper discharge of its functions and section 10 requires the Secretary of State to consult with it on proposals for a wide range of regulations. One of the matters of greatest interest for present purposes is that the consultation provisions require the Secretary of State to consider any report and recommendations made by the Committee on his or her proposals. In particular, he or she is obliged to lay before Parliament, alongside any regulations which he or she proposes, a copy of the Committee's report and to explain how far, if at all, he or she has given effect to the Committee's recommendations. Most importantly, perhaps, he or she has to give reasons for not following the recommendations where that is the preferred course of action. We shall leave aside the exceptions to the duty and a number of defects which could be identified to examine more closely the positive side of the provisions.

Some version of this structure offers considerable scope, in our view, for extending canons of parliamentary accountability. What we see here is a body capable of informing the mind of Parliament on vital issues which it is incapable of scrutinizing itself. The provisions also offer the potential for instituting a policy dialogue, with decision-makers being required to justify departing from recommendations based upon the same or similar evidence to which they have themselves attended. It should be observed too that the Committee in framing its own views is prepared to initiate public consultation and discussion although it must be said that the ministerial timetable presented to the Committee has not always allowed this process to be as extensive as might be thought desirable.[82] With amendment then, and in particular absorbing the lessons of Federal administrative law, this experiment could produce a significant contribution to informing the parliamentary policy-making process and bringing the rule of law up to date in addressing contemporary executive discretion and power.

The SSAC is also involved in wider social security issues than the scrutiny of draft regulations, not least where the minister wishes to consult over broad policy changes. The Committee will not necessarily vigorously oppose firm government policy with which it is ill at ease if government commitment seems unyielding.[83] None the less, the SSAC has been prepared to commission studies on options in green papers, made significant criticism of proposals from the Secretary of State and, in general, has been prepared to issue reports on subjects which it prioritizes. In this latter frame of mind, it is willing and able to take evidence from a very extensive range of sources. Before developing the further constitutional potential of these provisions we wish to express one major caveat. The provisions of section 10 of the 1980 Act provide only a parliamentary method of redress where the Secretary of State offends the 'reasoned assessment' standard. Valuable though that is we are not satisfied that it is adequate, given the pressure on the parliamentary timetable and for other reasons expressed earlier. What is required is *judicial* supervision of this rational discourse requirement, enforcement of such being one of the foremost duties of a constitutional court which claims to give meaning to a revitalized concept of the rule of law.

Conclusion

Let us summarize, albeit at a high level of generality, what we see as the potential for institutions like the SSAC. Accountability (through Parliament at the end of the day) is primarily a matter of constituencies and one of the ways in which the whole nation may be rendered a proper account is through Parliament having a coherent dialogue on discrete issues presented to it through the mediation of some representative, specialist body. However much improvement in parliamentary scrutiny may be achieved by reform of its own procedures, we believe that it will continue to need assistance from other sources. An extension of bodies such as the SSAC would be a major means of structuring executive discretion. If, however, they are to be more than tokens then it must be possible for interested parties to object, through the courts if necessary, to the adequacy of ministerial response to policy-sensitive information. Furthermore, such bodies could be empowered to call for departmental annual reports or policy statements for the purpose of subjecting them to examination when they decided that issues so highlighted should have a high priority.

In this way, it should be possible for such bodies to examine important issues which had not been the subject of positive ministerial action. This should prove of particular importance in helping to expose the links between executive power and interest groups, 'private' governments and quasi-polities which are in need of urgent constitutional attention. We are in no doubt that what is required is a British Administrative Procedure Act dedicated to producing open discussion, natural justice and rational planning processes. Within central government itself, and without prejudice to the importance of the issue of reformed parliamentary procedures, we believe that some intermediary bodies should assist in informing the mind of

Parliament and the nation at large. The constituencies for accountability are the major focus for constitutional reformation. The nature of their conduct and relationship to the legal order form the subject matter of our next two chapters.

References

1 For which see briefly Peter H. A. Lehner, 'Judicial review of administrative inaction', *Columbia Law Review*, **83** (1983), pp. 627–89 at 640.
2 See e.g. P. Birkinshaw, *Grievances, Remedies and the State* (Sweet and Maxwell 1985), Alan Page, 'Legal analysis of economic policy', *Journal of Law and Society*, **9** (1982), p. 247.
3 P. Nonet, *Administrative Justice* (New York: Russell Sage Foundation 1969), p. 6.
4 Most notably see Peter Bachrach and Moreton S. Baratz, *Power and Poverty: Theory and Practice* (Oxford University Press 1970), esp. ch. 3.
5 ibid., pp. 43–6 and cf. R. A. Dahl, 'Power', in *Encyclopaedia of the Social Sciences* (NY 1968), vol. XII.
6 ibid., pp. 47–51.
7 See the very useful article by one of the few academic lawyers to take an interest in these issues. N. Green, 'Crisis in the MMC: Anderson Strathclyde and other recent developments', *Business Law Review*, **4** (1983), pp. 303–6. On monopolies see R. Merkin and K. Williams, *Competition Law: Antitrust Policy in the United Kingdom and the EEC* (Sweet and Maxwell 1984), p. 18.
8 See on this point D. Trubek, 'Complexity and contradiction in the legal order', *Law and Society Review*, **11** (1977), 529 esp. p. 562.
9 D. Ashford, *Policy and Politics in Britain* (Blackwell 1981), p. 263.
10 See generally Lehner (note 1 above).
11 United States Code, Title 5, Section 551 (13).
12 For the cases where the courts *have* reviewed non-implementation see Lehner, p. 627 note 3. Most recently see *Hecker v Chaney* 105 S.Ct 1649 (1985), and Cass R. Sunstein, *University of Chicago Law Review*, **52** (1985), p. 653.
13 The literature is too formidable to list, but see e.g. J. Pierce and A. Shapiro, 'Political and judicial review of agency action', *Texas Law Review*, **59** (1981), p. 1175.
14 Lehner, p. 635.
15 See e.g. K. Middlemas, *Industry, Unions and Government* (Macmillan 1983).
16 Michael Moran, 'Finance capital and pressure-group politics in Britain', 11 *Journal of Political Studies*, **11** (1981), p. 381.
17 ibid., pp. 399, 387.

18   See P. Nonet and P. Selznick, *Toward Responsive Law* (New York: Harper and Row 1978), G. Teubner, 'Substantive and reflexive elements in modern law', *Law and Society Review*, **17** (1983), pp. 234–85.

19   Moran, 'Finance capital', p. 402.

20   L. C. B. Gower, *Review of Investor Protection, A Discussion Document* (HMSO 1982).

21   J. S. Fforde, 'Competition, innovation and regulation in British banking', *Bank of England Quarterly Bulletin* (September 1983), p. 363, at 368.

22   Annoted comments of F. R. Ryder, on the Banking Act 1979, *Current Law Statutes* (Sweet and Maxwell), see also Sir Harold Wilson, *Report of the Committee on the Functioning of Financial Institutions* (Wilson Committee), Cmnd. 7937 (HMSO 1980), esp. para. 1073.

23   Banking Act s.4. *Annual Report of the Bank of England* (1984).

24   R. Stewart, 'The reformation of American administrative law', *Harvard Law Review*, **88** 1667 (1975), p. 1761.

25   cf. *Greater Boston Television Co. v FCC*, 444 F.2d 841 (DC Cir. 1970. 403 US 923, 1971).

26   See *Study of Federal Regulation*, US Senate 95th Cong. Doc.95.71 (July 1977), p. 8.

27   e.g. J. Habermas, *Theory and Practice* (Boston: Beacon Press 1973), ch.1, 'The classical doctrine of politics in relation to social philosophy'.

28   P. Self, *Administrative Theories and Politics* (Allen and Unwin 1972).

29   See Duncan Kennedy, 'Cost–benefit analysis of entitlement problems: a critique', 33 *Stanford Law Review* 387; Brian Wynne, *Rationality and Ritual* (British Society for the History of Science 1982), esp. pp. 172–6.

30   D. Pearce *et al.*, *Decision-making for Energy Futures* (Macmillan 1979).

31   See e.g. J. Choper, *Judicial Review and the National Political Process*, (University of Chicago Press 1980); R. Dahl and C. Lindblom, *Politics, Economics and Welfare*, 2nd edn (University of Chicago Press 1976), and L. Rieselbach, *Congressional Politics* (McGraw-Hill 1973). In Britain, see e.g. R. Hadley and S. Hatch, *Social Welfare and the Failure of the State* (Allen and Unwin 1981).

32   Self, p. 289 and see generally 285–9.

33   For an interesting suggestion along these lines see the sadly neglected report by Justice, *Administration Under Law* (Stevens 1971), bearing the hallmark as it does of the French *Principes généraux de droit*.

34   For the latter two sets see Norman Lewis, 'Who controls quangos and the nationalised industries?', in J. Jowell and D. Oliver (eds.), *The Changing Constitution* (Oxford University Press 1985). (The Centre for Criminological and Socio-Legal Studies is at the time of writing engaged upon a major research project on complaints mechanisms in local government with a view to making recommendations on the optimum level of complaints machinery in that area.)

35   See Employment Protection (Consolidation) Act, 1978 s.1 (4).

36   *Study of Federal Regulation*, Committee on Governmental Affairs, US Senate S. Res.71 vol. III, *Public Participation in Regulatory Agency Proceedings*, July 1977, ch. 9, and see the study commissioned by the Office of Consumer Affairs, *Technical Assistance Research Programme, Feasibility Study to Improve Handling of Consumer Complaints*, Evaluation Report Contract No. HEW–05–74–292 (April 1975) (TARP).

37   K. C. Davis, *Discretionary Justice* (University of Illinois 1971).

38   USC ss. 553, 556, 557.

39   See R. Baldwin, *Regulating the Airlines, Administrative Justice and Agency Discretion* (Oxford University Press 1985).

40   Nonet and Selznick, *Toward Responsive Law*, pp. 108–10.

41   *New Local Authorities, Management and Structure* (HMSO 1972), and see R. Greenwood and J. D. Stewart (eds.), *Corporate Planning in Local Government* (1975).

42   See R. Greenwood, Hinings *et al.*, *In Pursuit of Corporate Rationality: Organisational Developments in the Post-Reorganisation Period* (Inlogov 1976), esp. pp. 18–19.

43   N. Lewis and I. Harden, 'Law and the Local State', *Urban Law and Policy*, **5** (1981), pp. 65–86.

44   See e.g. D. Winchurch, 'Political values in corporate planning', *Corporate Planning Journal*, **7**, 27 (1980); *idem*, 'Politics and policy planning', *Corporate Planning Journal*, **5**, 37 (1978).

45   NEDO, *A Study of UK Nationalised Industries* (HMSO 1976).

46   *The Nationalised Industries*, Cmnd. 7131 (1978).

47   Tony Prosser, *The Nationalised Industries, Government and Public Scrutiny* (Blackwell 1986).

48   The *Guardian*, 2 October 1984.

49   The *Guardian*, 11 May 1983.

50   See also the Report of the Monopolies and Mergers Commission on the CEGB, H.C. 315 (1981), and Report of the Energy Select Committee on Nuclear Power H.C. 114 (1980–1).

51   See for one of the few sophisticated treatments of accountability in British literature E. L. Normanton, 'Public accountability and audit: a reconnaissance', in B. L. R. Smith and D. C. Hague (eds.), *The Dilemma of Accountability in Modern Government* (Macmillan 1971), ch. 14.

52   Normanton, p. 312.

53   ibid., pp. 314–15.

54   5 USC 552b.

55   D. Welborn, W. Lyons and L. Thomas, *Implementation and Effects of the Government in the Sunshine Act*, Draft Report for the Administrative Conference of the United States (Washington 1984).

56   See M. Posner 'Theories of Economic Regulation', *Journal of Economics and Management Science*, **5** (1974), p. 335.

57 *Report of the Committee on the Civil Service* 1966–1968, vol. 1 (Cmnd. 3638 1968) para. 292.
58 James V. DeLong, 'Informal rule-making and the integration of law and policy', *Virginia Law Review*, **65** (1979), p. 329.
59 Fulton, paras. 188–90.
60 ibid., para. 293.
61 More generally see R. A. Chapman, *The Role of Commissions in Policy-Making* (Allen and Unwin 1973).
62 See M. Kogan and T. Packwood, *Advisory Councils and Committees in Education* (RKP 1974), p. 78.
63 ibid., p. 86.
64 *Errington v Minister of Health* [1935] 1 KB 249 and see also *Steeples v Derbyshire County Council* [1984] 3 All ER 468.
65 Though see e.g. James Q. Wilson, *The Politics of Regulation* (New York: Basic Books 1980); Schuch, review of Wilson, *Yale Law Journal*, **90** (1981), p. 702 for references.
66 See generally Senate *Study of Federal Regulation* (n. 26 above).
67 ibid., pp. viii–ix.
68 For a summary of the case law see *A Guide to Federal Agency Rule-Making*, Office of the Chairman, Administrative Conference of the United States (ACUS 1983), ch. 7, 'Ex parte Communications and Rule-Making'.
69 ibid., pp. 165–6 and *Recommendations and Reports* (ACUS 1980), pp. 27, 30.
70 See ACUS, *A Guide to Federal Agency Rule-Making*, pp. 166–9.
71 *Senate Study of Federal Regulation*, ch. 10; see also M. H. Cardozo, 'The Federal Advisory Committee Act in Operation', *Administrative Law Review*, **33**, 1 (1981).
72 Self, p. 157.
73 See though e.g. Beer, esp. pp. 109, 406–7.
74 See e.g. Shirley Williams, in Norman H. Ornstein (ed.), *The Role of the Legislature in Western Democracies* (American Enterprise Institute 1980), pp. 128–9.
75 See the *Guardian*, 20 November 1984.
76 Maurice R. Garner, 'Auditing the efficiency of the nationalised industries: enter the Monopolies and Mergers Commission', *Public Administration*, **60** (1982), p. 427.
77 Note 45 above and see Lewis, 'Who controls quangos and the nationalised industries?'.
78 See e.g. *Senate Study of Federal Regulation*.
79 *Associated Provincial Picture Houses v Wednesbury Corporation* [1948] 1 KB 223.
80 *Consultation Document on Supplementary Benefit Review* (DHSS May 1984).
81 See the *Guardian*, 11 October 1984.

82   See e.g. *Second Annual Report of the SSAC* 1982/3 (HMSO 1983), esp. para. 3.3.

83   See e.g. *First Annual Report of the SSAC 1980–81* (HMSO 1982), e.g. para. 2.19 and *Reply to the First Report from the Social Services Select Committee on Arrangements for Paying Social Security Benefits*, Cmnd. 8106 (HMSO 1980).

9   A hard look

This chapter is premised on the belief, expressed in Part One, that the political system needs to be open at all times if choice is to be meaningful at any time. A democracy, of whatever variety, is a normative system informed by certain master ideals. Quite aside from the content of any particular laws, rules or norms, the way that they come into being has to take its colour from larger sentiments. Those larger sentiments almost certainly embrace some affection for the idea of 'experiments in living' and for a society taking a hard look at different ways of doing and believing.

As Habermas has argued, democracy is not about an *a priori* preference for any particular organizational imperative. Organization is in a sense a highly contingent matter provided always that the unforced choice of the protagonists is the end result. The attempt to arrange a society democratically can only be a self-controlled learning process.[1] This conforms well with our immanent critique, for we are arguing both that present constitutional arrangements are an acceptable and possibly desirable channel for effecting improvements and that the methods for overcoming the problems inherent in relating our belief system (explored in Part One) to the operational reality (Part Two) should not be foreclosed prematurely.[2]

We have discussed the issue of accountability and stressed the need for informed constituencies to bring scrutinized information before the people and their representatives. We have now to speak to the quality of that information and ways in which it might be garnered. A little more must be said about the need for freedom of information and considerably more about the need to ensure that the information which emerges is not tarnished or sullied and is capable of operating as the staple diet of rational discourse. The hard look doctrine is a standard of review which has been demanded by the American Federal courts from time to time and we shall be recommending its adoption in Britain in appropriate circumstances. However, we use the expression also as a general pointer to the need for ensuring that the representative side of our democratic beliefs is given larger expression. If the electorate is to take a harder look at its instruments of government than is frequently the case then many of the more important issues and policies which concern it will need to be broken down and closely examined outside the hustings. A harder look at individual programmes and especially major policies becomes an institutional necessity if an open society is to be assured.

Without freedom of information – subject to the standard set of exceptions in the interests of, for example, national security – democratic government is a contradiction in terms. Not only is choice rendered a matter of hunch but communication is always potentially distorted when one side fails to disclose to another. The matter seems to us to be beyond argument: either rational discourse is optimized or it is not. Conventionality and convenience are ultimately irrelevant. Furthermore, the means of securing a free flow of information must be as strong as possible and must ultimately be in the hands of someone other than those who claim the right to suppress. As an Australian Senate standing committee put it:

The essence of democracy lies in the ability of the people to make choices: about who shall govern: or about which policies they support or respect. Such choices cannot be properly made unless adequate information is available. It cannot be accepted that it is the government itself which has determined what level of information is to be regarded as adequate.[3]

Open government then is the principle that information held by government departments on which policies are based and decisions taken should be available for public scrutiny. This is not a new idea and indeed is inherent in the rule of law itself, even in its Dicean formulation. It is clearly evident in the idea of legal autonomy where law is the independent arbiter of when allegiance to promise has been infringed and when not. It is indispensable to Dicey's insistence that the rule of law would be infringed if our polity were not characterized by the existence of clearly visible rules known in advance so that citizens could order their affairs so as to take the rules into account. Freedom of information then is not simply a matter of modish chic, it is the logical extension of everything respectable which was ever claimed for the rule of law. Older versions of the genre simply overlooked the growth of the administrative and the extended state and by adopting a narrow concept of law blotted out the largest part of the decision-making process. The sentiments and ideals which characterize *the* rule of law, as opposed to *a* rule of law, presuppose freedom of information in the setting of the state activity we described in Part Two.

The logic of this argument is that constitutional forms must evolve to keep pace with change. This understanding is frequently accommodated by the flexibility of modern written constitutions, but is a more urgent requirement in Britain which clings as it does to old forms when the nature of the state has altered so dramatically. Given our expanded concept of law it must follow that as polity evolves, the legal order expands in scope and depth. When that occurs the law will be asked to undertake different and more facilitative tasks as its central legitimation characteristics are re-examined. The openness and fairness characteristics in particular, always a feature of *gesellschaft* claims, must correspondingly be addressed in light of new legal forms and new legal tasks. Thus, where decision-making takes place in the heart of the administration, and where policy-formulation becomes contested on technical, economic or social grounds, then legal forms require re-examination to provide subtler concepts of public responsibility than formerly. The law will need to partake of the flavour of a surrogate political process, not for engaging and arbitrating the claims of competing social values, but for assuring the larger constitutional values inherent in the rule of law to promote rational civic discourse through a hard look at the thornier of problems. We will elaborate on the nature of a revised rule of law in the next chapter: here we wish only to make the point that a hard look at major policy issues is bound to involve extended notions of civic participation both as learning process and to ensure that important public values are properly addressed. Citizen involvement in community self-determination is desirable without reference to canons of efficiency or concern for the general reduction of popular clamour. Public values are sharpened during the process of examination, advocacy and response. They are not simply 'reflections of individual preferences or of an exogenous structure of entitlements'.[4] This is learning process with added nutrients.

Representative institutions, however self-reformed, need assistance in coming to conclusions on complex issues and more generally on account of 'agenda overload'. To this end, freedom of information is indispensable, not just for the ultimate decision-makers but for those intermediary bodies established to help them inform their minds. That process of informing depends upon information being subjected to rigorous debate and scrutiny – not through the standard of the *Wednesbury* test, but through a more demanding hard look criterion. The mechanism of the hard look will depend on the context and on the significance of the issue at hand. It is ultimately for the courts to guarantee the higher standard by demanding reasoned decision-making and to determine what manner of procedure is appropriate to achieve the standard in any given case. The rest of this chapter will consist of pursuing this theme in detail.

Democracy, information and hard look

Both traditional democratic claims and the substantive nature of rule of law ideology make demands of a constitutional nature about open decision-making and listening to the various sides of an argument. That, at the heart of the logic, is the justification for parliamentary government and for an independent judiciary. They are both now, as we have seen, incapable of satisfying those constitutional demands unaided.

The Wilkites' campaign in the latter part of the eighteenth century has been seen by some as the prelude to the campaign for parliamentary democracy and responsible government. That campaign forcefully advocated an open legislature as a necessary condition of democratic rule.[5] Now that would not have seemed a satisfactory resting-place for their objectives had executive power then assumed its twentieth-century proportions and in fact most commentators would now admit to the fact of British government being essentially closed. Clear principles as opposed to pragmatic accommodation have never really held sway in modern British government, which instead has relied on loose ideology, in which the rule of law ethic is pre-eminent. This does not address itself to the assessment of the pace of social change and its procedural accompaniments as effectively as would clear statements of constitutional belief. Thus, although the rule of law is associated with hostility to arbitrariness, its very timelessness in usage and culture cloaks the fact that the progressive reduction of arbitrariness knows no stopping-place and that commitment to such progressive reduction requires us to look at new ways of exercising authority and new modes of participation.[6]

Because of the deficiencies of our constitutional response to new ways of governing, both democratic expectations and cognitive development are in danger of being thwarted unless we attempt to fill the gaps that have arisen between the traditional system of electoral representation and the present reality of bureaucratic regulation. It is no doubt a feature of representative democracy more generally that a handful of actors come to play a dominant role in the affairs of nations, but the situation in Britain is particularly acute. In the field of welfare, for example, debate has been erratic and shallow, for

The political system . . . has rested upon competition between elites. This gives a premium to dramatising and simplifying the issues, to synthesising big problems and big solutions out of the shreds and tatters of everyday life, and to carrying over into the implementation of welfare programmes the gestures of the public debate.[7]

The failure to come to terms constitutionally with the existence of the extended or disintegrated state has two major repercussions. The first is that the danger of factional domination of decision-making processes by insiders is magnified when broad delegations of authority make specific power locations targets for the sustained and organized political pressure of powerful interest groups. The second is the institutional failure to deal with problems of a cognitive nature: the problems of learning processes.

Rationality, learning and scrutiny

Most observers of the political and industrial scene are now in some sort of accord that modernity presents general problems of cognitive competence. The fashionable expression to describe this state of affairs is that of 'rationality crisis', meaning that any given state of organizational arrangement based upon traditional ways of doing is likely to experience a failure of systemic comprehension concerning the complex tasks in hand. Indeed, the extravagant version of the claim is that the interdependent complexity of modern systems is such that rational planning may not now be possible. However, the common ground among most analyses of this issue is that considerable effort to design systems and institutions needs to be undertaken if the problem is to be overcome. Social and economic processes, it is argued, are simply too dense, complex and potentially contradictory to be handled by current mechanisms of political and legal control.[8]

Unfortunately the response to this level of complexity has often been the exact opposite of that which makes most sense. One might have thought that if rationality presented a genuine problem, then the more informed the input received, the more likely an acceptable resolution of the problem. Indeed from time to time organization theory within large private industry has canvassed this very solution, but unfortunately it has been less influential within the governmental system than might have been expected. Rather there has been a drift towards technicism, the natural accompaniment of an 'unprincipled' approach. The more complex decisions become, the more important it seems to some that decisions are left to 'the experts' and the more other views are excluded. Thus the ends/means dilemma is often resolved in charted examples of British policy-making by a search for 'efficiency'.

It is as though the term is taken to be universally understood and politically neutral. The assumption is that all that is involved is getting the best results at lowest costs. But the emphasis on *technique* which this focus encourages is only meaningful if there is a consensus about ends. In practice there is seldom agreement between the many interested parties on the fundamental issues as to what services should be provided.[9]

Several problems thereby become rolled into one. A substantial body of literature exists from Weber onwards which argues that the clear distinction between instrumental and value rationality, frequently made in the same tone as that between administration and policy-making and between policy-making and implementation, is ultimately incoherent.[10] Even where issues can be understood as technical, the sheer intransigence of some of the problems posed can only be lessened by informed interventions from the widest variety of sources.

To increase the cognitive competence of an organization it is necessary to make creative use of planning, evaluation and development staffs who would welcome and have the capacity to evaluate criticism. If planning is to be purposive, if it is to be goal-oriented, then authority must be open and participatory, consultation must be encouraged and consent to some extent taken as a test of rationality.[11] These arguments have now begun to win considerable allegiance. For example, the requirement under the US Freedom of Information Act that departments and agencies compile indexes identifying for the public any rules issued, adopted or promulgated has proved useful to the bureaucracies themselves.[12]

Policy and policy-planning is the area which most urgently needs

to be addressed by a revised legal order. Our contemporary jurisprudence is not, however, well-equipped to deal with purposive and
goal-oriented programmes, concentrated as it is upon the atomic
rather than the social. The legal process, if it is to address contemporary problems, cannot confine itself to restraining government
within the limits of rules, but must seek to structure opportunities
for participation and criticism, allowing interested parties the
opportunity to comment on and to influence policy. The legal
process offers an alternative model of governance where authority
is seen as nourished by effective criticism and enlarged by its ability
to respond to the demands of a constituency. Our polity presupposes effective criticism and civic participation but as we have
argued all through this essay, the old beliefs have fallen victim to
changed circumstances. Our constitutional jurisprudence is offered
the opportunity to redress the balance.

Our law, as we have seen, especially in Chapter 7, too easily drifts
into mere legalism with adjudication operating as the application of
unexamined policies. Law and politics form a continuum, as can be
seen quite clearly if subjecting discretionary activity to the scrutiny
of a hard look standard of review is accepted as a central feature
of the legal process. Administration cannot replace or make unnecessary civic participation, and participation through law may be
one way of ensuring that authority is not an unquestioned notion
and that lawful conduct means conduct subject to systematic scrutiny and open to extensive criticism.[13]

The functions of the institutions and patterns of accountability
outlined in Chapter 8 are to enable a hard look to be taken and to
cause decision-makers to defend the positions they adopt without in
any direct way affecting their ultimate authority to take decisions
and make policy. The institutions of accountability are the machinery
for updating the rule of law while the quality of their deliberations is
represented by the standard of judicial review which we describe as
the 'hard look doctrine'. The object of deliberation by the agents of
accountability is to achieve a probing, in-depth review of decisions
and policies as opposed to what has been called the 'crystal-ball
approach' which is to a large extent the standard of review represented by the *Wednesbury* test.

Freedom of information

The fact that British governmental practice is among the most secretive in the western world is perhaps the clearest single illustration

of the contradictory nature of claim and practice within the British constitution. There seems little point in our outlining the details of the official secrets legislation save to say that they are a constitutional outrage. Section 2 of the 1911 Act in particular has been so heavily condemned that we can add little to the intellectual force of the opposition argument. Lord Franks's report is the best and the most thorough treatment of the issue and curious readers are directed to re-examine it to see how all-pervasive is the British passion for secrecy.[14] The chequered history of attempts to reform the legislation and to replace it with a statutory right to know has not as yet culminated in the desired outcome. It is unlikely that public clamour for reform will abate in the near future and it is difficult to see how, in the longer term, the claims can be resisted. Debate normally draws lessons from the perceived success of the Swedish and the American legislation although in more recent times a number of common law jurisdictions, most notably Canada and Australia, have brought their constitutions into line with this central democratic requirement.

We shall spend little time on the details of foreign freedom of information legislation since the literature is extensive and fairly comprehensive.[15] We shall instead dwell on the defects of British practice and the ways in which freedom of information legislation is capable of contributing to the level of rigorous examination of public conduct which we believe long overdue. However, by way of introduction, some mention of foreign experience would be appropriate.

Open government is in essence the principle that information held by government departments on which policies are based and decisions taken is available, with certain limited exceptions, for public analysis. The term, as Dresner points out, is most widely used to refer to the public's access to government documents, such as background studies, records, rules and staff instruction manuals. However, the generic expression also refers to a second group of laws covering the individual's right of access to records held by government departments on him or herself and the right to correct or register a counter-statement where the information recorded is disputed. Such legislation has been adopted on a broad front among Western democracies in recent years, though the British foray into this territory in the form of the Data Protection Act 1984 is severely circumscribed and in consequence has been subjected to considerable criticism.[16]

As to freedom of information as a means of exposing the working of the governmental machine, it is something of a national humiliation that information directly touching upon areas of crucial concern to the British people has often been made available only through the use of foreign freedom of information laws.[17] Furthermore, the history of freedom of information in the United States has been a most interesting learning process, and the post-Watergate amendments made to the original 1966 Act should prove invaluable in working upon a British model. In particular there is a need to catalogue and index both decision-making structures and areas of substantive responsibility and to impose strict timetables for compliance with information requests. The American experience makes it apparent that the courts must be the ultimate arbiter of the workings of any such legislation, not least in deciding what constitutes a genuine exception to the disclosure requirements.

Although freedom of information is important across the whole range of public decision-making, it is especially so for the policy-forming process. Yet this is the very area where most official concern has been expressed regarding information tendered by advisers, including the civil service, in confidence to the decision-maker. The arguments pro and con have been particularly well-rehearsed and have special significance given the traditional British doctrine of ministerial responsibility to Parliament. American experience indicates that the understandable concern to retain confidence and trust in minister–civil servant relationships can live in tandem with disclosure of information necessary to contribute to the policy-making process. Federal legislation provides that an exception to disclosure requirements shall obtain for '. . . inter-agency or intra-agency memorandums or letters which would not be available by law to a private party in litigation with the agency'. The purpose of this exemption is to cover confidential advice given by staff to their superiors in an agency, on the assumption that if this were made publicly available there would be too much caution. Although in practice it is sometimes difficult to draw the line, case law has made a distinction in principle between pre-decisional material prepared to assist the making of a decision, which is exempt, and factual material and post-decisional memoranda which are not. Policy advice quoted or referred to in an agency's final decision on a matter must be released.[18] The courts have been prepared to insist upon the disclosure of policies delayed, policies refused, programmes rejected and other areas of non-decision-making. Cracks need to be made in the pre-decisional wall if discretionary decision-taking is to be adequately illuminated.

Freedom of information in Britain

The Thalidomide case, the decision to build Concorde, the attempt to suppress the Crossman Diaries and the decision to postpone a new child benefit scheme in the 1970s were all examples where the British government of the day decided that the traditions of government secrecy were more important than legitimate public interest in the information on which the decision was based.[19] There are other, well-documented *causes célèbres*: the Rhodesian oil embargo where information was not only not provided but actively concealed; an attempt by industrialists and civil servants to transfer Rolls Royce from public ownership to GEC without ministerial knowledge at a timely stage; the suppression of information regarding both the reliability of invalid cars and hygiene on board British ships (eventually obtained via American law) and so on.[20] Public indignation has been aroused in Britain from time to time by particularly prominent examples of governmental secrecy which eventually managed to make the headlines. Nevertheless, what must be appreciated is that secrecy is a constant and continual feature of our public life.

It is worth underlining the utility of freedom of information in exposing the constitutional relationships involved in networked decision-making in Britain. The danger of the 'cosy embrace' has been emphasized by the American courts even in relation to the regulation of financial institutions which are to a considerable extent exempted from the freedom of information requirements.[21] Open government of itself is no more likely to increase lobbying activity than does its opposite, since a degree of time-consuming information exchange already takes place in Britain between government and favoured interest groups who are requested to keep the consultative process secret. Secrecy on this view merely limits the consultative process and therefore operates as the enemy of the hard look doctrine. There has been a tendency in the US for freedom of information requests to cause policy decisions to be re-examined and potentially improved, and whatever the defects and limitations of freedom of information in a Federal setting it has had much to contribute in the war against *ex parte* lobbying and agency capture. The captured regulatory agency problem exists in the UK too:

An example was the Department of Transport, illustrated by a memorandum leaked to the Guardian in mid-1979, which argued in favour of a public inquiry which would enable the Road Haulage Federation to make its case better known. Another example was the Price Commission report on car components . . . which emerged with much information deleted, such as the finding that for sparking plugs the replacement equipment price is no less than 10 times the original equipment price. In both the USA and the UK, large companies sometimes play a part in drafting legislation which will regulate them. It is this type of information which British civil servants are reluctant to release and which the FOIA enables the public in the USA to obtain.[22]

Freedom of information and 'sunshine' legislation are clearly all of a piece, and both have much to teach the constitutional scholar in Britain. Thus, for example, where meetings are legitimately closed under the Government in the Sunshine Act there must be a full written explanation of the reasons, subject ultimately to review by the courts. This requirement has been the subject of complaint by agency officials within the Federal system[23] who no doubt would be much happier with the less than constitutionally buccaneering British courts who have been prepared, even in a local government setting, to marginalize statutory requirements for a full explanation of reasons for closing a meeting normally open to the public.[24]

Open government must be the starting point for a process of in-depth legitimation. This must, of course, extend to the right of a citizen to inspect his or her own personal file held by public authorities. This, after all, is the surest guarantee that the administration will provide accurate information and not operate on the basis of untested assumptions. The record of the legislation in practice overwhelmingly validates the argument. Dresner found for instance that in 1977 alone the US Department of Defense agreed to amend inaccurate records amounting to 99 per cent of cases requested, the Public Health Service 96 per cent of those requested and the Department of State 90 per cent.[25]

The case for freedom of information is so strong that its opponents are reduced to questioning the costs of its administration in default of respectable arguments against it. The implications of freedom of information need to be explored in the light of themes addressed earlier. Bargaining of the British variety and an attachment to 'marketism' are the natural enemies of taking a hard look at policy decisions and non-decisions. Furthermore, the invocation of clearly separate public and private spheres, of limited politics on the one hand and 'markets' on the other, must be calculated to drive out elements which insist on wider ranges of participation in decision-making. If a clear and large sphere is regarded as private then there is a natural inclination to deny the need for civic rights and for broader inputs into the decision-making process. The intricate links between executive power in the British state and the gamut of private and semi-private ordering are less visible and more prone to covert bargaining than would be the case if constitutional address were paid to the fact that the contemporary world cannot be comprehended by the economic theories of the late eighteenth century.

The hard look doctrine

The soft standard of judicial review associated in Britain with the *Wednesbury* test is inadequate to produce reasoned decision-making in the policy process, as American judicial experience, particularly during the 1970s, has shown. The dominant strain of that period came to be represented as the hard look doctrine which sought to ensure a standard of review which would demand serious policy analysis without producing administrative overload. The doctrine was aimed at providing a criterion somewhere between the 'kid glove standard' which left the decision-maker with almost complete discretion provided he or she did not disclose manifest absurdity during the decision-making process, and the 'substantial evidence' rule. The latter had been in some respects responsible for producing an unmanageable record for the court to review and a correspondingly onerous administrative workload.[26] Conventional 'kid glove' legal analysis on the other hand finds a decision process rational if a reason for the decision can be articulated and if the chain of logic leading to the conclusion can be discerned. In Britain the *Wednesbury* test, which demands no more than that a decision be not so unreasonable that no reasonable body could have made it, represents the general 'kid glove' standard for judicial review of policy decisions.

The hard look doctrine was first clearly articulated in 1970 in the case of *Greater Boston Television Co. v FCC*:

The function of the court is to ensure that the agency has given reasoned consideration to all material facts and issues. This calls for insistence that the agency articulate with reasonable clarity its reasons for decision, and identify the significance of the crucial facts, a course that tends to assure that the agency's policies effectuate general standards, applied without unreasonable discrimination.[27]

Throughout the 1970s the doctrine was becoming the prevailing standard of review of rule-making in cases where large policy judgements intersected with technical questions. The analytical and evidentiary materials relied upon by the agency to ground its rules would thereby have to be available to a reviewing court for it to trace the relationship between the materials and the rule – a paper trail of rational analysis. In spite of the setback to the reviewing standard delivered by a 1978 Supreme Court decision (in the *Vermont Yankee* case), the influence of hard look has remained extraordinarily strong in contemporary American administrative law.[28] The Freedom of Information and Sunshine Acts, and other developments which we shall shortly touch upon here, combined with the doctrine to ensure that an agency accumulates a fairly complete record of subjects that have become the object of its decision. The courts have thus been able to demand that an agency produce contemporaneous records sufficient to explain its data, methodology and reasoning. They have sought to ensure that conclusions reached are rational responses to the broad standard delegated by Congress and to the arguments and evidence received. Where the record has been found to be insufficient they have not hesitated to direct further proceedings requiring the agency to develop a more adequate record. It should be stressed, however, that the courts have shown a sensitivity to the problems of administrators and have not only tailored the hard look standard to the nature of the problem under consideration but have also left the agency considerable discretion as to what methods of scrutiny are employed to produce the hard look at argument and objections. Furthermore, the courts have rarely rejected a plausible agency explanation of action or conduct.[29]

We shall develop the general implications of hard look in our treatment of hybrid rule-making but before moving to that strand of the analysis we should tie together the relationship between this higher standard of review and what we have said about the role of intermediary constituencies in promoting participative discourse about *non*-decision-making.[30]

We showed in Chapter 8 how the Federal courts had periodically reviewed inaction, non-implementation and failure to enforce standards. This was facilitated by the increase in information and documentation more generally demanded through freedom of information and other open government developments which put agencies on notice to keep an up-to-date record of anything that may be of concern to the public. It is therefore increasingly possible to force an agency to give coherent reasons for its programmatic inaction, whether failure to initiate a rule-making proceeding, to complete agency tasks or to enforce promulgated standards. Federal courts have required agencies to implement and enforce regulatory statutes, or at least to explain their failure to do so, in a broad range of circumstances including, for example, decisions by the Secretary of Labor not to file a suit to invalidate a union election; by the Securities and Exchange Commission not to promulgate rules requiring disclosure of environmental and employment policies; by the Secretary of the Interior not to adopt rules governing traders doing business on Indian reservations; and by the Attorney-General not to conduct extensive investigation of a crime.[31]

The standard of review adopted in such cases has required reasoned articulation of the factors governing discretionary decisions. Courts have required the agency to provide relevant data and an explanation for inaction and have remanded for a more adequate statement of the agency's position than it had previously been prepared to offer. All this has occurred within a context of understanding the nature of competing interests, limited budgets and multiple responsibilities. The courts nevertheless have a limited capacity and whereas we believe that being the least dangerous branch they must ultimately be the trustees of the constitutional compact and its accountability demands, in assessing complex regulatory programmes the scope of judicial remedies must be limited in order to avoid serious disruption. The emphasis ought instead to be placed on non-judicial methods of controlling administrative authority. It is precisely for this reason that we have recommended experiment with the institutions of accountability outlined in the preceding chapter. These seem to us to represent a serious attempt to address the question of administrative performance and democratic entitlement. It is also for this reason that we shall have much to say in Chapter 10 in favour of self-regulation and other 'soft law' forms, provided always that a long-stop exists to guarantee a genuine and hard look at policy alternatives. The regulatory enterprise does involve choice among, and reconciliation of, competing public values with the ultimate choice residing in Parliament and its delegates – constitutional actors at large. The hard look doctrine is nevertheless justified as the most acceptable guarantee that all values are genuinely considered during the policy-making process. In order to stress these various components of our argument let us now turn to the hard look doctrine's procedural side: the hybrid rule-making procedures.

Hard look and hybrid rule-making

The model of decision-making which has informed the emergence of hard look has at its centre a concern that due consideration be given to all competing interests. This has entailed the belief that the public is treated unfairly when a rule-maker hides crucial decisions or the reasons for them or when there is a failure to give good faith attention to all the information and contending views relevant to the issues. Rule-making should be 'openly informed, reasoned and candid'.[32] If predictions constitute a substantial basis for a rule they must be available for study and criticism and an agency must make continuous disclosure of the facts and assumptions on which it intends to rely in promulgating the rule and give serious consideration to alternative rulings.[33] The premise then in all hybrid rule-making is that the challengers have raised questions about the agency's substantive action that are so serious that the agency must justify its position more adequately than it has. We are of course not speaking here of every minor rule and policy but of 'big problems in the mass justice area'[34] and especially where large policy judgements intersect with technical problems. The reviewing court must be able to find an intelligible answer to each major challenge mounted against the proposals, though in circumstances where the *agencies themselves* should be left to work out the most suitable procedure for each issue. In short they must be satisfied that a real give and take is fostered on the key issues.[35]

A range of flexible devices has been developed, including paper hearings; qualified cross-examination; inquiry conferences and lesser procedures involving selecting written statements for particular treatment; written questions directed at the agency panel; double notice-and-comment, and varying degrees of informal contact between agency officials and interested parties. The most important consideration is to grant timely access at critical points in the policy-making processes of the agencies. In Britain this has very occasionally been expressed in terms of the need for government departments to publish studies of policy options before positions have hardened.[36]

A detailed taxonomy of the hybrid experiment may prove useful. Let us begin with paper hearings: Richard Stewart has suggested the following elements in the light of his experience with agency practice.

1 Publication of proposed rules, together with a detailed explanation of the grounds for the proposed rules.

2 Public availability of the evidentiary and analytical documents prepared by or for the agency or utilized by it with respect to the proposed action.

3 The right of interested parties to submit written comments, together with relevant evidentiary materials in documentary form, which should be made publicly available.

4 Public availability of any documents containing additional evidentiary or analytical material developed or relied upon by the agency in response to comments.

5 Opportunity for a second round of public comments responding to comments previously filed.

6 Explanation of the rule adopted by the agency, accompanied by a detailed defence of the decision and the reasons why the agency fails to accede to any critical comments that were relevant and significant.[37]

As well as the above list one could add informal conferences between 'intervenors' and agency staff, discovery of documents, interrogatories, technical advisory committees composed of outside experts with differing perspectives, limited cross-examination, funding independent research by intervenors, detailed annotation of technical reports, surveys of existing literature, memoranda explaining methodology and so on.[38]

The Administrative Conference of the United States (ACUS) has also made recommendations in relation to hybrid rule-making which are particularly advantageous where the data relevant to a rule poses problems of complexity or where problems are so open-ended that the agency might benefit from the reception of diverse public views or where the potential cost to a range of the general public is high.[39]

Hybrid rule-making has been a response to the bipolar nature of due process in the USA: trial-type procedures on the one hand and mere notice-and-comment on the other. It would be difficult to argue that such bipolarity is not a problem in Britain as well save only that notice-and-comment is not itself as extensive a practice here. It is obvious that any of these hybrid forms might represent substantial overkill in any particular context but for decisions where dramatic economic or social issues are at stake they represent devices which merit serious attention in Britain where the conventional constitutional wisdoms have broken down. There will be objections on the basis of cost and delay but it has been remarked that, except for an initial shake-down period of agency adaptation, advantages have accrued through these newer procedures without debilitating cost, uncertainty or delay.[40]

Limits have been imposed upon both hard look and hybridization by the *Vermont Yankee* decision but in one form or another much of their substance remains intact.[41] Furthermore, the Regulatory Reform Bill of the 97th Congress was considerably influenced by these ideas and developments. It was passed by a unanimous Senate though not considered by the House of Representatives and it seems that much of its contents enjoy broad support. In particular the emphasis on 'regulatory analysis', which embodies much of the spirit of hard look and hybridization, indicates the importance with which attempts at providing genuine discourse in policy-making are regarded. We shall not repeat here in detail what we have said elsewhere[42] about the concept of regulatory analysis save to say that it requires a public demonstration of the agency's reasoning and its justification of its rule, focusing on identification of likely effects both desirable and undesirable, how the proposals will produce these effects and consideration of policy alternatives. These developments, including President Reagan's Executive Order on Federal Regulation (EO No. 12,292) have had the effect (intended or not) of producing a genuine public law framework for *deregulatory* decisions in which requirements of participatory procedure and public justification of policy apply – mere political rhetoric is not enough. At the time of writing this has particular bearing on developments in Britain.

A British hard look doctrine

British constitutional arrangements are inadequate to give sufficiently informed scrutiny to major initiatives and developments of major concern to the nation, a general conclusion abundantly illustrated by individual instances of vital policy concern which have come to light largely as a matter of accident. What we wish to suggest is that some version of the hard look doctrine might be explored with a view to repairing some of these deficiencies. The need is to ensure both that reasoned decisions and choices are made and that procedures are adopted to enfranchise potential and actual constituencies who might wish to contest proposals of a major sort. Specific examples will help to develop the argument.

Privatization

Whatever the general desirability or otherwise of privatization its potential repercussions are of enormous importance, as is the performance of those industries that remain nationalized. What is clearly not being done at the moment is to examine the likely social and economic implications of these proposed changes thoroughly and publicly before the elected government decides which choices it is prepared to make. The Civil Aviation Authority study of the proposed privatization of British Airways[43] is a possible exception but, valuable as this exercise was in many ways, involving active consultations with the industry and consumer interests, it suffered from numerous defects not least of which was the way it was treated in Whitehall. Since it upset a number of parties, including the management of British Airways, intense *ex parte* lobbying and ministerial trimming occurred which was never fully brought into the open.[44] A promising mechanism for sensitive debate was blunted by the absence both of legal restraints on covert brokerage and bargaining and of judicial authority to require ministerial justifications to Parliament to be based upon a reasoned response to the evidence received and the inferences drawn therefrom.

There are two major procedural repercussions of a decision to privatize a nationalized industry. The first relates to the justification of the decision itself and the second to the institutional relationship between the state and the newly privatized services which, almost by definition, are of particular importance to the nation at large.

These matters involve complex policy analysis. Thus, for instance, the Civil Aviation Authority in its examination of the effects of deregulation in the United States discovered that, whereas prices on busy trunk routes had dropped since deregulation, fares outside the main network had actually risen and some communities, exposed to the full rigours of free competition, had lost their air services altogether. The problems of competition and its effects where state industries are sold off require careful attention therefore, but the creation of private monopolies demands even more careful justification. British Telecom for example is a near monopoly, British Airways' dominant position had to be reasserted (despite the CAA's recommendations) in order to make it an attractive proposition for privatization and there are severe problems associated with providing competition in the gas and electricity supply industries, aircraft production and the like. If what is required as a consequence of the claims we make about our government is a policy system which would permit comparison of the consequences of different solutions to problems and the accumulation of critical experience, then British arrangements are seriously deficient.

After a decision to privatize has been taken then at the very least what is necessary is a set of watchdog authorities to oversee the monopolies, near-monopolies or heavy concentrations of economic power which result. The Office of Telecommunications (OFTEL) has been set up under the Telecommunications Act 1984 and already two portents, one specific and one more general, would suggest that little can be expected that would satisfy demands for a regeneration of the ancient ideals of the rule of law. The first is that OFTEL has been given an initial staff of fifty and an initial annual budget of between £2 and £3 million. The corresponding staff monitoring New York's telephone service alone is well in excess of 200.[45] We have argued that the conduct of the nationalized industries does not satisfy legitimation requirements but at least there are some conventions which exist for the monitoring of their performance by ministers. There is a strong likelihood that privatization will transfer effective control to large financial institutions in the City of London thereby adding to an already constitutionally worrying concentration of economic power.

The second concern about OFTEL, and about regulatory schemes in general, is that such intermediary bodies do not operate in a climate of open government, of citizen and group participation, and certainly not in terms of hybrid rule-making systems or hard look. If, after detailed public scrutiny, privatization is thought to be acceptable then bodies such as OFTEL will be needed. However, without the kind of mechanisms of accountability which exist in American Federal law, or something remarkably similar, there can be no expectation that such bodies will operate in a constitutionally acceptable fashion. The same must be said about the remaining

NATIONALISED INDUSTRIES WHICH FAIL TO PERFORM THE JOBS OF DISPUTE SETTLEMENT, RULE-MAKING + CORPORATE PLANNING IN AN ATMOSPHERE OF OPENNESS AND ACCOUNTABILITY.

nationalized industries which also fail to perform the jobs of dispute settlement, rule-making and corporate planning in an atmosphere of openness and accountability.

The nationalized industries

The absence of open scrutiny systems reflects not only an abandonment of constitutional principle but also a lost opportunity for corporate learning. It is a commonplace that the public corporations have been victims of lack of investment, lack of strategic objectives, ministerial interference and perpetual uncertainty over their fate. The fact that open conduct of the industries' affairs has not been characteristic has tended to disguise the degree to which planning has been hindered and simultaneously has prevented discourse on new directions for the industries. The proposals for reform recommended by the National Economic Development Office in 1976 were not well received by Whitehall or by ministers but they are outstandingly the most imaginative and innovative set of proposals yet produced for institution-building to create open and rational conduct of public enterprise in line with our master principles of legitimation.[46] The proposals envisaged a separate policy council and corporation board for each industry. The policy council's main functions would be to agree corporate objectives and the strategies to achieve them, to establish performance criteria appropriate to the individual industry, to endorse corporate plans and to monitor performance.

The board, on the other hand, would manage the corporation within the framework of these objectives, strategies and criteria and would put forward strategic policy options for consideration by the council, undertake the necessary planning and be fully responsible for the implementation of agreed policies. Government's concern for effective use of resources and for social, economic and regional policy would be exercised through the policy council on which it would be represented. It would not be able to intervene directly in the actions of the board but would be given the power of specific direction which would in extreme circumstances allow it to override the council. Such directions would be published and thereby subject to the normal democratic processes.

The report considered that such a system would foster improved performance and provide greater concertation of all major interests. Executive management's policy would be monitored against agreed objectives and criteria by the same body which was responsible for establishing them in the first place. The interests of the government should be brought to bear directly at the strategic policy level but in a public and open fashion in conjunction with broad constituencies.

More modest suggestions for taking a hard look at the policies and plans of nationalized industries have also come to grief in recent times. In particular the proposal for Nationalized Industry Consumer Councils (NICCs) to be given increased powers to make their industries consult them on policies affecting consumers included a statutory right to obtain information from industries, particularly on finance.[47] At present the Central Transport Consultative Committee, for example, enjoys no legal right to consider rail fares and charges or reductions in service. Such a right, frequently demanded, would not of course afford the Committee any executive decision-making authority but would allow it early access to proposals for and information surrounding, say, fare increases or line closures. This would be only a minimum version of any self-respecting hard look doctrine. It may be that in some industries there does exist the occasional (untested) right to receive such information. The Electricity Act 1947, for instance, lays upon area boards a duty to inform the NICC of their 'general plans and arrangements' for performing their statutory functions.[48] However, the uncertainty surrounding the meaning of the statutory formula has until now provided ample opportunity for boards to exploit artificial distinctions between general information which may be supplied and managerial information which may not.[49]

Social welfare
Large areas of social welfare policy pay eloquent and expensive testimony to the fact that the failure to provide an institutional duty to consider alternatives has had the most damaging repercussions for British public administration. Reorganization of the National Health Service in the early 1970s is as good an illustration as many. The Secretary of State's consultative document on reorganization in 1971 was not made generally available but was sent only to interested parties with a mere two months allowed for comments and opinions. There was no invitation to the public to share in the debate before the government's proposals were shaped into a white paper the following year. Meanwhile detailed planning for the proposed changes was already under way in the DHSS two years before the reorganization bill became law. As Hadley and Hatch have made plain, those considering reform in NHS

organization in the late 1960s and early 1970s could have explored a whole range of alternatives to the structure ultimately adopted. Unification under centralized control was by no means the only feasible solution for the problems which had been generally identified.

In summarizing the democratic and organizational failures of reform undertaken in three separate but strategic areas of social welfare Hadley and Hatch point to 'the high cost of moving directly from grand design to implementation without any serious attempt to pilot the changes':

> the assumptions on which major changes have been made in social services and local government institutions have more the character of a mythology than a set of principles founded on well-tested experience. In particular, the mythology is one which serves to insulate managers and professionals from the demands and criticisms of consumers and lower-ranking employees by arguing that the representation of interests is something that should be carried on through separate political institutions.[50]

This assessment leads to the last strand in our hard look overview, a return to the experience of the Social Security Advisory Committee whose functions we described in Chapter 8. Warts and all, the arrangements seem to us to offer considerable scope for development and for significant reform.

The notion of rational discourse, albeit contested and cloudy, has at least two clear components. To be rational means to have 'coherent, defensible reasons for action' and discourse requires constituencies of widely differing sorts to be taken into account before decision-taking, both for democratic and for learning purposes. The SSAC has some potential in relation to both of these aspects.

We have already seen that the Committee interprets its brief in such a way as to seek to consult interested publics, although the timetable imposed by the minister is not always particularly helpful in this respect. Nevertheless, at best it has performed this task with some credit,[51] and in its early years the Committee has enjoyed no little success in affecting the content of regulations, not least in light of the discussions it has had with interested and informed parties.[52] Furthermore, the statutory requirements go some way towards obliging the Secretary of State to take a hard look at objections and to defend his behaviour in detail. His conduct in this respect has been mixed. On occasions his rejection of SSAC recommendations has been clearly rationally defensible, on others he has obviously been compelled to change his position by being forced to listen to the SSAC's arguments. There have, however, been occasions when he seems to us not to have satisfied the statutory requirement at all in circumstances where a reviewing court would have been bound to remit the decision for further argument.[53] In our view, however, section 10 of the 1980 Act provides only a parliamentary and not a judicial remedy. Ultimately Parliament should retain decision-making authority but this has to be seen in the light of strengthened powers of hard look review by overseeing courts. There is no compelling reason why the minister should not have to rebut countervailing arguments with rational and coherent reasons to the satisfaction of the courts, who are used to performing this function at least in the field of land-use planning.

Conclusions

We have spoken of the need to reinstitutionalize discretion in the executive branch if the rule of law is to retain contemporary meaning. The standard of critical examination for the new institutions to meet must be something akin to the hard look doctrine, which together with the administrative adoption of hybrid type procedures, leads in the direction of providing coherent reasons for action based upon close attendance to the evidence and information adduced as criticism of executive proposals. Traditionally, the attributes of legality have been the search for truth, consistency of thought, logical analysis of evidence, and the examination of analogies which are potentially persuasive. Given the new tasks for law for which we have strongly argued during the course of this essay, a revised rule of law would partake of the institutional essence of universal reason. It would partake of the universal logic of rational assessment and scientific inquiry. Criticism, testing and change are required of and for social systems through mechanisms of institutional order, so that rather than rail against arbitrary conduct we should set ourselves the task of its orderly reduction. What lies behind the institutionalization of hard look is the capacity of the legal order to inform itself of the range of issues and interests it affects. More generally, rational discourse seeks to comprehend the group structure of society and seek out new constituencies to add energy to the working of legal institutions:

Thus the enlargement of legal participation goes beyond increasing the democratic worth of the legal order. It can also contribute to the competence of legal institutions.[54]

References

1   J. Habermas, *Communication and the Evolution of Society* (Heinemann 1979), esp. p. 186.
2   See also G. Teubner, 'Substantive and reflexive elements in modern law', *Law and Society Review*, **17** (1983), pp. 239–85, at p. 269.
3   Quoted by Rt Hon. David Steele MP in the foreword to D. Wilson (ed.), *The Secrets File* (Heinemann 1984).
4   R. Stewart and C. Sunstein, 'Public Programs and Private Rights', *Harvard Law Review*, **94** (1982), pp. 1193, 1280.
5   John Brewer, 'The Wilkites and the Law 1763–1764', in J. Brewer and J. Styles (eds.), *An Ungovernable People: The English and their Law in the 17th and 18th Centuries* (Hutchinson 1980).
6   P. Selznick, *Law, Society and Industrial Justice* (New York: Russell Sage 1969), pp. 18–19.
7   R. Hadley and S. Hatch, *Social Welfare and the Failure of the State* (Allen and Unwin 1981), pp. 106–7.
8   Teubner, p. 268.
9   Hadley and Hatch, pp. 65–6.
10 See e.g. J. Forrester, 'Bounded rationality and the politics of muddling through', *Public Administration Review*, **44** (1984) pp. 23–31, and Teubner who refers to the Habermas–Luhmann debate; on policy *v* implementation see Michael Hill, 'The Policy–Implementation Distinction. A Quest for Rational Control?', in S. Barrett and C. Fudge (eds.), *Policy and Action* (Methuen 1981).
11 See e.g. P. Nonet and P. Selznick, *Toward Responsive Law* (New York: Harper and Row 1978), pp. 99–100.
12 See S. Dresner, *Open Government: Lessons from America* (OCPU 1980), p. 13.
13 For a strong argument in this vein see Selznick, esp. pp. 6–9.
14 Departmental Committee on Section 2 of the Official Secrets Act 1911 Cmnd. 5104 (HMSO 1972).
15 In relation to the American experience Stewart Dresner's treatment is, in our view, one of the most useful. The other recommended is R. F. Bouchard, (ed.), *Guidebook to the Freedom of Information and Privacy Acts* (New York: Clark Boardman Co. Ltd 1984).
16 See e.g. Rodney Austin, 'The Data Protection Act 1984: the public law implications', *Public Law* (1984), pp. 618–34. As we go to press, the Local Government (Access to Information) Act 1985 must be seen as another nail in the coffin of secrecy.
17 See, e.g. The *Guardian*, 19 September 1984.
18 Dresner, pp. 50–2.
19 ibid., p. 1.
20 P. Kellner and Lord Crowther-Hunt, *The Civil Servants* (MacDonald Futura 1980), pp. 170, 188–9, 281.

21 5, United States Code, S. 552 (b) (8) and see *Consumers Union v John G. Heimann, Comptroller of Currency*, no. 77–2115 US Court of Appeals (DC Cir. 1978).

22 Dresner, pp. 82–3.

23 See D. Welborn, W. Lyons and L. Thomas, 'Implementation and effects of the Federal Government in the Sunshine Act', Draft Report to ACUS (1984), p. 41.

24 *R v Liverpool City Council, ex parte Liverpool Taxi Fleet Operators' Association* [1975], 1 All ER 379.

25 Dresner, p. 76.

26 See generally R. J. Pierce and S. A. Shapiro,'Political and judicial review of agency action', *Texas Law Review*, **59** (1981), p. 1175.

27 444 F.2d. 841 (DC Cir. 1970) 403 US 923 (1971), p. 851.

28 *Vermont Yankee Nuclear Power Corporation v Natural Resources Defense Council* 435 US 519, 55 L.Ed.2d. 460. See also Richard Stewart, '*Vermont Yankee* and the evolution of administrative procedure', *Harvard Law Review*, **91** (1978), p. 1805.

29 See P. H. A. Lehner, 'Judicial review of administrative inaction', *Columbia Law Review*, **83** (1983), p. 628.

30 See for development of this argument, James V. DeLong, 'Informal rule-making and the integration of law and policy', *Virginia Law Review*, **65** (1979), p. 247.

31 See Stewart and Sunstein, p. 1198.

32 Judge Skelly Wright, 'The courts and the rule-making process: the limits of judicial review', *Cornell Law Review*, **59** (1974), p. 375 at 379.

33 See *International Harvester v Ruckelshaus*, 478 F.2d. 615, 649 (1973), and *Pillai v CAB* No. 73–1408 (DC Cir. 22 August 1973), 18–24. cf. in England *Bushell v Secretary of State for the Environment* [1980] 2 All ER 608, discussed in Chapter 7 above.

34 Judge Henry Friendly, 'Some kind of hearing', *University of Pennsylvania Law Review*, **123** (1975), pp. 1267, 1316.

35 See Chief Justice Bazelon, *Natural Resources Defense Council v US Nuclear Regulatory Commission* 547 F.2d. 633 (DC Cir. 1976).

36 See e.g. *3rd Report of the Social Services Committee* (1980–1), para. 31.

37 See Stewart, *Vermont Yankee*, pp. 813–14 and also Pedersen, 'Formal records and informal rule-making' *Yale Law Journal*, **85** (1975), p. 38. cf. S. 10 Social Security Act 1980 and e.g. DoE Circular 14/75, *Housing Action Areas, Priority Neighbourhoods and GIAs*.

38 See e.g. Chief Justice Bazelon in the Court of Appeals: *National Resources Defence Council v US Nuclear Reg. Commission*, 547 F.2d. (DC Cir. 1976) at 653.

39 R. Stewart, 'The reformation of American administrative law', *Harvard Law Review*, **88** (1975), 1667 at p. 1759.

40 Stewart, *Vermont Yankee*, p. 1814.

41 See e.g. the Magnusson-Moss Act, Public Law 93–637 which applies to

l Trade Commission, and more generally DeLong, 'The
n of law and policy', pp. 275–6.

sation, de-regulation and constitutionality: some Anglo-
rican comparisons', *Northern Ireland Legal Quarterly*, **34** (1983),
207–229.

43 *CAP 500 Airline Competition Policy* (CAA, 16 July 1984).

44 See e.g. the *Guardian*, 3 August 1984.

45 See the *Guardian*, 25 October 1984.

46 *A Study of UK Nationalised Industries* (HMSO 1976).

47 See *NICCs, A Strategy for Reform* (Department of Trade 1982).

48 Section 7 (5).

49 See *Making the London Electricity Board More Publicly Accountable*,
A Report from the London Electricity Consultative Council (October
1983), ECC 930.

50 *Social Welfare and the Failure of the State*, p. 86.

51 See *First Annual Report*, Appendix 9 and *Second Report*, esp. paras.
3.2, 3.3.

52 See e.g. *Requirement and Resources Regulations, 1982, statement
under S. 10 (3) (4)*, Cmnd. 8598 (1982).

53 See e.g. *SB (Requirements, Resources and Single Payments) Regs.*
1983, reports under s. 10 (3) (4), esp. para. 14, para. 30, the *SB
(Requirements and Resources) Amendment Regs.*, 1984, reports under
s.10 (3) (4), Cmnd. 9296 (1984), and ibid., para. 24 Secretary of
State's response.

54 Nonet and Selznick, p. 98.

10   A revised rule of law

For all the failures of the past and the present, law and legal analysis have a considerable role to play in the collective order of things which we have described and which we envisage. They must, however, transcend their nineteenth-century forms and concern with the atomistic in order to liberate more substantial political sentiments and to afford them visible institutional expression. In this chapter we shall examine this task specifically and, in outline, address the set of roles which a suitably expanded concept of law could and should play.

The present 'autonomous' legal order espouses a model of rules, regards fidelity to law as strict conformity to positive norms, and believes that its own autonomy would be imperilled were criticism of official behaviour not to be channelled through existing political processes. Law is naturally separated out from politics as a matter of course, in spite of the clear mingling of the supposedly separate realms. This means that legal institutions at present lack the crucial capacity to promote critical reconstruction of outmoded or inappropriate policies, that they are unequipped to encourage public discourse, criticism and collective learning. And yet legitimate, independent, institutional integrity is necessary to promote those ends and to ensure that policy debate does not degenerate into prejudiced factionalism. Only law can hope to secure these ultimate constitutional guarantees, but law as a grander and more expansive social conception than the frailer creature that is its orthodox image.

To take the view that it is now necessary to design more competent legal institutions than currently exist is not to undervalue individual rights, but rather to claim that individual justice depends over the longer term upon supportive institutional conditions. Human institutions are paralysed by formalistic legalization dependent upon detailed rules and regulation. Such rules are rarely an effective device for directing energies to those places where they can be most creatively and effectively applied.[1] It is for this reason that we do not oppose self-regulation in principle, for, if law is equated with legitimate institutional power, the central issue for examination in discussions concerning the rule of law is legitimacy itself. If our claim for overarching principles that demand open and accountable conduct of government and public affairs has been convincing then the prime agenda issue cannot fail to be the design of competent legal institutions.

The rule of law in Britain has a long and frequently worthy pedigree. Its dependence upon common law, understood both as legal autonomy and the reflection of the collective beliefs of the people, render it a suitable vehicle to adapt to current conditions. It has after all been adapting for a very long time even if in more recent memory its protean impetus has been lost. We do not believe that it is impossible to relate common law and rule of law traditions directly to broadly defined statements of principle or the obligations of government. What has to be done to atone for our public sins and to restore our immanent expectations is to reinvigorate the legal order by causing it to address current problems directly, albeit against the instincts of more recent traditions. In particular it needs to place collective policy-making decisions at centre stage while retaining its integrity and refusing to pander to factionalism. The progressive reduction of arbitrary conduct being the central purpose, revised legal techniques need to move into the heart of the administration breathing collective and social notions of natural justice, open procedural address and structured debate. To live under the law, in modern conditions, we must engage in public rational debate and to this end our major legal energies should be addressed. This vein of thinking does not lead to the abandonment of *gesellschaft* legal forms, which remain of crucial importance. Rather, a mix of forms of law will be necessary to ensure the efficient and legitimate conduct of the state in the foreseeable future. Even so, traditional models are less relevant to the problems of the late twentieth-century British state than a revised model of administrative or public law which is more dependent upon procedural devices directed at producing a hard look standard of review.

To speak, as do many writers, of the central task of law in the modern bureaucratic state being one of regulation is liable to mislead, although less so than the orthodox view of law as an adjudicative process. Rather, a new model would involve the law testing alternative strategies for the implementation of mandates and reconstructing those mandates in the light of what is learned. Policy-setting procedures which seek to reduce arbitrariness and accommodate rule of law ideals will need to experiment with participatory decision-making forms as a source of knowledge, a vehicle of communication and a foundation for consent. Much more than rule-making is at issue here though rule-making procedures need considerable refinement and extension in Britain. From the perspective of the law-jobs discussed in Chapter 3, it should cause no surprise that the reformation of the rule of law involves more than amending the processes of making rules, unless that term be understood to embrace the whole corpus of policy and administration. Establishing performance criteria, operational goals and the setting of standards are of the utmost importance and need to be seen in the institutional setting which autonomous law can provide. To exclude these central policy areas, including the relations between government and the major private power configurations, would be to

deprive the 'non-legal' institutions of government from [sic] the benefit of the law's expertise in the practical and intellectual art of setting standards and ... deprive 'legal' agencies of 'non-legal' resources, thus confining them to a constricting, sometimes crippling model of regulation through legal orders.[2]

The developments we wish to foster would transform classical methods of legal inquiry into methods of social policy analysis, both within the governmental system itself and as between the disintegrated state, its clients and interests in the private or quasi-public spheres. The notion of dialogue has to be extended to decision-makers of all types as well as to interested publics. Such 'post-formalist' legal thought, to use the jargon of the American critical legal studies movement, must be inspired by the critical insights of formalist or traditional legal models in order to transform methods of public argumentation.[3]

A number of modern writers have in this context spoken of the evolution of legal forms. Among the most influential have been Nonet and Selznick who characterize three forms: 'repressive', 'autonomous' and 'responsive' law. The last mentioned represents the highest form, identified by its purposiveness and its commitment to creating larger social competences. Repressive law is logically prior in point of development in that it seeks to resolve the fundamental problems of establishing political order, a condition without which the legal and political system cannot move on to higher pursuits. Autonomous law, the Dicean rule of law model, builds upon that achievement primarily by seeking institutional integrity and separating out law from politics.[4] Responsive law transforms the rigid structures of autonomous law into open-textured standards and result-oriented rules. As we shall see, responsive law is not the only conceptualization of post-Dicean, post-*gesellschaft* legal development available.

The theoretical basis of all such evolutionary social types is somewhat unsatisfactorily elusive but Nonet and Selznick, in particular, correctly identify one of the salient functions of developmental models in social policy generally and not least in legal science. That is, to help diagnose the capacities and weaknesses of institutions and assess their potential for the realization of values. This is the key, we believe, to coming to terms with a revised rule of law. For by engaging in immanent critique the very task we have set ourselves is to identify the values upon which the British constitutional compact is based and to diagnose the capacities and weaknesses of our constitutional institutions, to mark their progress in supporting and buttressing those values. Indeed, we would go further and speak to their potential for *promoting* those values in a changing world.

Law as a phenomenon is thus considerably broader than the important but narrow *gesellschaft* model would suggest. In viewing law as a socially necessary set of tasks aimed at normative integration through a system of shared values we liberate its potential for institution and constitution building. We have already indicated, albeit in broad terms, the capacities and weaknesses of our institutions for conducting public business so that we are now well placed to argue for a revised, reconstructed rule of law which maintains the libertarian virtues of orthodox autonomous law while supplementing them with newer and different constructs for engaging policy problems. What we are led to adopt is a mix of relatively firm institutional proposals for a number of major areas of difficulty and an experimental innovative programme of institutional adaptation elsewhere. This programme is in harmony with modern concerns to delegalize, or more accurately to deregulate, and to move decision-making capacities to differing sets of constituencies. Open systems will be compelled to justify outcomes to larger audiences whose influence might thereby be expected to increase leading to further, though patterned, disintegration. This brings us back to the question of law as participation and learning.

Law and learning

It is necessary for democratic institutions to adapt their workings to cope with modern governmental agendas for

Should this fail to occur, democracies may fail to sustain acceptable standards of executive performance, or alternatively power will seep away to hidden bureaucracies or to some type of 'business government', leaving political institutions increasingly formalistic.[5]

Given the secular drift towards seeking technical, professional solutions to problems it becomes increasingly likely that unchallenged expert wisdoms will dominate and that ideological conclusions developed independently of argument and analysis will be swallowed wholesale by administrators who, when confronted with opposition, merely engage in damage-limitation exercises. In these circumstances, for the administrator's genuine organizational talents to be brought into play, some external direction will be required.[6] In our view such external direction would be best provided by hybrid procedures requiring a standard of rigorous examination of competing policy options. It is necessary to emphasize that what is required is not only that decision-takers give coherent reasoned explanations for proposals and actions, and similar responses for refusing to adopt alternative proposals, but also that there is a positive attempt to construct arguments for unrepresented but interested or affected publics. To this extent the administrative lawyer's appeal to participatory devices for collective learning responds to the concern of, for example, Bachrach and Baratz about the 'mobilization of bias'.

Self remarks that architects encounter only weak consumer resistance to the imposition of their ideas upon the tenants of subsidized housing schemes. Others have made similar, well documented, points concerning the impact of planners at large upon inarticulate consumer constituencies.[7] The failure to provide opportunity for consumer input to these decisions has almost certainly contributed to the widespread failure of major socio-spatial experiments. Thus what are essentially democratic and human concerns usually mesh fairly precisely with considerations of efficacy.

There now exists a substantial weight of evidence that the complexity of modern and technical systems is such as to require public learning processes which may, at any given juncture, require in a legal setting a relatively light regulatory touch and the adoption of the occasional reactive rather than proactive style. In the areas, say, of information technology, cable and financial services and the like, a properly responsive legal order would see social discourse as both a source of knowledge and an opportunity for self-correction. Such an approach to decision-making is inspired by a very different set of assumptions from the pure marketist ideology, though some markets make public sense for no other reason than that a centralized public bureaucracy cannot adequately garner the information to take decisions of its own momentum or initiative. Freedom of contract may in certain circumstances represent a socially necessary degree of decentralization of decision-making. However, as the Gower Report and later developments in the field of investor protection indicate, major markets are not only often highly artificial but overriding considerations of public policy necessitate that their learning be in the context of larger public purposes. Supervision may be light but it must demand rigour, critical discourse and close examination of overall performance.

Be that as it may, contemporary developments all point in much the same direction and learning as a response to novelty, uncertainty and complexity has now come to be widely recognized as requiring institutional encouragement. This can be seen, for example, in the government's response to the Gower Report where it is claimed that excessive regulation would prevent or delay new services and products being developed in response to market opportunities and that flexibility must be encouraged. The regulatory framework needs to be clear enough to guide but not to cramp structural and other changes in the markets and it must have the resilience not to be overrun by events.[8]

The logic of this position is that one frequently cannot and should not regulate in detail where the landscape is unfamiliar. Instead general principles (investor protection, health and safety, a satisfactory level of transport services etc.) should inform the collective enterprise for which government, directly or at a remove, must take responsibility. Thus whereas Nonet and Selznick have spoken of the need to construct and emplace a system of responsive law, which has at its heart a concern with purposive civic direction, others have discerned the appearance of a 'soft' or 'reflexive' type of law. Such law avoids obsession with regulatory detail and concerns itself instead with overseeing quasi-voluntary regimes which nevertheless partake of a public interest flavour. Self-regulation is part of this phenomenon but it is not the whole of it, for policy-making in the public interest requires the uniting of a number of different institutional techniques for scrutinizing the costs and benefits of alternative policies and programmes.

Reflexivity, soft law and self-regulation

The relationships between private governments or quasi-polities and the public interest, between learning processes, cognitive competence and decentralization, and between self-regulation and the standard of judicial review required to balance open accountability with flexible adaptation are all illuminated by recent developments within the sociology of law.[9] For present purposes it will be convenient to concentrate upon Teubner's work which is a useful synthesis but also contains certain important innovative ideas.

The interventionist welfare state takes over responsibility for defining goals, selecting normative means, prescribing concrete actions and implementing programmes. Substantive or regulatory law is the main instrument by which the state modifies market-determined patterns and structures of behaviour. Following Weber such developments are often characterized as a 'rematerialization' of law in which the logic of substantive rationality replaces and undermines the formally logical rationality of *gesellschaft* law. In recent times, the pace and nature of regulation has come under attack, and not only from the libertarian right which would seek to reinstate *gesellschaft*.

Teubner speaks in this context of a reflexive tendency in legal evolution in which law might become a system for the co-ordination of action within and between semi-autonomous social subsystems. This in part directs legal energies to creating, shaping, correcting and redesigning social institutions that function as self-regulating systems. Instead of taking over responsibility for concrete social results, the law in this manifestation is restricted to structuring mechanisms for self-regulation such as negotiation, planning and organized conduct. Similarly, the necessary politicization of law imports a different set of social conflicts and integrates different interests without commanding the specific results that substantive rationality would require.

Reflexive rationality has emerged only recently in the crisis of the welfare state. It is as yet an undeveloped and not fully defined alternative to the regressive tendencies of the reformalization of substantive law. It shares with substantive law the notion that focussed intervention in social processes is within the domain of law, but it retreats from taking full responsibility for substantive outcomes.[10]

Although the language is very different, the 1985 White Paper on Investor Protection makes substantially the same point, even if it may be engaged in special pleading. The government proposed two overseeing bodies with the general remit of underwriting standards and protecting the interests of the public, while encouraging innovation and competition. There should be loose regulation, it was argued, with significant practitioner involvement not only in devising and enforcing the rules but also in encouraging the observance of high standards of conduct.[11] The White Paper also envisaged that the Secretary of State would be empowered to delegate his or her statutory responsibilities to one or more regulatory bodies, provided always that he or she was satisfied on the composition and constitution of the bodies concerned. To provide for a statutory power of authorization and regulation to be given to a private sector body is unprecedented in that it will be able to make rules with the force of law and to ensure that businesses comply with them. Nevertheless, the government felt confident that the practitioner-based system would not work without maximum freedom from detailed government intervention.[12]

It is difficult to comment specifically on the balance of these arguments without seeing the enabling legislation, which at the time of writing is some way off. However, the concerns expressed in the White Paper and the loose regimen proposed are firmly in line with the prescriptive mood of most of the reflexive law literature. Without prejudice to context there is much to be said for the state engaging in the business of institution-building to further public objectives. In so doing there may, from time to time, be much to be said too for building upon voluntary or practitioner-based arrangements to ensure that general social and political goals are taken into account while the quasi-polities or private governments continue to take the ordinary, regular and judgemental decisions themselves. Providing that the overseeing mechanisms are effective and can summon the necessary information, monitor achievement, comment upon programme planning and from time to time adjust the balance of public and private assessment, this may well constitute a very important form of legal development in the years to come.

We recall that the omnicompetent British Parliament may act, in constitutional theory, against any private power configurations it sees fit to confront. Again, it is not obliged to, and the constitutional significance of governmental inaction has already been discussed. In any event, private governments exist in so far as large corporations and configurations make decisions of major national significance. They set national policy in significant areas of concern, and are frequently the agencies of administration for government. Now quite apart from the machinery which we have begun to suggest to make government accountable for its relationships with such quasi-polities, the relationships themselves may often best be conducted through some variant of reflexive law.

If governments wish to distance themselves from intervention in the affairs of large social units or subunits they are of course free to do so. They may wish to support social autonomy by pleading a faith in markets, invisible hands or other metaphors, though the experience of the Stock Exchange in Britain in the 1980s would not indicate that such a stand could be easily defended. The important question in distinctly constitutional terms is what mechanisms exist through which government can be called upon to justify publicly its relations with these social units or polities. Most of the advocates of reflexive law, however, anticipate and recommend a different approach from the pure hands-off philosophy. Instead, they espouse regulated autonomy and seek to design self-regulating social systems through norms of organization and procedure.

The role of reflexive law is to structure and restructure semi-autonomous social systems, by shaping both their procedures of internal discourse and their methods of coordination with other social systems.[13]

The task of 'reflexion structures' is to resolve conflicts between function and performance by imposing internal restrictions on given subsystems so that they are suitable as components of the environment of other subsystems.[14] Now all of this may seem some way away from the rule of law and the British constitution, but we think it not to be so. The formulation of these issues in the language of systems theory must not disguise the fact that we are here discussing how the law-jobs are to be performed. The central insight of the theorists of reflexive law is to add to our stock of concepts which describe potential social mechanisms through which the law-jobs can be carried out. By giving extended meaning to the concept of law and by asking for open and accountable conduct in our collective affairs we are seeking the rational democratization of British public and quasi-public life. In particular, this is the primary requirement in the policy-making field where there is a necessity not only for greater participative input but also for learning and for progressively reducing the imposition of preconceived solutions to problems which are becoming increasingly intractable. Central–local government relations offer a useful illustration. Recent history has shown a startling naïveté within central government about the complexity of policy, particularly when execution and evaluation must take place under diverse circumstances.[15] The Central Policy Review Staff, even before the controversial central government interventions of recent times, claimed that central government does not in fact comprehend the overall position of local authorities at any given time, being restricted for the most part to examination of particular service areas. Central government is simply unable to make an effective assessment of the cumulative impact of its own policies and it remains unlikely that, should a local authority develop a corporate response to its problems, central government would be in a position to evaluate it.[16]

The logic of our broad immanent critique requires that central government reinstitutionalize the rule of law in its dealings with other subsystems, public or private. It should be obliged to lay down at least the ground-rules for constitutional action while encouraging and monitoring institutional learning processes which expand civic participation. This is to adopt at least that part of the reflexive law argument which is directed to the proceduralization of the legal order as a whole. The legal system thereby provides the structural premises for self-regulation of larger or smaller entities, such premises being concerned not only to guarantee the autonomy or relative autonomy of the subsystems but also to work for the democratization of those orders. The dialectical logic of the critique is that open and accountable behaviour should characterize public life, quasi-public life and all those private configurations of significant power which affect large numbers of citizens. But this is perhaps to seek to go too far, too fast.

Whether decisions should be left where they now lie must ultimately, in the absence of a Bill of Rights or other substantive attempts at giving legal force to moral issues, be a matter for central government and for its considered judgement. What cannot be left to debate is whether open and accountable decision-making should characterize government *per se* and in its dealings with other social actors. Relative degrees of institutional autonomy are precisely what hybrid rule-making has been about, what lies at the heart of the new investor protection scheme, and what must in future be effectively overseen by reviewing courts if the progressive reduction of arbitrariness through rational discourse is to occur within a climate of cognitive development.

All distinctly legal orders which place value on autonomy, whether at a purely institutional level or also through allegiance to substantive belief systems, partake of a belief in rational debate, in adducing argument, in the need to rebut demonstrable falsehoods and to repel dictation and undebated direction. To these generalities must be added the necessary conditions of rule of law claims: openness and accountability of the sort we have outlined within the British tradition.

In the post-formalist period, law, whether responsive or reflexive, may be thought of as a necessary tool for the purposes of cultural reproduction. As a mechanism which can facilitate both communication between policy actors and mutual learning it seems one of the most potentially useful legitimation devices available. It needs, in order to reproduce the essential life of the rule of law paradigm, to assume major responsibility for setting the parameters and the style of comprehensive planning processes. That the present legal system is deficient in this respect is not in issue. That a reformed legal order can make a major contribution is perhaps a less evident truth which needs to be asserted.

The law and the constitution

Society and politics have been made and can be imagined in various ways. They are neither given nor preordained and in so far as they are susceptible to change it makes no sense for a legal order to claim that it is simply following events and to neglect to analyse what has been happening, what developments have occurred or what needs to be retained in face of change and what jettisoned. Politics, the contest over the control of the state, has become to a large degree, in Britain as in many other places, a struggle between various coalitions of interest groups, some more stable than others. This is not to say that the state has fallen hostage to a faction or factions but neither is it to describe a condition where all live under the equal protection of the law, or where arbitrary conduct is diminished to the point of banishment or where what is done in the name of the state is written in bold type for all citizens to mark.

Legality ultimately requires, through its association with the rule of law, a rich doctrine of justification which appeals to public purposes and underlying expectations. When that is accepted

the principle of legitimacy shades into a political philosophy. The polity becomes the touchstone, not the legal order treated as a realm apart. . . . [A] living constitution is subject to interpretation in the light of social needs and circumstances. Its authoritative clauses are given new content as new understandings and necessities emerge. But this does not reduce the constitution to a handy barometer for registering social forces or the changing sentiments of judges. A living constitution can rise to the height of the times, not by mindless adaption but by progressive fulfilment of its own promises.[17]

Our constitution is not in this sense a living one. Various sorts of politics wax and wane but our constitution shows little sign of restoring its ancient purpose and readdressing purpose to newness. Changes in the nature of decision-making structures mean that rules, policies and programmes are no longer legitimate in the ancient sense simply because they emanate from authority. This is because the *way* they emanate from that authority has ceased to correspond to the original ground-rules for justification. We can no longer really see what is happening and when we can we are unable seriously to question it. We know too little about plans and intentions and too frequently are excluded from the pre-decisional processes which shape ultimate outcomes. Constitutional reform requires at a minimum that rules, policies and programmes be legitimated not only by emerging to the light of day through Parliament and via public actors but also in the manner of their formulation, in the way that they are applied and in their fidelity to overall purposes and promises.

In defining precisely the obstacles to the realization of democracy in each major locus of decision-making, central and quasi-government, the relations between public and private actors and so on, we seek the re-establishment of an historical conviction that power must be made biddable, tractable and apparent. In various fashions (and here we perhaps adopt and extend the argument of Sir Douglas Wass in his 1983 Reith Lectures) the institutions of government need to be expanded to ensure that for every aspect of the social order, public and private, there should be some instrument for controlling and challenging the use of state power.[18] In other words, wherever the functions of governance are exercised there should be corresponding restraints on the exercise of authority.

We are not yet as a nation committed to the constitutional idea of fundamental human or collective social rights and correspondingly are presumably unwilling to emplace an arbitrative mechanism to override political decisions in the name of larger civic virtue. We are not then about to establish a legal order which has the constitutional right to trump the substantive choices of elected governments. What is, however, the minimum necessary for the rule of law to be more than a sham is that political judgements should be genuinely contested and positively defended, by rational means and through participative mechanisms. Constitutional law must now serve the polity.

Towards constitutional reform

The rule of law as an atomistic, *gesellschaft* system, whatever its achievements and whatever its residual role in the modern state, has been substantially overtaken by events. The virtues and principles for which it has stood retain their transcendent significance but require transformation to deal with the problems of policy planning in the modern state and with the networked relations between the institutions of the modern state and configurations of private power.

In making the test of the legal order its contribution to the effective functioning of collective life, we are conscious that the nature of the legal profession must alter somewhat, even allowing for the traditional legal order remaining undisturbed in many of its salient particulars. Quite apart from the requirement of a judiciary to guarantee overarching standards of review, the fact is that in the contemporary constitutional world legal doctrine must be continuous with and not counter to other modes of normative argument. It cannot be separated off from policy and politics but instead should provide the framework for the proper conduct of these activities. Thus, the legalistic colonization of argument in major policy decisions (the extended planning inquiry for example) needs to be abandoned if a genuine search for dialogue about policy is to be encouraged and experimentation with a range of procedures and processes undertaken. This can only occur through rejection of the notion that law's contribution to the administrative state is primarily rule-dependent adjudication. Adjudication is in fact the least pressing concern and policy structuring the most pressing.

Legal discourse in Britain has not yet come to see the legal order as purposive. It does not seek to examine underlying conceptions of state and society with a view to refining the desirable forms of human association. Still dominated by *gesellschaft* thinking it makes no contribution to debate over whether, for example, reflexive law forms constitute a feasible or desirable mode of achieving public purposes in principle, or in particular concrete circumstances. Nor have the limits to the cognitive and legitimating powers of public institutions pursuing substantive goals and objectives in complex environments entered legal consciousness in a systematic way. This is no doubt in part precisely because the issue of constitutional reform has not been seriously examined as a matter of extended national debate and instead there has been a series of pragmatic responses to the major and minor crises of different periods of political history.

The legal system is currently not geared to undertaking such functions, in spite of the fact that courts are required with increasing frequency to make significant constitutional interventions. They are asked to arbitrate between contending versions of nationhood and political obligation in circumstances where their operating assumptions and presuppositions are not exposed and consequently not subject to the test either of immanent conformity or developmental suitability.[19] Court decisions can only make sense in terms of the adoption of *some* theory of what comprises the British constitution, but we are not vouchsafed access to judicial beliefs in this regard and it simply will not do to take a positivistic, unschematized approach to matters of a contestable nature and then to claim that no constitutional issues are involved. However we examine present arrangements, there seems to be little mileage either in carrying on as at present or expecting coherent constitutionalism from the judiciary as now constituted and instructed.

We have no doubt therefore that the capacity of our governing institutions to learn, to change in ways consonant with the pursuit of traditional values in changed conditions, can only be unlocked by the enactment of a major new constitutional or administrative law statute. Before we offer a tentative sketch of its contents, let us summarize very briefly the central problems to which it must be addressed and the guiding principles which it must embody.

Private interests and public purposes in the modern state

Many of the most important themes pursued in this essay converge on the central issue with which any constitutional reassessment must deal: the role of constituencies. We have seen that interests, organized in a variety of forms, play a major role in the policy process in modern Britain. They do so in circumstances where their participation is constitutionally unstructured and almost invisible because the constitutional orthodoxy simply fails to recognize a set of phenomena which cannot be admitted by its categories of analysis. Attention is focused only on powerful interests which, systematically or on occasion, do not function smoothly according to the rules of the game of the British mode of governance and which thereby elicit responses from the visible political system. Such responses, moreover, generally appeal implicitly or explicitly, to the constitutional orthodoxies as appropriate criteria.

Relationships between public actors and private interests take place partly in and around the institutions of the disintegrated state – quasi-government and quasi-non-government – and partly through informal, *ex parte* contacts. Secrecy, exclusivity and imprecision of responsibilities create a context in which varieties of power rather than legitimate authority are too often decisive and the pursuit of a distinctively public interest too often goes by default.

The development of networked decision-making in Britain was a response to the inability of the state to function exclusively through the forms inherited from the nineteenth-century constitution. Both legitimation needs and the information requirements of effective decision-making called for the long-term and relatively stable integration of constituencies into policy-making. These considerations remain as pressing as they ever were, if not more so. The complexities of the modern world join with the requirements of democracy to demand participative learning mechanisms with an even greater role for constituencies, albeit one that is structured, open and non-exclusive.

Rule of law principles

The rule of law connotes the exclusion of arbitrariness: the minimization of the contribution of naked social, economic and physical power to public life. It seeks to ensure that decisions and non-decisions are both publicly visible and rationally defended and is therefore at one with the theoretical requirements of effective policy planning. Rule of law values then deny any ultimate division between the principles of citizenship and the requirements of effective government.

Accountability is not a luxury that can be afforded in times of national success and which must be sacrificed in times of failure and decline. It is an indispensable precondition for success in the achievement of public purposes and goals. Closed, hierarchical administration, a separation of policy-making from implementation and an exclusive focus on 'efficient' management are guarantees of policy failure and planning disasters.[20] Although there is indeed something of this strain in British policy processes much more characteristic is the partial and secretive accommodation of favoured or powerful constituencies through networked decision-making. While avoiding certain kinds of failure and disaster this results in an incremental, reactive style of governance which lacks the capacity for innovation and adaptation and which imposes the resulting cumulative costs disproportionately, though not entirely, on excluded groups.

The preservation of a sphere of private autonomy, although essential, as we have emphasized at numerous points, is not in itself sufficient to ensure accountability for public decisions. Conversely, the imposition of rule of law values on the existing sphere of public autonomy would not pose any threat to the protection of individual rights. On the contrary, the realization of rule of law values demands the creation of mechanisms of accountability to ensure that a hard look is taken at policy options and proposals, including those which would affect individual liberties – something which is by no means guaranteed to happen under present arrangements.

Accountability, the hard look standard and the courts

A British Administrative Procedure Act (APA) would need to require and facilitate a number of procedural and institutional developments in order to achieve the implementation of the hard look standard across the whole range of public policy-making.

Open decision-making is the first prerequisite and so freedom of information and 'sunshine' legislation are a basic need. Policy-making must be observed by arc-light and not by lightning. There is much precedential material available from the United States, Sweden and Commonwealth countries concerning freedom of information and the details of implementation have been thoroughly argued by others in work to which reference has already been made.

A limited British precedent for government in the sunshine has existed for some time in the Public Bodies (Admission to Meetings) Act 1960 but its requirements are, as we have seen, limited in relation both to the range of bodies to which they apply and the ease with which they can be avoided. The Local Government (Access to Information) Act 1985 now extends the 1960 Act's sunshine requirements to local authority subcommittees and to some quasi-local-government bodies. It also provides for a degree of freedom of information at local government level. Whatever the difficulties that may attach to central government departments, there seems little reason why the deliberations of the generality of quasi-government bodies and official advisory committees should be less open to public gaze than the proceedings of local government and quasi-local-government, or indeed of Parliament.

In the United States, the Federal Advisory Committees Act imposes procedural and other constraints on those advisory committees which contain at least one member who is not a government employee. The rationale for the legislation is that bodies which contain private sector representatives but which are established or utilized by government should be subject to provisions of the kind which the Sunshine Act imposes on purely governmental bodies and which are designed to avoid arbitrary and ill-considered action.[21]

The experience of FACA and the Sunshine Act needs to be incorporated into a British APA, although there is room for considerable debate, of a kind which has already occurred in the US, about how far such provisions should extend to bodies established by the private sector and to 'one-off' meetings of *ad hoc* groups.[22] Such debate is now urgently required in Britain in order to begin to establish a known and defensible framework for public/private relationships.

Over and above these requirements is the need to institutionalize participative politics to provide a genuine legal framework for rule-making, policy review, corporate planning and standard setting. The hybrid procedures to suit different types of decision-making would have to be worked out in their own contexts, but much material is available both within and outside British settings to provide useful comparisons and analogies. The purpose of such hybrid developments must be to address in clear constitutional fashion the informal consultative practices of British political conviviality, to limit *ex parte* contacts and give enforceable rights to interested publics. The standard to be demanded of the decision-takers in hearing and responding to the views expressed should be something approximating to the American Federal courts' hard look doctrine, for nothing else will have the remotest chance of securing genuine discourse in our executive and administrative machinery.

A British APA would have to ensure that some properly equipped court of law operated as the ultimate quality control mechanism of our public life by overseeing and guaranteeing administrative mechanisms for genuine participative dialogue, reasoned decision-making and early access to policy thinking. For all their defects and inadequacies, only the courts with their long tradition of autonomy have the authority necessary to ensure that these constitutional guarantees are delivered: at the end of the day they alone can ensure that political actors respect the canons of honourable discourse. At present the courts remain attached to the old constitutional orthodoxies and unwilling to develop the common law creatively to uphold rule of law values in those areas of constitutionally significant activity which Dicey ignored. Not only have they done little to reclaim immanent constitutional expectations in terms of, for example, the behaviour of quangos and the nationalized industries, but as we saw in Chapter 7 they have on occasion gone out of their way to sell the constitutional pass altogether in this respect.[23]

None the less it is essential that there be some autonomous, impartial and disinterested body to oversee the implementation of constitutional guarantees of a procedural kind. Such a body is by definition a 'court' and, if the courts that currently exist are not those we would install on a green field constitutional site, that is neither here nor there. The doctrine of parliamentary supremacy requires the courts to apply any enacted statute, an APA no less than any other. The common law developments which from time to time the courts have seemed about to undertake, only to resile later,[24] would seem to indicate that it is the felt lack of a legitimate institutional role and inadequate theoretical resources, rather than any fundamental antipathy to the infusion of rule of law values into the modern state, which explains their traditional supine position *vis-a-vis* executive power.

Throughout this essay we have been at pains to emphasize that rejection of the claims of the *gesellschaft* legal type to embody the essence of law does not entail the rejection of rule of law values. That is the central message of our immanent critique. It should also be clear therefore that by attempting to inject rule of law values into the modern fragmented and extended state we are not seeking to do so through *gesellschaft* methods. We are not, in other words, recommending the imposition of rule-bound or trial-type adjudication on the policy-making process. If adjudication on the basis of rules and principles is not the essence of law, however, it comes close to being the essence of the judicial function. Thus the role of courts in a revised rule of law, although indispensable, must necessarily be residual. Human rights aside, courts are inappropriate institutions for making policy and for second-guessing the substantive decisions of policy-makers. As the American Federal courts have demonstrated, the potential role of the judiciary in a new constitutional settlement would be to oversee the procedural guarantees of participative policy-making institutions and processes. A British APA would thus need to have at its core the development of institutional mechanisms through which participative policy-making to hard look standards could be undertaken, and would have to define the relationships between such institutions and the traditional foci of constitutional attention: Parliament and central government departments.

The institutions of accountable policy-making

In Chapters 8 and 9 we examined the Social Security Advisory Committee (SSAC) and, with reservations, recommended it as a model for the creation of policy dialogue between constituencies and central government, with the potential to provide to Parliament a hard look standard of information on policy. Our reservations concerned the vulnerability of the SSAC to the imposition by the minister of unreasonably short timetables for reporting and, a not unconnected matter, the reliance on exclusively parliamentary procedures to evaluate the adequacy of the policy dialogue and the minister's response to critical comment. None the less the SSAC already functions more openly and comes closer to achieving a hard look at policy than do institutions in many other fields. In relation to the setting of external finance limits for nationalized industries for example, or the territorial distribution of resources in the National Health Service, no such intermediary bodies exist. The same is true of local authority Housing Investment Programmes (HIPs):

> HIP submissions have ... evolved in concept from broad and forward-looking planning documents concerned with local strategies, local needs and four year forward investment programmes to a more narrow function covering a limited and centrally determined range of needs, informing on progress on implementing Government policies, and setting out short-term investment plans.[25]

The evolution of HIPs from a planning system to a central control mechanism has occurred without any structured policy debate or hard look at the policy objectives of the system. Some intermediary body of the SSAC type, reporting to Parliament on the operation of HIPs and to whose policy analysis the minister would have had to respond, could at least have ensured some level of rational debate of public policy towards a key area of social infrastructure. In another area of housing policy, the allocation of public finance to housing associations, the intermediary body emplaced between the voluntary sector associations and the Department of the Environment is the Housing Corporation. Rather than stimulating publicly visible debate over priorities and objectives, however, current arrangements ensure only a closed corporatist arrangement involving the Department, the Corporation and the National Federation of Housing Associations, in which there is no public discussion of policy alternatives.[26]

A very different institutional arrangement results in a similar absence of a hard look standard in competition policy. Although the procedures of the Monopolies and Mergers Commission are extremely rigorous and the Director-General of Fair Trading provides independent policy advice to the minister, the latter can reject the Director's advice and/or refuse to follow M&MC recommendations without any cogent reasoning. In these circumstances it is unclear whether any coherent public policy exists at all, albeit that there are 'institutional constraints on ministerial discretion'.[27]

Our general conclusion is that there is a need both for the creation of new intermediary organizations to enfranchise existing or potential constituencies with relevant interests and expertise, and for such bodies as are created or which currently exist to use hybrid type procedures to achieve a hard look standard of policy development.

Such a constitutional programme would itself require a consider-able investment of administrative resources in order to design institutions and procedures appropriate to particular contexts. Furthermore, this would not be in any sense a one-off task. There would be a need for a continuing reappraisal and here, as elsewhere, learning capability would be essential. We are led therefore to suggest that an important part of the institution-building task of a British APA would be to create a standing body specifically charged with the role of addressing and monitoring the institutional and procedural patterns of a new constitutional settlement.

The primary function of such a body – which we might provision-ally label a Standing Administrative Conference (SAC) by analogy with the Administrative Conference of the United States (ACUS) – would be to harness and co-ordinate the existing and potential policy-making resources of various constituencies to stimulate open, rational learning processes. The terms of reference of ACUS provide a useful point of departure, though of course they are not directly transferable to the British context. ACUS may

study the efficiency, adequacy, and fairness of the administrative procedure used by administrative agencies in carrying out administrative programs, and make recommendations to administrative agencies ... and to the President, Congress, or the Judicial Conference of the United States, in connection therewith, as it considers appropriate;

[and] ... collect information and statistics from administrative agencies and publish such reports as it considers useful for evaluating and improving administrative procedure.[28]

Details of the composition of ACUS and its operation in practice need not concern us. The point is that a British SAC would need a similarly wide-ranging, roving brief but with a specific statutory mandate to examine self-regulatory as well as non-departmental public bodies and, perhaps most controversially, the conduct of policy development by central government departments. Its role would be to consider areas of policy with a view to giving advice on how to improve the institutional and procedural framework of policy analysis.

Such a specifically constitutional remit would distinguish the SAC from, for example, the Standing Royal Commission proposed by Sir Douglas Wass, who envisages an independent mechanism for policy evaluation and assessment with terms of reference which would allow it freely to deliberate and pronounce upon any issue with a political or constitutional content.[29] Our general analysis leads us to favour all practicable proposals for adding to national resources for generating hard look standard policy and so the idea of a Standing Royal Commission undertaking substantive policy analysis and acting as 'a vehicle for "externalising" experience that is now internal to government',[30] has much to commend it. The SAC, however, would be charged with the duty of taking a hard look at the framework of policy analysis itself.

Relationships between the SAC and the courts, and between it and the executive, would require careful delineation, but there are no insuperable obstacles of constitutional principle to the intended role of the SAC. As a body without legislative, judicial or executive authority the SAC would be unable to clash directly with the executive. In relation to the courts, the SAC should itself be subject to their jurisdiction as well as having standing to seek judicial remedies when it considered that a hard look standard of policy had not been achieved, whether as regards executive response to its own reports or otherwise. Its wide-ranging remit would thus enable it to relieve the courts of the burden of primary responsibility for overseeing the new constitutional settlement, leaving them a residual and interstitial role as the final arbiters.

As regards Parliament matters are perhaps more complex. If the SAC functioned effectively the result should be an immeasurable improvement in the flow of hard look standard information on policy and policy alternatives to Parliament, deriving from the structured participation of constituencies in the policy process through intermediary bodies and from reports of the SAC itself. There would be no constitutional problems involved in writing provisions into an APA that would prevent administrative decisions or delegated legislation being made on the basis of procedures which were found to be inadequate by the courts. It is trite constitutional law that, even when approved by Parliament, both administrative decisions and delegated legislation can be challenged in the courts on grounds of procedural or substantive *ultra vires*. The same is not, of course, true of primary legislation.

Executive dominance of Parliament means there is a real danger that an APA structure of hard look decision-making and mechanisms for guaranteeing rational discourse might be pre-empted by the enactment of primary legislation. Within the constitutional framework that takes parliamentary legislative omnicompetence as axiomatic no easy solution to this problem is available. The issue might eventually become a marginal one, for if the new constitutional settlement were to succeed in significantly improving the participative rationality of the policy process the political price to be paid for reverting to older ways might, with time, become unacceptably high. In any event, as a limited procedural obstacle to executive outflanking of hard look debate, Parliament might wish to change its standing orders to prevent a first reading being given to a bill which dealt with matters on which the SAC was due to produce a report. This would at least require a minister to speak in defence of a decision to suspend the standing order when proposing a motion to that effect.

Conclusions

Our brief account of the contents of a British APA raises many more questions than it answers for our intention has not been to lay down a detailed blueprint but rather to indicate the objectives that an APA should seek to achieve. To create rational discourse over policy issues in the conditions of the modern state is an immensely complex task. If this essay has succeeded in its purpose it will have convinced the reader that orthodox constitutional theory, and the narrow concept of law that informs it, have little to contribute to promoting rational policy debate and that rule of law values need to be freed from *gesellschaft* associations.

Our analysis of the nature of rule of law values and of the operation of existing procedures and institutions of policy-making leads necessarily to the positive goal of seeking a new constitutional settlement. The central feature of this must be the development of hard look standard policy by the structured and open participation of constituencies, conducted through intermediary bodies using hybrid type procedures and with the courts as the ultimate quality control mechanism. Only through genuine participation and accountability is it possible to produce government which has the learning capacity to formulate and achieve public objectives. Only through genuine participation and accountability is it possible to produce government which is democratic and in accord with rule of law values. Effectiveness and legitimacy are not antithetical: on the contrary in the modern state each is a necessary precondition of the other. The details of how to implement freedom of information, 'sunshine' and hybrid-type procedures, the design of intermediary institutions, the structuring of accountable self-regulatory bodies and further exploration of the potential worth of something like a Standing Administrative Conference seem to us to form the necessary agenda for contemporary constitutional debate.

We are none the less conscious of the many gaps and omissions in our treatment of the rule of law and the British constitution. We have already explained our reasons for setting to one side the issue of human rights. The absence of any detailed discussion of local government also seems to us theoretically defensible since what we have had to say about policy-making at the national level bears upon the most salient aspect of the matter at the time of writing – the nature and conduct of central government policy towards local authorities. The possibility of rational public debate of the broader issue which underlies the present conflicts, that is the appropriate extent and form of local autonomy in the modern state including regionalism and devolution, depends in our view upon the revised constitutional framework we are seeking to promote.

Many would no doubt also wish to argue that constitutional address to the behaviour and structures of political parties be made. Such arguments would find us a sympathetic audience but the necessary analysis would require another essay, another volume.

Perhaps the least defensible omission from our essay has been the constitutional impact of the European Economic Community. Here we can only plead that the EEC shows few signs as yet of being about to supersede the *Europe des patries* and, in Britain at least, one of the most crucial constitutional effects of the EEC has been further to reduce public accountability for the decisions and non-decisions of *British* public actors. More generally, if as a nation we cannot even begin to tackle the problems of constitutionalizing our own state we cannot expect to contribute much to the constitutional arrangements of a supranational entity.

Let no one imagine that we believe that the constitutional revisions we have proposed would, if implemented, achieve all their intended effects. Deeply engrained patterns of expectation about how the business of governing should be conducted are not easily disrupted and actual social institutions always represent to some extent the unintended consequence of actions rather than the realization of conscious design.[31] None the less, if at a theoretical level we have come close to an accurate portrayal of the essential nature of the British constitution, there is a good chance that the effects of a new constitutional settlement would be dialectical rather than random. In any event, to do nothing in the face of change is the biggest gamble of all.

References

1   Lon Fuller, 'Two Principles of Human Association', in J. Roland Pennock and John W. Chapman (eds.), *Voluntary Associations* (New York: Atherton Press 1969), pp. 13–14.

2   P. Nonet and P. Selznick, *Toward Responsive Law* (New York: Harper and Row 1978), pp. 108–9.

3   e.g. D. Trubek, 'Complexity and contradiction in the legal order', *Law and Society Review*, **11** (1977), 529–69 at 563–4.

4   Nonet and Selznick, pp. 24–5.

5   P. Self, *Administrative Theories and Politics* (Allen and Unwin 1972), p. 292.

6   ibid., p. 295.

7   See e.g. E. J. Eade, 'Town and country planning', in M. Harrison (ed.), *Corporatism and the Welfare State* (Gower 1984).

8   *Financial Services in the United Kingdom, A New Framework for Investor Protection*, Cmnd. 9432 (HMSO 1985), paras. 1.5, 3.1.

9   See e.g. J. Habermas, *Communication and the Evolution of Society* (Heinemann 1979); N. Luhmann, *The Differentiation of Society* (New York: Columbia University Press 1982); G. Teubner, 'Substantive and reflexive elements in modern law', *Law and Society Review* **17** (1983) 239–83.

10 Teubner, p. 254 (emphasis in original).

11 Cmnd. 9432, paras. 5.2, 5.3.

12 ibid., ch. 5.

13 Teubner, p. 255.

14 N. Luhmann, quoted and translated by Teubner, p. 273.

15 See Ashford, p. 173.

16 CPRS, *Relations between Central Government and Local Authorities* (HMSO 1977), para. 9.1.

17 P. Selznick, *Law, Society and Industrial Justice* (New York: Russell Sage Foundation 1969), p. 31.

18 And see e.g. R. M. Unger, 'The critical legal studies movement', *Harvard Law Review*, **96** (1983), 561–675 at pp. 592–3.

19 See e.g. the highly charged and contentious decision of *Bromley LBC v Greater London Council* [1982] 1 All ER 129, discussed in Chapter 7 above.

20 See P. Hall, *Great Planning Disasters* (Weidenfeld and Nicolson 1980).

21   M. H. Cardozo, 'The Federal Advisory Committee Act in operation', *Administrative Law Review*, **33** (1981), p. 1, at p. 3.
22   ibid., pp. 20–8.
23   As in relation to the Independent Broadcasting Authority in e.g. *Cinnamond v British Airports Authority* [1980] 2 All ER 368.
24   See especially *Padfield v Minister of Agriculture* [1968] AC 997.
25   P. Leather, 'Housing (Dis?) Investment Programmes', *Policy and Politics*, **11** (1983), pp. 215–29 at p. 223.
26   See above, Chapter 6.
27   See N. Green, 'Crisis in the M&MC: Anderson Strathclyde and other recent developments', *Business Law Review*, **4** (1983), p. 303.
28   5 United States Code s. 574.
29   Sir Douglas Wass, *Government and the Governed* (RKP 1984); 'A Constitutional Commission for Britain', paper presented to a Royal Institute of Public Administration seminar, 3 April 1985.
30   Wass, 'A Constitutional Commission', p. 3.
31   K. Popper, *The Poverty of Historicism* (RKP 1961), p. 65.

Select bibliography

Ashford, D., *Policy and Politics in Britain* (Blackwell 1981).

Atiyah, P. S., *The Rise and Fall of Freedom of Contract* (Clarendon 1979).

Bachrach, P., *The Theory of Democratic Elitism: A Critique* (University of London Press 1969).

Bachrach, P. and Baratz, Moreton S., *Power and Poverty: Theory and Practice* (New York: Oxford University Press 1970).

Bagehot, W., *The English Constitution*, with an introduction by R. H. S. Crossman (Fontana 1963).

Barker, A. (ed.), *Quangos in Britain* (Macmillan 1982).

Beer, Samuel H., *Modern British Politics*, 2nd edn (Faber and Faber 1982).

Beyleveld, D. and Brownsword, R., 'Law as a moral judgment *vs* law as the rules of the powerful', *American Journal of Jurisprudence*, **28** (1983), p. 79.

Bickel, A., *The Least Dangerous Branch* (New York: Bobbs Merrill 1982).

Bickel, A., *The Supreme Court and the Idea of Progress* (New York: Harper and Row 1970).

Birkinshaw, P., *Grievances, Remedies and the State* (Sweet and Maxwell 1985).

Boddy, M., *The Building Societies* (Macmillan 1980).

Brewer, J., and Styles, J. (eds.), *An Ungovernable People: the English and their law in the seventeenth and eighteenth centuries* (Hutchinson 1980).

Cardozo, M. H., 'The Federal Advisory Committee Act in operation', *Administrative Law Review*, **33**, 1 (1981).

Cawson, A., *Corporatism and Welfare* (Heinemann Educational Books 1982).

Collingwood, R. M., *An Essay on Metaphysics* (Clarendon 1940).

Crossman, R. H. S., *The Diaries of a Cabinet Minister*, 3 vols. (Hamish Hamilton and Jonathan Cape 1975–7).

Dahl, R. A. and Lindblom, C. E., *Politics, Economics and Welfare*, 2nd edn (Chicago: University of Chicago Press 1976).

Davies, A., *What's Wrong with Quangos?* (Outer Circle Policy Unit 1979).

Dicey, A. V., *Introduction to the Law of the Constitution*, 9th edn (Macmillan 1939).

Dicey, A. V., 'The development of administrative law in England', *Law Quarterly Review*, **31** (1915), pp. 148–53.

Dresner, S., *Open Government: Lessons from America* (OCPU 1980).

Dworkin, R., *Taking Rights Seriously* (Duckworth 1977).

Dyson, K., *The State Tradition in Western Europe* (Martin Robertson 1980).

Ely, J. H., *Democracy and Distrust* (Harvard University Press 1980).

Emden, C. S., *The People and the Constitution*, 2nd edn (Clarendon 1956).

Gewirth, A., *Reason and Morality* (Chicago: Chicago University Press 1978).

Gower, L. C. B., *Review of Investor Protection, Report Part 1*, Cmnd. 9125 (1984).

Grant, W., and Nath, S., *The Politics of Economic Policymaking* (Blackwell 1984).

Gray, A. G. and Jenkins, W. I. (eds.), *Policy Analysis and Evaluation in British Government* (RIPA 1983).

Griffith, J. A. G., *Parliamentary Scrutiny of Government Bills* (Allen and Unwin 1974).

Habermas, J., *Legitimation Crisis* (Heinemann 1976).

Habermas, J., *Communication and the Evolution of Society* (Heinemann 1979).

Hadley, R. and Hatch, S., *Social Welfare and the Failure of the State* (Allen and Unwin 1981).

Hague, D. C., Mackenzie, W. J. M. and Barker, A., *Public Policy and Private Interests, The Institutions of Compromise* (Macmillan 1975).

Harrison, M. (ed.), *Corporatism and the Welfare State* (Gower 1984).

Heclo, H., and Wildavsky, A., *The Private Government of Public Money*, 2nd edn (Macmillan 1981).

Hill, Christopher, *Intellectual Origins of the English Revolution* (Oxford University Press 1965).

Hood, C. C., 'Keeping the centre small: explanations of agency type', *Political Studies*, **26** (1978), pp. 30–46.

Horwitz, M., *The Transformation of American Law 1780–1860* (Harvard University Press 1977).

Jennings, Sir Ivor, *The Law of the Constitution*, 5th edn (Cambridge University Press 1966).

Johnson, Nevil, *In Search of the Constitution* (Methuen 1977).

Jowell, J. and Oliver, D. (eds.), *The Changing Constitution* (Oxford University Press 1985).

Justice, *Administration Under Law* (Stevens 1971).

Kamenka, E. and Neale, R. S. (eds.), *Feudalism, Capitalism and Beyond* (Edward Arnold 1975).

Keegan, W. and Pennant-Rea, R., *Who Runs the Economy?* (Maurice Temple Smith 1979).

Kellner, Peter, and Crowther-Hunt, Lord, *The Civil Servants* (MacDonald Futura 1980).

Lehmbruch, G., and Schmitter, P. (eds.), *Patterns of Corporatist Intermediation* (Sage 1982).

Lehner, H. A., 'Judicial review of administrative inaction', *Columbia Law Review*, **83** (1983), pp. 627–89.

Lewis, N., 'Towards a sociology of lawyering in public administration', *Northern Ireland Legal Quarterly*, **32** (1981), pp. 89–105.

Lewis, N. and Harden, I., 'Law and the local state', *Urban Law and Policy*, **5** (1982), pp. 65–86.

Lewis, N. and Harden, I., 'Privatisation, de-regulation and constitutionality: some Anglo-American comparisons', *Northern Ireland Legal Quarterly*, **34** (1983), pp. 207–29.

Lewis, N. and Harden, I., 'Sir Douglas Wass and the constitution: an end to orthodox fairy tales?', *Northern Ireland Legal Quarterly*, **35** (1984), pp. 213–30.

Lewis, N. and Harden, I., *De-Legalisation in Britain in the 1980s*, Working Paper No. 84/125 (European University Institute, Florence 1984).

Lewis, N., and Wiles, P. N. P., 'The post-corporatist state?', *Journal of Law and Society*, **11** (1984), pp. 65–90.

Llewellyn, K., 'Law and the social sciences – especially sociology', *Harvard Law Review*, **62** (1949), pp. 1286–1305.

Llewellyn, K., 'The normative, the legal and the law-jobs', *Yale Law Journal*, **49** (1940), p. 1355.

Maitland, F. W., *The Constitutional History of England* (Cambridge University Press 1955).

May, Erskine, *Treatise on The Law, Privileges, Proceedings and Usage of Parliament*, 20th edn by Sir C. Gordon (Butterworths 1983).

Middlemas, K., *Politics in Industrial Society* (Andre Deutsch 1979).

Middlemas, K., *Industry, Unions and Government* (Macmillan 1983).

Miller, A. S., *The Modern Corporate State, Private Governments and the American Constitution* (Greenwood Press 1976).

Moran, M., 'Monetary policy and the machinery of government', *Public Administration*, **59** (1981), pp. 47–66.

Moran, M., 'Power, policy and the City of London', in R. King (ed.), *Capital and Politics* (RKP 1983).

Morawetz, Thomas K., *The Philosophy of Law* (Macmillan 1980).

National Economic Development Office, *A Study of UK Nationalised Industries* (HMSO 1976).

Nonet, P., *Administrative Justice* (New York: Russell Sage Foundation 1969).

Nonet, P. and Selznick, P., *Law and Society in Transition: Toward Responsive Law* (New York: Harper and Row 1978).

Offe, C., *Contradictions of the Welfare State* (Hutchinson 1984).

Pateman, C., *Participation and Democratic Theory* (Cambridge University Press 1970).

Pierce, J. and Shapiro, A., 'Political and judicial review of agency action', *Texas Law Review*, **59** (1981), p. 1175.

Pliatzky, Sir Leo, *Getting and Spending* (Blackwell 1982).

Poggi, G., *The Development of the Modern State* (Hutchinson 1978).

Prosser, T., *The Nationalised Industries, Government and Public Scrutiny* (Blackwell 1986).

Redwood, J., and Hatch, J., *Controlling Public Industries* (Blackwell 1982).

Richardson, J. J., and Jordan, A. G., *Governing Under Pressure* (Martin Robertson 1979).

Schmitter, P. and Lehmbruch, G. (eds.), *Trends Towards Corporatist Intermediation* (Sage 1979).

Self, Peter, *Administrative Theories and Politics* (Allen and Unwin 1972).

Selznick, P., *Law, Society and Industrial Society* (New York: Russell Sage Foundation 1969).

Smith, B. L. R., and Hague, D. C., *The Dilemma of Accountability in Modern Government: Independence versus Control* (Macmillan 1971).

Stewart, R., 'The reformation of American administrative law', *Harvard Law Review*, **88** (1975), pp. 1667–813.

Teubner, G., 'Substantive and reflexive elements in modern law', *Law and Society Review*, **17** (1983), pp. 239–85.

Trubek, D. M., 'Complexity and contradiction in the legal order: Balbus and the challenge of critical social thought about law', *Law and Society Review*, **11** (1977), pp. 529–69.

Unger, Roberto M., *Law in Modern Society* (Collier Macmillan 1977).

Unger, Roberto M., 'The critical legal studies movement', *Harvard Law Review*, **96** (1983), pp. 561–675.

Verkuil, P. R., 'Judicial review of informal rulemaking', *Virginia Law Review*, **60** (1979), pp. 185–239.

Wass, Sir Douglas, *Government and the Governed* (RKP 1984).

Index